Luminos is the Open Access monograph publishing program from UC Press. Luminos provides a framework for preserving and reinvigorating monograph publishing for the future and increases the reach and visibility of important scholarly work. Titles published in the UC Press Luminos model are published with the same high standards for selection, peer review, production, and marketing as those in our traditional program. www.luminosoa.org

A

Angloscene

The publisher and the University of California Press Foundation
gratefully acknowledge the generous support of the
Philip E. Lilienthal Imprint in Asian Studies, established
by a major gift from Sally Lilienthal.

Angloscene

Compromised Personhood in Afro-Chinese Translations

Jay Ke-Schutte

UNIVERSITY OF CALIFORNIA PRESS

University of California Press
Oakland, California

Suggested citation: Ke-Schutte, J. *Angloscene: Compromised Personhood in Afro-Chinese Translations*. Oakland: University of California Press, 2023.
DOI: https://doi.org/10.1525/luminos.146

Library of Congress Cataloging-in-Publication Data

Names: Ke-Schutte, Jay, 1980– author.
Title: Angloscene : compromised personhood in Afro-Chinese translations /
    Jay Ke-Schutte.
Description: Oakland, California : University of California Press, [2023] |
    Includes bibliographical references and index.
Identifiers: LCCN 2022025037 (print) | LCCN 2022025038 (ebook) |
    ISBN 9780520389816 (paperback) | ISBN 9780520389823 (ebook)
Subjects: LCSH: African students—China—Social conditions—21st century. |
    College students—China—Social conditions—21st century. | Students,
    Foreign—Social aspects—China—21st century.
Classification: LCC LB2376.6.C62 K47 2023 (print) | LCC LB2376.6.C62
    (ebook) | DDC 378.1/982996051—dc23/eng/20220629

LC record available at https://lccn.loc.gov/2022025037
LC ebook record available at https://lccn.loc.gov/2022025038

32   31   30   29   28   27   26   25   24   23
10   9   8   7   6   5   4   3   2   1

To my departed friend Yalong (Allen) Chen 陈亚龙, who saw the value of this work before anyone else, but who left us too soon to see its completion. We miss you.

CONTENTS

ACKNOWLEDGMENTS

I would first like to thank Xiao Schutte-Ke, my partner and mediator, without whom this would have been a very different book. I would also like to express my gratitude to my former teachers, Constantine Nakassis, Julie Chu, and William Mazzarella, whose respective engagements with this research prompted my analysis in many of the directions presented in this book. At the University of California Press, I would like to thank my editors Reed Malcolm, LeKeisha Hughes, Francisco Reinking, and Christopher Pitts who were exemplary in their professionalism while handling this project. Gratitude is also due to Asif Agha, Dilip Menon, Darryl Li, and Ryan Jobson for their insightful suggestions, and to the two anonymous reviewers whose feedback pushed the final writing of many sections in important ways. Michael Silverstein, Susan Gal, Kristina Wirtz, Charlene Makley, and Judith Irvine have all, at different times, read, commented on, and discussed the formulation of my ideas at class and at the annual Michicagoan graduate student conference.

I want to acknowledge and thank Routledge Press and *positions: asia critique* for granting permissions to make use of previously published materials, which are cited in relevant chapters. I additionally want to thank the members of the University of Chicago Social Theory and Semiotics workshops; the CA/AC network; Afrikaners Against Racism Network; Graduate Students United (UChicago); Wits Institute for Social and Economic Research (WISER); Wits Anthropology Seminar; #RhodesMustFall; #FeesMustFall; the Society for Linguistic Anthropology (SLA); Media For Justice; Southwestern Minzu University Department of Anthropology; Peking University Department of Foreign Languages; the University of Chicago Beijing Center New Generation China Scholarship; the University of Pennsylvania Semiotics Workshop; the Colorado State University Departments of Anthropology and Communication Studies; as well as the University of Chicago Gender and Sexuality Studies Working Group. These institutions and groups generously provided forums in which many of the ideas in this book were tested.

To my informants in Beijing, I owe an enormous debt for your time and patient indulgence of my interview methods and questions. I also want to acknowledge members of my writing group at Colorado State University—Adrienne Cohen, John Pippen, and Jessica Luna—for brief but highly generative exchanges. Thank you also to the Stefan Landsberger Collection and International Institute of Social History, Amsterdam, for maintaining their excellent archive, materials from which appear in this book and are indicated accordingly. The permissions for the cover image of this book were generously granted by the studio of William Kentridge, and graciously arranged by Katherine Baloyi of the Marian Goodman Gallery. Finally, I want to thank a list of individuals who—in one form or another—provided indispensable friendship, mentoring, inspiration, and peer support: Sneha Annavarapu, Joshua Babcock, Robert Blunt, Corneel Booysen, Andrew Carruthers, Sharad Chari, Alex Chen, Yalong Chen, Lindelwa Dalamba, Greg Dickinson, Drekpa Sherab, Bernard Dubbelt, Wade Goodwin, Grigory Gorbun, Andrew Graan, Ha Guangtian, Elina Hartikainen, Kristin Hickman, Julia Hornberger, Ana Huang, Mingwei Huang, Huatse Gyal, Daniel Hutchinson, Yuan Ji, Moemedi Kepadisa, Ujin Kim, Lai Sumin, Erik Levin, Li Anshan, Li Jin, Liang Yongjia, George Paul Meiu, Dilip Menon, Kelly Mulvaney, Mawethu Ncaca, Kristina Nielsen, James O'Mara, Jessica Peng, Jessica Pouchet, Suvi Rautio, Mary Robertson, Sanggay Tashi, Geshe Sangpo, Gillian Schutte, Gerhard Schutte, Stefan Schutte, Derek Sheridan, Swami Iswaramayananda, Swami Karunananda, Raffaella Taylor-Seymour, Marius Vermaak, Joshua Walker, Wang Bo, Hylton White, Hai (Allen) Xiao, Dali Yang, Zeng Yukun, Zhuang Shuting.

Much of this book was written during a long period of extreme emotional distress and personal difficulty following decades of extensive familial violence, neglect, and abuse. In the academic context, these conditions were compounded by unnecessary and unwarranted systemic as well as interpersonal cruelty by administrators, teachers, and peers across the universities where I trained. Much has to change in a context that should nurture ideas rather than destroy the bodies that produce them. The individuals on this list, with small acts of kindness during important times, helped in ways that they will never realize. For this I will be eternally grateful. Any errors or omissions in this book are my own.

LIST OF ILLUSTRATIONS

BRICS	Brazil, Russia, India, China, and South Africa
CCTB	Central Compilation and Translation Bureau (Zhongyang Bianyi Ju)
CFL	Chinese as a Foreign Language
CI	Confucius Institute
CPS	Central Party School (Zhonggong Zhongyang Dangxiao)
EFL	English as a Foreign Language
FOCAC	Forum on China–Africa Cooperation
GRE	Graduate Record Examination
Hanban	Office of Chinese Language Council International (Guojia Hanyu Guoji Tuiguang Lingdao Xiaozu Bangongshi)
HSK	Hanyu Shuiping Kaoshi (Standard Test of Chinese Proficiency)
RP	Received Pronunciation

Introduction

In February of 2018, the Chinese national broadcaster, CCTV, televised the annual Spring Gala concert. One segment of the show would go on to make unprecedented waves in the Euro-American media, which rarely, if ever, mentions one of the largest televised events in the world. The BBC described the segment as follows:

> The controversial sketch was part of the four-hour CCTV New Year Gala—also known as the Spring Festival Gala. . . . By some estimates, the show is the most watched entertainment program on earth. The skit begins with a routine by a group of African dancers in "tribal" attire and people dressed up as zebras, giraffes, lions and antelopes. This is followed by a comedy skit where a young black woman asks a Chinese man to pose as her husband when meeting her mother. While the young woman is played by a black actor, her mother appears to be an Asian actor in black-face make-up, donning a traditional outfit complete with huge fake buttocks. She walks on stage carrying a fruit plate on her head and is accompanied by what is thought to be . . . a black actor in a monkey suit, carrying a basket on his back.[1]

To contextualize this description, it is useful to understand that the Spring Gala concert is watched, actively or passively, in almost every Chinese home, forming a kind of backdrop to one of the most important national holidays in China, the Spring Festival. In the days following the broadcast, excerpts from the Gala concert are replayed on television, accompanying extended family gatherings that play out over days of family visits and shared meals, with few Chinese actively paying attention to the rebroadcasts. This was certainly the case in my in-laws' home near Wuhan, where the casual holiday atmosphere had stretched out over a number of days—a lull between the travel arrangements that bookend the festival period. Like large festivals that entail family gatherings in the rest of the world, the Spring Festival sets in motion annual mass migrations across and beyond the Chinese nation-state. These movements form a counterpoint to the mass-media calibration of national and nationalist affect that the Spring Gala concert undertakes through mass-mediated spectacle. For many outside viewers, the content of this media event might appear to have the character of an ethno-racial pantomime. At times, it has produced various portrayals and stereotypes of ethnic minorities that have been debated as offensive within China. For this reason, the Spring Gala event is consistently received ambiguously, but seldom generates an uproar around its portrayals of black African people. One reason is that black Africans are not official "ethnic minorities" (*shaoshu minzu*) in China, and are almost never featured in the event's proceedings.

In this sense, the February 2018 broadcast should have stood out for its inclusion of Africa and Africans, an inclusion that also should have prompted epistemic questions around whether the inclusion of Africans suggested shifts in China's own ethno-racial epistemologies of alterity and territory. For instance: Are Africans now Chinese ethnic minorities? How would such a framing reorder China's spatialization on the one hand, and Han ethno-nationalism on the other? These are some questions that could have been posed within and beyond China. However, these pertinent inquiries were occluded by another: Why was the Chinese state broadcaster CCTV engaging in such obvious racism? This question and its entailed criticisms emerged from two theaters—western media audiences and cosmopolitan, middle- and upper-class liberal Chinese viewers. In the latter case, commentary was often voiced in English—"this is racism"—or mediated through the Chinese gloss, *zhongzuqishi*.[2]

Both groups identified two elements of the show as most troubling: first, the donning of blackface on the part of a Chinese actress playing the mother of a black actress; and second, the co-presence of animals in the scene, particularly the part played by a monkey, who appeared to be a henchman or familiar of the mother in blackface. The former was denounced not only as racist, but fundamentally unnecessary given that a Chinese-speaking black actress could have played the mother's part. The representation of the monkey drew criticism for depicting Africans' closeness to nature, seemingly evoking an older bio-racial trope of racial colonialism (Opondo 2015). The accusations thus turned on treating the acts of donning blackface and juxtaposing black bodies with animals as racist in themselves, rather than asking what kinds of Chinese subjectivities and receptions were being transfigured in doing so. Racist acts not only made racists out of their perpetrators, but additionally attributed agency to black skin as the catalyst for racism. This idea, that the existence of black persons in volatile settings causes racism to happen, has been trenchantly critiqued by Karen and Barbara Fields (2012).

[blackness + animality] + Chinese blackface = racism. The speed of these associations elides important questions: Can Chinese actors enact equivalent racisms compared to their white counterparts elsewhere? Are Chinese subjects able to equally inhabit whiteness to the degree that they are able to reenact Euro-American racio-colonial violence? The blanket ascription of racism on the part of the western media and its presumed audience seemed to reveal a familiar sleight of hand playing out beneath the trapdoors of a far-from-decolonized global modernity, albeit in an out-of-the-way place.

This book begins its investigation within the educational encounter between Africa and China with an ethnographic analysis of African and Chinese students' language- and race-mediated interactions in the universities within Beijing's higher education district, Haidian. What I will show, however, is that these interactions have ramifications far beyond this bounded space-time. By the time of publication, readers will have experienced a global epidemic that unfolded in a counterpoint of volatile political assertions and social reorderings—these were demonstrated to be both intersectional and transnational. The mediations of race and language, and indeed the status of personhood, have not only been shown to be interconnected concerns in a political landscape that extends well beyond monolingual settler-colonial states. The very language of universalism and relativism, with its archetypes of rational personhood, have been compromised (D. Li 2019; Jobson 2020). Writing from the precipice of a political and intellectual crisis in the social sciences, my own intervention is an ethnographically situated one. I focus on the intersectional relationship between whiteness's vectors of English, cosmopolitanism, and unmarkedness in the shadow of "third world historicity." I will demonstrate how this relationship mediates the interactions between African educational migrants and Chinese actors, and will argue that this mediation is enabled through a semiotic nexus I term the Angloscene. In undertaking this task, I depict how seemingly familiar colonial tropes become reconstituted in novel but ultimately limiting ways in Sino-African encounters. As such, *Angloscene* affords an opportunity to reapproach the analytics of intersectionality and postcolonial translation from a context once expected to have cathartically invoked "the Third World [starting over] a new history of man" (Fanon 1963, 238). The arguments I make throughout the course of the following chapters address two primary concerns. The first is an analysis of how current Sino-African encounters contest or recontextualize, perpetuate or fetishize the persistence of Anglocentrism, cosmopolitanism, and whiteness as historically imbricated manifestations of western hegemony.[3] The second is a demonstration of the ways in which an ethnographic study of encounters in actual micro-interactions can restage the stakes of postcolonial translation by revealing the interactional emergence of ideological concerns with power, historical stratification, and their relationship to discourse that have plagued various genealogies of postcolonial, deconstructionist, and critical race theorists.[4] Thus, this manuscript grounds its methodological approach in the study of interactions—considered as dialectically contingent on, and constitutive of, the historical and material conditions of their contextualization. What follows undertakes a critical semiotics of postcolonial translation at an important breakdown point of both western liberal postracialism and its identitarian radical antagonists—the Afro-Chinese encounter.

FROM HAIDIAN TO JOHANNESBURG AND BACK

Wudaokou, a university neighborhood in Haidian district, is a place many Chinese students in Beijing refer to as "the center of the universe." Beginning around 2010, the nightclubs, restaurants, and coffee shops saw an increasing presence of African students exploring Wudaokou's cosmopolitan possibilities. To many of them, China's significant soft power investments in their respective countries seemed like the fulfillment of dreams of educational mobility—where an education in China emerged as an alternative horizon to the exclusions of the Euro-American academy—an exclusion that (for many African students) persistently favored an elite class of "globalization people." China, they were told, was the future—the new center of an alternative globalization. Many believed it until they had to start tutoring English to their Chinese classmates and the children of middle- and upper-class Beijingers who themselves aspired to either attend, or send their children to, Oxbridge and the Ivy Leagues.

In 2008, before beginning my graduate studies in the United States and China, I was working as a part-time English as a Second Language (ESL) lecturer, teaching a course called English for Medical Purposes at the University of the Witwatersrand in Johannesburg, South Africa. This was my home city, and the home city of a few of my future informants in Beijing as well. My class consisted of a group of doctors and medical students from Senegal, Rwanda, Angola, and Mozambique, as well as one each from Pakistan and Cuba. A number of universities in South Africa still offer bridging courses like these as a way of bringing qualified professionals into the state medical infrastructure. On a Friday in June of that year, Peter, one of my students from Senegal, was forced to withdraw from my course after being attacked and severely injured during his commute through the city. He was followed after taking a taxi to campus and then stabbed by a group of South African assailants who heard his foreign accent while negotiating a taxi fare. This was at the tail end of one of the first waves of xenophobic violence in the 2000s—a still-persistent political tension in South Africa. At the time, a number of opportunities to study in China had emerged for increasing numbers of educated African students in search of better learning and professional opportunities. Taking a few Confucius Institute (CI) Chinese courses in their universities facilitated academically talented African students' relatively easy passage into Chinese university programs. This option was increasingly on the minds of many (non–South African) students like Peter. I left Johannesburg in 2009, but met him and other classmates for a coffee at one of Wits University's cafeterias, and asked how he was doing. "I am okay. I think I will go to China for study soon," he said. Guessing my next question, he continued: "It will be really difficult, but . . . "

Peter didn't need to complete his sentence, not with so many non–South African Africans being killed on the streets of Johannesburg with little consequence. Almost anywhere would have been better for an "other-African" educational migrant in South Africa. Indeed, talented but neglected students like Peter—if they survived an ordeal such as his—were increasingly becoming disillusioned by a stifling world order. One that offered remarkably few opportunities to a continent with a growing population of talented and resourceful young people who find themselves crushed between selective global austerities and short-sighted local gatekeeping.

Five years after this encounter, I found myself beginning an ethnographic project on the streets of northwestern Beijing, in pursuit of a graduate degree in anthropology. Making friends with and moving among the massive range of African students enrolled in seventeen of Haidian's universities, I encountered many older graduate students like Peter: educational migrants attempting to study in China for as long as possible while waiting out a variety of "difficult situations" in their home countries. While many were longing for a better tomorrow, some had learned that the memorization of one particular phrase became necessary in order to account for their presence in the Chinese capital—especially in conversations with working-class Chinese, who could often be simultaneously discriminatory toward and jealous of African students attending "their" universities. This phrase was *disanshijie datuanjie*: "third-world solidarity." When strategically used in the right context, it could even evoke a grudging smile from the most xenophobic street vendor: *Bang ni de disan xiongdi ba!* ("Please help your third-world brother!")

Third world and third worldism mean different things in Euro-American and Afro-Chinese contexts. I know this, because my own use of this term in American and European academic conversations, workshops, and conferences encountered significant obstacles, a result of significant historical biases in US, British, and European higher education. After my return from China, it became immediately apparent that most of my Euro-American colleagues had internalized "third world" as a derogatory word. Most of them remain ignorant of the term's origin first in Maoist China, and then later in the Global South, following the 1954 Bandung conference. The fact of a shared history of third worldism in China and much of the Global South (Frazier 2014; Okihiro 2016)—a constellation of meanings that is not derogatory, but politically empowering—is fundamentally ignored in American and European intellectual audiences to whom many Global South students must address themselves. Outside of ethnic or Africana studies, the Euro-American social sciences rarely teach that the third world—as a conceptual category—was initially invoked as a horizontal call to political unity among decolonizing nations, before it became appropriated as a vertical and derogatory term for underdevelopment in area studies and the development-oriented social sciences. This shift from horizontal to vertical meanings of third worldness owes much to the writing and institutional labor of American intellectuals like Walter Rostow, Melville Herskovits, and Wilbur Schramm, all of whom devoted their careers to producing conceptual alternatives in development, area, and communication studies that

FIGURE 1. *Revolutionary Friendship Is as Deep as the Ocean*, Stefan Landsberger Collection, International Institute of Social History (IISH), Amsterdam.

could counter the appeal of communism in China and other newly decolonizing countries in Africa, Asia, and Latin America.[5] My use of "third world" in the account that follows recognizes this older, horizontal genealogy of third worldism and attempts to contextualize its reemergence as aspirational history and social fact in contemporary Sino-African encounters (Ke-Schutte 2019). In doing so, I will argue that the reemergence of third-worldist awareness, made explicit in the invocation of *disanshijie datuanjie* ("third-world solidarity"), is symptomatic of the persistence of another horizon of value that chimerically compromises the cultivation of decolonized personhood: the Angloscene.

Here, some key questions emerge: Is a return to the revolutionary forever of Afro-Asian internationalism a more acceptable reality than negotiating a world typified by a naturalized anti-blackness—a racial-capitalist infrastructure mediated through the politically correct prose of a persistent, global Anglocentrism? Are many of Beijing's African students projecting utopian pasts onto histories that never came to fruition? Or at least, histories that are so remote from the lives of eighteen-year-old Kenyan, Angolan, or Zimbabwean Africans as to be considered medievalist futurism: a kind of Pan-Africanist Star Wars. Consider the following image, posted on the dorm room wall of Fidel Mapfumo, a Zimbabwean exchange student in Beijing.

This particular poster was pasted on the wall next to his bunk bed in his university residence. I found out, through the course of my fieldwork, that it had, in fact, been given to him (after being downloaded from chineseposters.net) by an older roommate (Ke-Schutte 2019). The characters on the image read *Geming youyi shen ru hai* ("Revolutionary friendship is as deep as the ocean"). It was designed by well-known propaganda artist Guo Hongwo, and depicts a variety of African travelers—men and women—who have presumably come to China, posing with Chinese workers in front of Chinese-made modern farm equipment. When I asked a nineteen-year-old Fidel about the image, he noted: "[It] reminds me of the good old days." The frequent sharing of such media objects suggests a pragmatic awareness of a history that should or would have been. As sign vehicles, such media objects appear to tap into a contemporary "structure of feeling" (Williams 1965) that might be interpretable as a signpost to more explicit reimaginings of third-world solidarities that once may have animated Afro-Asian relationships—where these relationships were based on actual historical alignments to an anti-colonial proletarianization of the non-western world.

How do African and Chinese subjects' historically inspired invocations of anti-imperialism, as well as aspirations to unmarked cosmopolitan modernity, come to compromise the very voicing of history and aspiration as horizons in the fashioning of emancipatory postsocialist and postcolonial personhood? Why do the unmarked aspirations and historical invocations of postcolonial subjects in China constantly seem to fail? Or, alternatively, how do such aspirations and invocations generate contradictory results for the very persons attempting to enact their own emancipatory self-definition? In trying to understand these initial compromises and contradictions, I encountered a "point of breakdown" or "friction" at the edge of a substantial social problem: a counterintuitive contradiction where "social facts" emerge (Durkheim [1897] 1979; Tsing 2005). In my case, this problem emerged as a constitutive relationship between a neutral language and an unmarked cosmopolitanism—where the celebration of English's linguistic neutrality and cosmopolitanism's racial unmarkedness became the contradictory conditions of possibility for articulating both histories of third-world solidarity, as well as the precarious future of a genuinely postcolonial personhood as emergent in Sino-African educational encounters. A familiar compromising logic underpins this articulation: after all, isn't English just a language, and whiteness just a race?

Initially, the obstacle to exploring this social problem appeared to be one that had been defined, at considerable length, by generations of critical race theorists and anti-colonial thinkers in an array of disciplinary contexts: The forces of global twenty-first-century racial capitalism, Euro-American cultural hegemony, and transnational intersectional oppression had clearly persisted, despite the purported victories of cultural relativism, global anti-racism, and liberalism as internalized, transnational political values since the end of the Second World War. In fact, these "irrational" forces appear to have been integrated into the very political economies of value that sustain the infrastructures of "rational" actors.[6] In light of such contradictions, it remains surprising how often Euro-American intellectuals who are concerned with decolonization frequently fail to discuss the broader intellectual theaters from which global anti-imperialist arguments once emerged.

As a former graduate student and educator in the American higher-education context, I witnessed and was frequently surprised by a pervasive Eurocentric commonsense in teaching the relevance of Marxist and leftist intellectual genealogies in the American social sciences. This was surprisingly widespread among many instructors and students in top research universities: what was frequently being taught as "*the* Marxist Perspective" owed its prominence to the Frankfurt school's coincidental relocation to California. As a student initially trained in the Global South, I was outraged by an omission of facts.

The fact of third worldism's southern global front threatening an encompassment of US and European postwar hegemony. The facts of Asian, African, and Latin American Marxisms emerging as the primary conceptual modes through which to bring about postwar global decolonization, which still seems uncompelling among many professors and students alike. Rather, funny PowerPoint slides of Theodor Adorno enjoying the California sunshine and the tragedy of Walter Benjamin's suicide while fleeing Nazi Germany in an attempt to join him are preferred. These narratives keep smart, aspiring educational elites captivated as they are able to relate to the whimsically tragic cycle of such intellectual protagonists: clever, privileged men engaged in brave, intellectual pursuits, caught in traumatic historical misfortune. At the time of writing, none of the graduate or undergraduate students I encountered were presented with any information about the theoretical imperatives of third worldism, the Bandung Conference, the various Pan-African congresses, or the nonalignment movement that created a political urgency for engaging socialist thought beyond Europe. Nor did they know about the shift in global political polarities that these events represented, which contributed significantly to the establishment of Marxism as a methodological perspective in American social sciences training.

The stratifying contours of biopolitics, empire, multitudes, expulsions, cruel optimism, cultural capital, and intersectionality as key terms, which many contemporary Euro-American intellectuals have gone to great pains to delineate in their contemporary writings, were already entailed in the writings and thoughts of many non-European thinkers: early Chinese Marxist-feminist He Zhen (or He-Yin Zhen); pragmatist sociologist and innovator of critical race theory, W. E. B. Du Bois; political thinker and statesman, Mao Zedong; as well as revolutionary and decolonial theorist, Frantz Fanon.[7] All revealed the empirical dimensions of what these keywords would later depict. Fundamentally developing their own respective genealogies, they made their political and intellectual projects intelligible through their transnationally aligned yet contextually particular recastings of Karl Marx's ideas in relation to the colonial and decolonizing worlds they were writing in. How did these genealogies become so compromised in the elite intellectual theaters of the Global North?

Indeed, compromise has a long history in third-word revolutionary thought. Here, we can define compromise in the sense of making a participatory presence at the cost of truncated citation or distorted translation, like signing an unequal contract, or making an unfair deal, whether the signing subject is aware of the structural mechanism that engenders the compromise or not—Audre Lord's ([1984] 2007) master's tools and Lauren Berlant's (2011) cruel optimism are two profound examples of compromise in this abstract sense. At a political scale, one is able to discern these dynamics of compromise in Afro-Chinese histories of nonalignment. Scaling back its explicit support for Pan-Africanist initiatives, China's deals with Nixon and the United States shifted the dynamics of the Cold War (Segal 1992). In South Africa, Nelson Mandela and the African National Congress's (ANC) relatively moderate demands guaranteed ascendency over other, more politically radical movements. This followed from political sanctions that were imposed on the apartheid government when the South African Defense Force's disruption of Pan-Africanist and other socialist movements in the Global South became unnecessary to NATO states (Onslow 2009). This came at the tail end of decades of assassinations and political subterfuge that all but obliterated the legacies of Nkrumah, Senghor, Sékou Touré, Machel, and Hani, to name a few.

The sequential western media coverage of the Tiananmen protests in 1989 and Mandela's release from prison in 1990—after the fall of the Berlin Wall— rhetorically bolstered America and the liberal west's claims to world leadership and its contingent moral authority to guide the world into a Star Trek-esque united federation: a postnational order at the dawn of a new millennium (Evans 2016). A transnational supply chain of compartmentalized labor, unchecked extraction, and free-flowing capital would support of a horizon of aspiration and consumption that promised unconstrained and unmarked cosmopolitan mobility for the right kind of global citizen (Ke-Schutte 2019). As Arjun Appadurai has suggested, we can understand this ideological shift at end of the Cold War as the awakening of a global *imaginaire*—what he terms a "constructed landscape of collective aspirations" (1996, 31). This was certainly the romantic narration within the educated Anglospheres of the Global North. However, as some have noted, many "out-of-the-way" places did not, and still do not, experience the process of globalization and the formations of its ideal personhoods in this way at all. As Achille Mbembe has demonstrated in his work, Africa and Africans become frequent political conscripts for maintaining the indispensable nightmarish underbelly of this *imaginaire* (Mbembe 2001, 2003).

In Afro-Chinese encounters, I suggest that the relationship between globalization's utopian *imaginaire* and its dystopian underbelly is very much still relevant, yet has been rendered significantly more elusive with the rise of a simultaneously neo- and (il)liberal China (Vukovich 2019). The countervailing social forces of China's aspirationally liberal and ambitiously nationalist "middle classes" are contributing significant labor to the transformation and maintenance of this global "work of the imagination" (Appadurai 1996).

Aligning with an urgent need for intellectual decolonization in anthropological genealogies (Allen and Jobson 2016, Jobson 2020), I will argue that contemporary educational encounters between Chinese and Africans reveal contradictions in the construction of such global *imaginaires:* that their landscape of collective cosmopolitan aspiration not only fails subjects who are disproportionately stratified in the hills and valleys of "modernity," but that the very act of aspiration toward these *imaginaires* generates the ideological gravity that stratifies the aspirational subject in relation to it. Additionally, I will show that the rhetorical unmarkedness of the "work of the imagination" ultimately masks-while-recruiting its racio-linguistic and intersectional horizon: a white space-time with English subtitles that ideologically and discursively stratifies all non-heteronormative, non-white subjects in ultimately unequal ways, even within a non-western encounter.

ENGLISH AND WHITENESS

The ethnography that follows will show that the experience and recruitment of English and whiteness in interactions among African students and their Chinese interlocutors is not one of discreet subtypes of language and race. Instead, English and whiteness are mutually entailed in a larger ideological process that compels recourse to a simultaneously third worldist and cosmopolitan double-consciousness. What pragmatist sociologist and early critical race theorist W. E. B. Du Bois (1903, 1–9) once termed "double consciousness" can certainly be understood as reflective of the ways in which marginal subjects—within the broad social context of white monopoly capitalism and colonialism—have a greater interactional burden than less-marginal members of a society. Du Bois's argument not only persists within the protracted global moment, but becomes equally visible within smaller-scale interactions in out-of-the-way places—both in terms of the limited range of participant roles that black subjects are able to adopt (no matter where they go), as well as the degree to which they must always adopt more than one of these limited roles in every interaction. As demonstrated in the subsequent chapters, this experience is acutely traumatic for the majority of African students in Beijing, as blackness—in the racio-political sense—is not an initially foregrounded vector of identity in the way it is for black Americans who must negotiate the Anglo-centric vagaries of white settler-colonial space-time in order to merely become intelligible public persons. In what follows, the interactions between, and reflections of, most black African students in Beijing revealed contours and experiences of transnational racialization in ways that are uncannily reminiscent of what Du Bois once called the Color Line: a historically and mass-mediated political horizon of value that (still) functions as a commensurator of global racial capital. Most of my informants, though coming from different national and linguistic backgrounds, shared a coming-to-awareness of their blackness mostly as a result of the continental racializations (Africa = black people) they were recruited into when coming from their home countries into an "African" student community in Beijing, engendering a kind of Pan-Africanism by default—though some may have described it as more of a hostage situation. Among black African students I interviewed, the vast majority of whom described their experiences of racialization, most perceived the often ugly manifestations of the Color Line as a trade-off toward becoming educational migrants in pursuit of cosmopolitan futures—a horizon that, like the Color Line, demarcates a point separating earth and sky, but which can neither be mapped nor reached.

What I present is an ethnographic study of language and education reception in the context of African and Chinese mass mobilities—thus, an inquiry into the imbricated politics of language and education discourse from the perspectives of those receiving and translating these in a transnational setting. The material that follows demonstrates the strengths of long-term ethnographic participant observation undertaken from a South-South perspective. Building on seven years of ethnographic and historical engagement among African students and their Chinese interlocutors, as a South African researcher, student, and classmate in the Chinese university system, I was able to gain insights that might be counterintuitive to both my Euro-American and Chinese colleagues. Following the movements of informants between Africa, China, and the United States, I came to see a contrapuntal relationship between the experiences of African university students traveling to China and the cosmopolitan aspirations of their Chinese peers and teachers. This relationship between expectation and experience became visible in ways that would have been impossible when following the imperatives of conventional proposal-based, object-centered, or single sited ethnography. Through supplementing this approach with archival work conducted on four continents, I was also able to explore how an ethnographic counterpoint of mobility entails both a "third-world" history of global class consciousness and decolonization down to the present, as well as a postsocialist, postcolonial embrace of "cosmopolitan desire" informing contemporary educational aspirations in urban China and the African diaspora (Chakrabarty 2005; Snow 1989; Rofel 2007; Okihiro 2016; P. Liu 2015). My arguments emerge out of this dialectic of encounter and its historical-material conditions. It is also for this reason that I will frequently refer to the experiences of African students more broadly. While every African student in Beijing comes from a country with its distinct history of sovereignty, many or most are compelled to identify with the subject position of being an African student, as continental scale exchanges are the political terms of engagement underpinning their educational endeavors. It is not surprising, then, that some kind of explicit Pan-Africanism or less formal inter-African climate of association emerges among students from a continent whose destinies have at least as much in common as they do apart.

My intuition at the outset of the research was that Sino-African encounters presented an opportunity to recontextualize translation outside of its usual "west-and-its-others" ethnographic space-time—given the contrapuntal mobilities and historicities converging through these African and Chinese educational endeavors. This certainly proved to be the case, but in simultaneously contradictory and constraining ways. In mapping these contradictions and constraints, I provide a detailed analysis of the productive tensions emerging between them: The persistence of English as a discursive unit of ideological commensuration in Sino-South encounters since the Bandung Asia-Africa conference in 1954. The prominence of whiteness and English language-ness as a kind of ideological gravity animating African and Chinese cosmopolitan aspirations. The crises of personhood and value generated by the participation in a Chinese social setting where signs of English and whiteness become the only available forms of cultural capital to actors who have been historical others to these discourses. And the precarious and costly translations that African and Chinese educational migrants must undertake in their affective commitments to mass mobility: a state emerging in response to physically, racially, and linguistically constrained encounters with a "globalism" that promises precisely the opposite. Toward uncovering such contradictions, I drew on analyses of informants' interactions—with each other and their environment. In distilling such analyses, I relied methodologically on anthropological theories of meta-pragmatics and aesthetics; language and mediation; and mobility and cosmopolitan aspiration. However, neither the analysis nor the writing could have been possible without a protracted period of participation and observation that enabled an awareness of the citation, circulation, and invocation of media discourse as key components of Afro-Chinese interactions.

IS ENGLISH REALLY NEITHER HERE NOR THERE?

At the time of my research, there were around ten thousand African students in Beijing pursuing Chinese higher education, many of them hedging their bets between China as the future superpower and China as a detour to the fulfillment of a deferred cosmopolitan aspiration. This moment, for many, perhaps begins with the conclusion of the first Forum on China–Africa Cooperation (FOCAC) meeting between China and various African nations in 2010, as well as a series of other key agreements following this event (Li et al. 2012). In these agreements, China guaranteed African governments educational access and development in exchange for natural resources. As my African student informants arrived in Beijing, however, they came to discover that many of their Chinese classmates not only placed their faith in foreign Euro-American institutions, but that Chinese students were, in fact, able to attend Oxbridge and the Ivy Leagues in vast numbers. At this realization, many continue to wonder as one frustrated informant did: "Why do I have to *come here*, while the Chinese can *go there*?"

For African and Chinese students in China, "coming here," "going there," and "going far" are possibilities that an ability to speak English either facilitates or forecloses. If we are to understand English as a means of interdiscursive and interpersonal teleportation, some questions arise: What makes English—ideologically and discursively—more than "a language"? What allows English to transcend its proposition as merely an arbitrary lingua franca? What makes it *the* means to affect destination, arrival, and an unmarked horizon of aspiration? Why can some travel further than others? Why, even when English fails them, are so many African and Chinese students still compelled to commit to it?

To be sure, my ideological engagement with language and race emerges out of Silversteinian linguistic anthropology—a genealogy that, as with the work of W. E. B. Du Bois, extends and politically contextualizes the project of pragmatist semiotics. From this perspective, no language exists in a vacuum nor has a materiality that is innocent of its destructive political potential in its cultural context. Sticks and stones can break your bones and words can certainly kill you—particularly in the juridical sense. The case with English, in this light, should be of particular concern to the analyst of ideology, intersectionality, and inequality. First, the space-time that English encompasses at this point in history is considerable, given the technological means that have allowed for its amplified mediation, including nuclear imperialism, the internet, Anglo-medicalization, and American information technology and software monopolies. Second, English has also existed in Africa and China—since the end of World War II—as *the language* in relation to which all other languages are measured and standardized. As such, English is a volatile vehicle for its Chinese and African occupants, indexing a curious contradiction between imperialist nightmares and liberal dreams: a theme poignantly explored in the extremely popular Chinese film *American Dreams in China* (dir. Peter Chan). In the American academy—among my graduate school peers, professors, and students at top-tier universities—English is, of course, *just a language*. But international students—struggling frantically to keep up with the popular culture references and shibboleths of their American peers—must maintain the performative pretense of English's "arbitrariness," lest they are admonished: "Subaltern, please shut up!"

These concerns also arise in contemporary Beijing, where most African students attend classes in English, with many also teaching English to their Ivy League–aspiring Chinese classmates after hours. Within this skewed political economy of language, African subjects find themselves having to undertake double translational labor. They must help Chinese students to translate their Chinese dreams into Ivy League aspirations, and yet must simultaneously find a way to translate future African subjects of Chinese education into an aspirational horizon that is as yet unintelligible. Upon witnessing these dynamics, two related questions emerged during the early phases of my research: First, why is the ideal African subject of a Chinese education such an elusive enigma? Second, why must

African students help their Chinese peers become ideal subjects of an English, cosmopolitan education when African students themselves are still marginalized by this very "global" English educational complex? Later, I came to realize that there was, in fact, no enigmatic ideal subject of Sino-African education, nor did African students have any choice but to help their Chinese classmates. This was because the promise of an equal encounter in the absence of white colonial bodies was always compromised by ideological and pragmatic conditions that stratified Chinese and African subjects in relation to a spectral horizon of whiteness, English, and cosmopolitan mobility.

This tension between a folk semiotics of arbitrariness and sociopolitical realities of stratification suggests that interactions for differently situated actors are indeed less open-ended for some than they are for others. This was apparent to sociologist Erving Goffman (1983) and later theorists of interaction. This principle is further demonstrated in the ways that the only imaginable future for the marginalized modern and decolonizing subject is still only thinkable in relation to an unmarked aspiration that defaults toward whiteness as encompassing horizon of value—despite the "porosity and enmeshment of interactions" or the "collisions of actants" (Lempert 2016; Latour 2005). Interactions, I will demonstrate, neither allow for the unfinalizability of personhood to be equally inhabited by all subjects of an interaction (Agha 2007b; Butler 1997), nor are the imbricated processes of language enregisterment and "performative" stratification of race, gender, sexuality, and class tenable as purely arbitrary propositions.[8] A revised interactionist perspective demonstrates that power is not simply a function of who has it. Rather, it reveals under what conditions power becomes available or recruitable to differentially stratified subjects, often regardless of their volition—as a robust, methodological extension of the process Louis Althusser (1971) once dubbed "interpellation."

Demonstrating such interactional dynamics is methodologically complex. It entails a reckoning with the complexities of spatiotemporal and historical imbrications in the empirically delineable real time of micro-interactions. On the one hand, this necessitates a postcolonial revision of ethnographies of language and interaction where history does not simply emerge in the interactional here-and-now (Spivak [1988] 2010). On the other, such a methodological revision must also situate interactional insights within dialectical materialist arguments that contextualize contemporary Sino-African encounters within a transnational history of third-world solidarity and nonalignment (Chakrabarty 2005; Okihiro 2016; D. Li 2019). The stakes of such a historical-interactionist recasting are important since third worldism and nonalignment were originary transnational aspirations to a genuinely global, socialist internationalism between decolonizing nations in the wake of overt European colonial and subsequent neocolonial projects. These historical moments of transnationalism were ultimately sabotaged and subsumed by the postwar *nation-state* as proxy for developmentalism and later post–Cold War neoliberalism: a succession of connected events and associations that ultimately led to the nation-state's failure to commensurate equity among imperialist, colonial, and decolonizing nations that were never equal (Chakrabarty 2005).

PROBLEMS WITH "MORE COMPLEXITY"

"How can we not know that in the names Machel and Neto, Sankara and Nujoma, there is already, by the historic force of ideological proclivity, the name Lumumba inscribed in the very utterance of those other names?" asks Grant Farred in his recent essay, "Not the Moment After, but the Moment Of" (2009, 583).[9] Here, Farred explicitly draws on Fanon's commentary on the dialectical nature of both history and anti-imperialist revolution: "For no one knows the name of the next Lumumba. There is in Africa a certain tendency represented by certain men. It is this tendency, dangerous for imperialism, which is at issue" (Fanon 1964, 191). In his meditation on a socialist internationalist history that connects Patrice Lumumba's Congolese revolution to "the long ten days" of Lenin and Trotsky's October Revolution, Farred points to the ways in which historical and material conditions constitute and are constituted by the still-revolutionary present: "[T]he power of the revolution, as much as or more than anything, occupied the twentieth century and ours, if only to a less obvious degree, even if the socialist experiment did not survive for one hundred years" (2009, 582). There is an obvious reference to the wordplay of several historians (Hobsbawm 1962, 1975, 1987; Braudel 1972; Arrighi 1994), where "long" or "short" as adjectives satirically challenge their ontological-time-indexing nouns. In doing so, Farred follows a number of influential dialectical materialists in attempting to disrupt linear, event-based histories that would otherwise ontologize time as isolated from social historical experience. Farred, like many critical theorists writing in this tradition, draws attention to the asymmetrical scale of history-making and its constant, politically precarious maintenance in the historicizing present.

In alignment with Farred's argument, I propose that a critical analysis of interactions methodologically enriches a traditional historicist approach to excavating the postcolonial historical present. This is because historicizing the present is ultimately contingent on interactional events connecting here-and-now interactions across time: where such interactional events not only emerge as historical and history-entailing space-times in themselves. Such interactional events are also contrapuntally discursive events; that is, they mutually entail related events that occur both in parallel and across time. Consider the metaphor of a scene in a play that has its own space-time, but also must cite simultaneous, future, or past scenes in the same play, as well as the material realms the audience occupies beyond the theatrical event. In a similar way, interactions—though seemingly fleeting—become socially and politically portable through the same dramaturgical entailments of language and meta-linguistic technologies (see Agha 2007a; Goffman 1959). As with the theatrical scene, the traceability and memorable character of a sociopolitical scene of interaction arises from its speech-based dimension that coordinates and weaves together adjacent or nonlinear interactional events. The further portability of such scenes is additionally contingent on their mass-mediation via their intersubjective transmission both trans-temporally (by actors communicating with or through one another across history) and contrapuntally (among subjects in the present). This is explicitly demonstrated in the fact of your reading this account in this book.

Such a revision of interactionism as method requires an attentiveness to the recruitment of history into emergent, intersubjective ideological constructions like those animating African-Chinese interactions in contemporary Beijing. There are certain objects of critique that the traditional resources of critical theory—the physical archive in its most literal understanding—find challenging to analyze: living discourse in, of, and through social interactions being an important case. To be sure, traditional historical discourse objects are themselves usually formed through the very archival modalities—Weberian, Rankean, and so on—that treat them as vital and originary.[10] Often, such historical objects are presented as relativistic or "more complex" accounts of ideological phenomena. Modernization theory, which—in China-Africa studies at least—still looms large, is one such counter-history that relies on semantic relativism in its treatment of historical objects in order to undermine postcolonial critiques. Its masterwork—an ur-text and meta-narrative of modernity theory's Cold War–era "take off" developmentalism—is Walter Rostow's canonical *The Stages of Economic Growth: A Non-Communist Manifesto* (1960). The afterlives of this meta-text—where colonialism is an event isolated in historical space-time, and hermetically sealed off from an economically pragmatic, developmentalist present—are as much a feature in key texts of China-Africa studies (Brautigam 2009; French 2014) as they are in contemporary treatments of English's "arbitrary" presence in East Asia, on the part of a number of "global English" scholars (Pennycook 2007; Pan 2015).

In *Global Englishes and Transcultural Flows* (2007), Alastair Pennycook voices what has become a somewhat canonic position on the globalization of English: "[English] cannot be usefully understood in modernist states-centric models of imperialism or world Englishes, or in terms of traditional, segregationist models of language. Thus, while drawing on the useful pluralization strategy of world Englishes, I prefer to locate these Englishes within a *more complex* vision of globalization" (5).[11]

The "more complex" globalization that so much of this kind of work proposes is seemingly bored with narratives of colonialism that would suggest a continuity of capitalist-imperialism from the rise of industrial colonial empires through to Cold War geopolitics. This boredom, however, has a notable and beneficial impact on the thriving global ESL industry. Like many stakeholders invested in this "more complex" narrative of the globalization of English, Pennycook aims to "understand the role of English both critically—in terms of new forms of power, control and destruction—and in its complexity—in terms of new forms of resistance, change, appropriation and identity" (5). Without acknowledging the deficit between power and resistance, many like Pennycook propose that "*we* need to move beyond arguments about homogeneity or heterogeneity, or imperialism and nation states, and instead focus on trans-local and transcultural flows" (5–6).[12]

The interactions, histories, and contextualizations described in this book all challenge two assumptions that are latent in the global Englishes as well as the developmentalist positions. The first is the assumption of a scholarly *we* that is equally situated so as to give up on passé projects of decolonization so *we* can focus on what is "more complex" in the circulation of English. The second is the assumption that "new forms of power, control and destruction" as well as "new forms of resistance, change, appropriation, and identity" are somehow antithetical to theories of decolonization, and are even intelligible beyond them.

In the first instance, non-western (and often non-white) scholars are frequently and unproblematically included—by default—within the ambit of this scholarly "we." Here, the double translational burden of their work—particularly in disciplines like anthropology, literary studies, and sociolinguistics—is once again being erased. Bilingual, non-western critics inevitably find themselves trying to account for the local in a situated disciplinary poetics that is everything but, while having to account for the far-from-decolonized global they almost certainly encounter daily. In the second instance, global Englishes and western developmentalist advocates relegate decolonization to a "past event" within a historical epistemology that would treat space and time as linear, flat, ultimately arbitrary semiotic formations that obstruct a common-sense "present" where "real change" can be enacted. From this understanding of history (for the privileged analyst of global English), linguistic "globalization"—captured by concepts like "superdiversity" (Vertovec 2007) and "linguistic superdiversity" (Jacquemet 2005; Blommaert 2010; Arnaut et al. 2016)—can be represented in endless, ultimately equally tenable modes. Modes within which the differential of power and resistance is erased, and subaltern subjects are burdened with agency that they do not have. From this relativistic treatment of English's still historicizing present, Anglo-imperialism is dismissed in what is naïvely imagined to be a provincialization of colonial legacies through invoking "more complex" engagements—as if decolonization were a simpler analytical matter. And yet, the only intellectual provincialization achieved by such a move is the marginalization of colonial and postcolonial language critiques—sustaining the analytically neutral proposition that English has become unmoored from its colonial and imperial history.

In the globalization of English, an important debate precedes Pennycook's: that between Chinua Achebe (1965) and Ngũgĩ wa Thiong'o (1986). Achebe's "The African Writer and the English Language" was published first as a highly influential essay that was (at the time) very optimistic about the possibilities of tooling a colonial language toward creative expression on the part of decolonizing writers, so as to produce works of art in the English language that could be African—a reasonable expectation in a climate of decolonizing African nations seeking equal participation in a world of interacting nations. Here, Achebe notes: "Those of us who have inherited the English language may not be in a position to appreciate the value of the inheritance. Or we may go on resenting it, because it came as part of a package deal that included many other items of doubtful value, especially the atrocities of racial arrogance and prejudice which may yet set the world on fire. But let us not, in rejecting the evil, throw out the good with it" (1965, 28).

A retrospective reading of Achebe's position may prompt the impatient reader to brand him a shameless Uncle Tom for speaking of "the good" of colonialism. This would be reductive, since the good that Achebe appeared to be referring to was not in fact colonialism, but the observation of an affordance for (at the time) a strategic assimilation in the wake of several African revolutions and new sovereignties: "So my answer to the question, 'Can an African ever learn English well enough to be able to use it effectively in creative writing?' is certainly, 'Yes.' If on the other hand you ask, 'Can he ever learn to use it like a native speaker?' I should say, 'I hope not.' It is neither necessary nor desirable for him to be able to do so. The price a world language must be prepared to pay is submission to many different kinds of use" (29).

In his observation of the waning white or European body as inhabitant of the English language, Achebe was not alone in his optimism in 1965, as both African nationalism and African socialism were still on the ascent across Africa. There was a wave of decolonization sweeping the continent and several potential allies in the non-western world were positively disposed toward emerging African states. Dynamic leaders like Kwame Nkrumah and Ahmed Sékou Touré emerged as prominent voices advocating a Pan-Africanism that aimed to demonstrate productive dialogue between socialist and democratic reform. In the hubris of decolonization, the third world—in an optimistic coming-of-age that was announced at the Bandung Conference in 1955—seemed set not only to provincialize Europe but to set an example for it. This hubris was short-lived. After a string of coups and economic expropriations in Africa and Latin America, dreams of third-world solidarity and Pan-Africanism seemed to give way to nightmares in which African futures lived-on only in rusted infrastructures that evoked optimistic pasts. The context from which Ngũgĩ would later challenge Achebe was one in which English was no longer an appropriable register through which to facilitate an unburdened, third-world cosmopolitanism among diverse intellectuals who could engage on an equal footing. The picture had changed drastically after 1976. In the space-time of NATO's ascendancy, and following the end of the Chinese Cultural Revolution with the death of Mao Zedong, Ngũgĩ argued that English (and other languages of colonization) had come to compromise—rather than liberate—the African writing subject: "How did we as African writers come to be so feeble toward the claims of our languages on us and so aggressive in our claims on other languages, particularly the languages of colonization? In my view, language was the most important vehicle through which that power fascinated and held the soul prisoner. Language was the means of the spiritual subjugation" (Ngũgĩ [1986] 1994, 286).

For Ngũgĩ, there is nothing arbitrary in the capacity of languages to stratify, liberate, or inveigle their speakers, nor are languages equally situated to do so. To be sure, this position is also supported by a number of linguistic anthropologists. Context matters, and in this regard the contexts in which Ngũgĩ and Achebe posited their respective dystopian and utopian arguments differed fundamentally. These two thinkers have been type-cast as standing on opposite sides of a debate about language and decolonization despite the fact that their arguments in these canonic documents are separated by more than twenty years. A dialectic emerges between them that draws attention to the third and perhaps most encompassing assumption informing Pennycook's argument: the scale of the global as an analytic of commensuration.

Both Ngũgĩ and Achebe remind us that decolonization continues to obstruct the outlook of globalization as an all-commensurating horizon of postmodern personhood—that decolonization still mediates similarly dialectical "global" futures (Mazzarella 2004; Ferguson 1999; Piot 2010). To be sure, Achebe and Ngũgĩ are making very different arguments about the possibilities of languages of command being recruited to projects of decolonization. Decolonization—historical and present—persistently troubles the possibilities of jumping scale to the global—while for Pennycook a "more complex" globalization of English retrospectively occludes the colonial. These arguments are far from equivalent. They reveal that arguments for globalization or decolonization—and indeed arguments of any kind—depend on commensurating scale.

This understanding resonates to some degree with linguistic anthropologists Summerson Carr and Michael Lempert's (2016) recent discussion of the "pragmatics of scale" as an indispensable concern in virtually all linguistically mediated social interaction. Scaling, as a special kind of commensurative semiosis, is defined as a broad social practice that can be studied across an array of contexts where subjects must make the scale *of something*—always in spatial and temporal terms—intelligible *to someone*, in some way. Obvious examples include doctors explaining diseases to nonmedical personnel through shared analogies; scientists explaining ontological observations to laypeople through mutually available metaphors; or religious ritual specialists conveying complex precepts using accessible parables or poetic juxtapositions. Many forms of scaling, however, do not emerge in an open-ended sense, but rather in dialectical interactions where the play of structure and moment-to-moment maintenance elides neither "structuralist" nor "dialectical" concerns in the way Lempert himself describes (Carr and Lempert 2016). Drawing on postcolonial theory and an older pragmatist semiotics—particularly in relation to the ideas of Frantz Fanon and Erving Goffman—it is this less open-ended kind of interaction I will be concerned with. Here, I will argue that the interplay between structure and agency, as well as the moment-to-moment of interactions and their histories, are not simply bypassed through the naïve postmodern accusation of structuralism. Rather, I propose that considerations of structure should be taken as fragile and precarious, yet indispensable propositions—particularly when they are voiced by our informants—and as such should be understood as entailing significant social labor and the recruitment of an array of stratified subject positions to maintain. Once we adopt such a stance, many of the analytical archetypes for discussing various permutations of political stratification can be productively synthesized: "*homo sacer,*" "the precariat," "the abject," and "the subaltern" among them (Agamben 1998; Standing 2011; Butler 1990; Spivak [1988] 2010).

SPACE-TIME(S) OF MY RESEARCH

In many ways the scholarly biases in contemporary anthropology—a far-from-decolonized discipline—mirror these political dynamics of ordering and marginalization observed among African and Chinese informants in Beijing: assumptions of equality that ultimately stratify, and assumptions of historical linearity that convert colonialism into a series of passé events that become obstacles to new possibilities of personhood—possibilities that are ultimately deferred in all too familiar ways. The ethnographic texture of these dynamics, as presented here, emerged out of a number of methodological phases during the last eight years, in the development, implementation, and recasting of this project. My preliminary research in archives in the United Kingdom, South Africa, China, and the United States was important in contextualizing contemporary encounters in Beijing, which became my primary research site. During shorter phases of fieldwork, I was either conducting follow-up interviews in China, or pursuing archival research in Southern Africa and the United Kingdom (during summers and in transit between China and the United States). The bulk of my research, however, was conducted as a student in Beijing. In this capacity, I took classes, attended social gatherings, and lived in the same conditions and neighborhoods as most of my informants during my time in China—sometimes on- and sometimes off-campus as was the case for many African and Chinese students I attended classes and social events with. This participant observation was supplemented by archival and historical work that I undertook at a few research centers in Beijing during my fieldwork.

Beijing, my primary field site, remains an important educational metropole from the perspective of both Chinese and African learners, although for different reasons. For African students, the process of arriving in Beijing is heavily mediated through Confucius Institutes (CIs), which have a strong presence on the African continent through their support within African educational systems—from elementary school through university and vocational schools. In this regard,

CIs not only provide Chinese-language education but often play an important brokering role in facilitating students' passage into Chinese universities both through scholarships and the establishment of interuniversity networks between Chinese and African institutions. The Chinese government ministry that oversees CIs throughout the world—the Hanban (or Guojia Hanyu Guoji Tuiguang Lingdao Xiaozu Bangongshi)—is also located in Beijing. For Chinese students from all over China, Beijing becomes an educational center by virtue of the fact that the city has the highest concentration of top-tier Chinese institutions. Even within Beijing, governmental and educational administration are spatially concentrated, with government districts located within the city's inner two rings, and an entire educational district, Haidian, mostly within its fourth ring.

For these reasons, Haidian is the nexus of both Chinese and African educational cosmopolitanism in China, and the place where I lived and sourced the majority of my informants during my research in the Chinese capital. While being enrolled as a Chinese philosophy student at one university, I was able to align myself to what the majority of my African and Chinese classmates and informants spent their days doing—participating in reading groups, engaging in sporting activities, hanging out, and sitting in on classes across more than seventeen major campuses and research institutes in and beyond Haidian. Given the close proximity of campuses, students from all over Africa were able to form considerably large communities of common interest groups. These were fairly diverse, ranging from Pan-Africanist to national, linguistic, and tribalist alignments. A variety of social and political activities facilitated much of the interaction among these sometimes overlapping, sometimes discreet communities of African students. Given the concentrated region within which my informants were living and learning, as well as their concerns with anonymity, I have provided pseudonyms for them and their affiliated universities, but have kept the national origin of students and their chosen gender designations consistent. The pseudonyms were usually created with the informant or were chosen to mirror—in the case of Marx Moji and Mao Mapfumo—actual given middle names that indexed intertwined political histories and kinship alignments. Given the sheer volume of subjects that had socialist middle names or nicknames, there is no risk of revealing their identities as they appear here. In some cases, there were place names, organizations, and actual dates of interviews and focus groups that may have placed an informant at risk—since I would be a rather conspicuous foreigner on CCTV footage in coffee shops and other locations. I changed these accordingly. Furthermore, making a connection between a person or organization mentioned and actual informants and institutions will be unlikely, given the number of informants I spoke to (more than one hundred), formally and informally, over a period of seven years, and the number of student-driven initiatives afoot in Beijing.

While all the universities in Haidian are Chinese-language universities, the dominant language among African students, as well as the primary language used between Africans and their Chinese peers and teachers, was English. This was also recognized by the Chinese institutions, all of whom offered classes in English while requiring students to pass a Chinese proficiency test by the end of their studies. Most African students only took English classes and their compulsory Chinese lessons; exceptions included either highly talented Chinese-language learners or long-term visitors in China. This situation and the escalating numbers of international students in Chinese universities have created a greater demand for English-language classes, a demand that places many Chinese-educated faculty at a disadvantage, as they have to teach their field in a foreign language within their own country. This is an obstacle that also negatively impacts African and other international students who complain about receiving an "economy class education," without its emancipatory association. There is a historical context that lends some nuance to this widespread complaint. Many within the foreign student community are acutely aware that the Haidian district universities have played host to African and other international students since the days of Maoist China—precisely as a gesture of socialist emancipation through third-world, internationalist, and communist solidarity. This followed the Maoist centralization of Chinese education, focusing their educational development initiatives—and their subsequent regulation—in one district: Haidian.

During my research, I came to be recruited to various spheres of social interaction through identities I could adopt in relation to different informants. As an Afrikaner South African, I had to learn to perform—when necessary—a species of cosmopolitan "English" subjecthood, which varies depending on my audience but is nonetheless facilitated by an expectation that I can carry off this performance in an American or European setting. In Beijing, and within this diverse milieu of Chinese, African, and South African students, I found myself enlisted in a wider range of roles depending on my interactions with various Chinese and African actors in Beijing. For most Chinese students, I passed as a generic white (American) exchange student from a US university. For other Africans, I was a white South African of a certain kind: a recognizable category to African students from most of the continent. And for South African students, I was a random Afrikaner in Beijing. This latter category, in particular, puzzled elite, black South African students, many of whom held stereotypes of Afrikaners as fairly prosaic, barely literate, country bumpkins—in short, the antithesis of themselves and the emerging cosmopolitan class in South Africa.

To most of them, an Afrikaner—especially one interested in the lives of African students—seemed somewhat out of place and worthy of initial suspicion. In overcoming this obstacle, I was fortunate that I had already known a handful of Zimbabwean informants who had attended university in South Africa before coming to China via Confucius Institutes in their home country. Following my later university enrollment, which I undertook as part of my fieldwork, I attended classes and shared meals with these students, since—initially—the black South

African community in Beijing was difficult to forge relationships with. Through my Zimbabwean informants and classmates' more obvious openness to Pan-African conversations, I came to know increasing numbers of African and Chinese students while taking classes in a few different universities in Haidian district where the random auditing of classes across campuses is a fairly common activity among both international and Chinese students. Through these more encompassing interactions, I came to observe a political economy of cosmopolitan aspiration where African students were coming to Chinese universities and teaching English as means of survival, while Chinese students were frantically acquiring English skills to try and study in educational destinations in the United States and Britain. It was this observation that prompted me to consider the relationship between language, race, and mobility in a far from equal relationship between Chinese and African interlocutors—both operating in an interactional space-time that continues to valorize a cosmopolitan aesthetics of Anglocentric, unmarked whiteness.

ROADMAP

Having laid out the implications of the arguments and engagements that will make up the body of the manuscript, I will briefly sketch a roadmap of the content chapters, which are arranged into two parts.

Part I explores personhood as a fundamental discursive battleground in Sino-African postsocialist and postcolonial translations. Chapter 1 defines what I mean by the Angloscene and outlines its pragmatic dimensions. I do so by demonstrating stratification and conditions of value that imbricate language and education reception among contemporary African students visiting Beijing. In this chapter, I reveal some of the constraints that African students experience in their pursuit of an unmarked cosmopolitanism in contemporary Beijing. In support, I provide a detailed analysis of important contours of these constraints: the persistence of English as the unit of commensuration in Sino-South encounters where signs of English and whiteness become the only available forms of cultural capital for actors who have been historical others to this semiotic field. In showing how language is not disarticulable from its surrounding *indexicalities* (M. Silverstein 1976) and material historical conditions (Marx 1972)—like the signs of race and cosmopolitan mobility—I hope to draw attention to the limits of cosmopolitan aspiration, when its units of commensuration, like "neutral" English, become compromised by the ideological vectors of whiteness and stratified mobility. Drawing on the ideas of the Russian formalist thinker, Mikhail Bakhtin, I propose an analytic through which to interpret an articulated relationship between English and its indexically associated signs of race and mobility. I term this the Angloscene. Doing so, I suggest, draws attention to the regime of evaluation or arbitration within which Sino-African postcolonial "translation" unfolds.

Analyzing the gendered and sexual relationships between, and among, men and women in Chinese and African student communities, chapters 2 and 3 reveal the ways in which the Angloscene is sustained "performatively." How the discursive silencing of subalterns, the micro-political contradictions of identity politics, and compromised units of translation—what Audre Lorde ([1984] 2007) referred to as "the master's tools"—persist as marginalizing concerns in contemporary Beijing, and also how they persist precisely through a cruel optimism toward the emancipatory horizons of the Angloscene (Berlant 2011). Making use of analytical and methodological approaches in postcolonial Marxist and black feminist theory as well as linguistic anthropology, these chapters reveal, respectively, how this stratification through aspiration can be simultaneously understood as racially intersectional (Crenshaw 1991, 1989) and linguistically enregistered (Agha 2005). As such, Afro-Chinese educational encounters reflect not only a productive confluence of these critical and semiotic analytics, but also an important recontextualization of their respective arguments beyond the bounded national-linguistic settings within which these processes are conventionally identified.

In part II, I explore the contradictory compromises that the pursuit of a Sino-African postcolonial personhood entails. In chapter 4, my concern is with the Angloscene as a zone of translation and site for the alienating calibration of the affective fields of sensual social life—the *translation* of (an)aesthetic orders of social stratification (Buck-Morss 1992). Here Sino-African aspirational mobilities represent one such affective field. I will suggest how the tension between fashioning unprecedented futures and imagining utopian pasts—entailed in the intersubjective maintenance of the Angloscene—remains unresolved at the level of sensual, intersocial, and nonconscious domains of encounter. Exploring the recruitment of "nature" tropes and their associated compromised personhoods in the mediation of racialized and racializing alterities in Afro-Chinese encounters, I give an account of dangerous mediation and translational attunement. As opposed to the "culture," "habitus," or "milieu" within which intersubjective, durable formations of practice are grounded and given meaning, my aim is to account for the *in-translation* aspects of personhood and their simultaneously sensual and semiotic building blocks—and then how such translational affordances are extracted for the construction of compromised futurities.

As a counterpoint, chapter 5 meditates on the indispensable pragmatics of translation that are intelligible and referable discursive phenomena in the world as well as political and cultural realities to African and Chinese actors that are unavoidably imbricated in a mutually transformative encounter. To this end, I explore the indispensability of translation as social practice not only in the particular instance of Afro-Chinese interactions, but in the broader context of non-western encounters beyond the settler-colonial encounter. Demonstrating a pragmatics of postcolonial translation, I analyze the reflexive, intersubjective mediation of Southern African and Chinese culture concepts, *Ubuntu* and *guanxi* as my primary example for discussing potential avenues for negotiated Afro-Chinese identities even in a context where the conditions for the making of personhood may initially appear compromised.

Laying out what I call the liberal-racism complex, chapter 6 concludes with a number of key concerns: Within what regime of evaluation or arbitration does a Sino-African translation unfold? What are the mechanisms through which the cultural capital of English persists as not only the common denominator of all other global languages but the standard measure of cultural value regulating Chinese and African interactions? How is the arbitrariness of English or whiteness tenable, when both signs not only become primary mediators between people who have been constituted as their historical others (non-white, non-English-speakers), but also in a context where their hegemonic influence is assumed to be absent—as black or Chinese subjects of a Chinese education? Grappling with these, I undertake a novel form of conclusion—an anticipatory theoretical engagement with current and adjacent literatures around critical race perspectives and their relationship to postcolonial theory and anthropology, exploring their respective limits and impasses in the contexts of Afro-Chinese encounters and beyond. As opposed to an occluded recapitulation of the introduction, this chapter represents a novel theorization of translation as ethnographic metaphor, synthesizing a path between pragmatist semiotics and the deconstructive dialectics of postcolonial theory.

PART I

Personhood

Chronotopes of the Angloscene

What cultural, historical, and other representational materials are available for synthesizing a future African subject of China-Africa educational encounters?[1] Postcolonial theorist Frantz Fanon once noted that the postcolonial subject's nightmares have a time and a place—a *socius* of the colonial encounter that haunts and recontextualizes the future of the colonized eternally within that shape-shifting nightmare (Fanon [1952] 2008, 84–85). This chapter—exploring the cosmopolitan aspirations of African students in Beijing—recasts Fanon's observation and explores how dreams of efficacious personhood, like nightmares of compromised subjectivity, imbricate the same spatiotemporal tension between aspirational horizons and their compromised conditions of mediation. At issue are the semiotic infrastructures that constitute affordances and "props" for the emergence and recruitment of both aspirational and available figures of personhood under conditions of twenty-first-century transnationalism.

Personhood—as analytical proposition—has become diffuse, stratified, and provincialized in many contemporary anthropologies of the Anthropocene (Haraway 2016; Tsing 2015; Latour 2005). Much of this literature inadvertently presumes dualisms between human vis-à-vis nonhuman, actant vis-à-vis network, and individual agency vis-à-vis social structure. Though much of this literature has often been understood as doing precisely the opposite, the contradictions of presupposing the object of negation—in this case the dualisms at issue— nonetheless protracts the discursive life of a given semantic tension. This is perhaps largely due to the ways in which elements that make up personhood's semiotic infrastructure—like language, media, and conditions of mobility—have been treated as discreet semantic problems requiring an endless divergence of methods as well as the compartmentalization of political engagements. As such, several disciplinary accounts of twentieth- and twenty-first-century social life—particularly those involving mobile subjects like migrants, global citizens, or refugees— often show little overlap between communicative practices, media landscapes, and conditions of mobility as integrated phenomena that impact contrapuntally, rather than unitarily, on their subjects' reception and legibility of being.[2]

This book is by no means solving that problem, but represents an attempt to situate personhood as neither an individuated social unit nor an overarching social, or even human, concept. Aligning with pragmatist and critical theoretical genealogies in contemporary anthropologies of personhood (Carr 2011; Comaroff 1999; Munn 1986), I understand personhood as the event, eventual, and eventuating horizon of reflexive social and intersubjective life. In this understanding, personhood entails time and place—historical and futurist; individual and collective; intimate and public; aspirational and traumatic. To demonstrate personhood's contingency on spatiotemporal contextualization necessitates an exploration of personhood as emergent and emerging—yet always relied upon as prior or above—within both durable social institutions as well as fleeting social interactions. Pursuing this imperative, I explore the contingency between personhood and space-time by reconciling three ethnographic dimensions of interaction—media propinquity, language, and conditions of mobility. What I term the Angloscene emerges at the confluence of these ethnographic dimensions, in face-to-face social interactions that must simultaneously presume upon available space-times of personhood, even while personhood is being remade through these interactions.

GETTING OFF THE OCCIDENTAL SCHOOL BUS

"What is that?" asked Eniola Eco, my classmate and a Nigerian international relations student at Da Hua University in Beijing. We were looking across a crowded intersection, having just come out of class for an off-campus lunch at a cut noodle (*dao xiao mian*) shop right around the corner. I followed Eniola's gaze to the other side of the road, but seeing nothing of particular interest, I replied, "What's up?"

"The bus," he answered. "Where have you ever seen one of those?" I understood at that moment that he was pointing toward an American-style yellow school bus, which did seem out of place in Beijing. I suggested that we walk across the road and take a look. As we did so, an enormous "ABCD English School" sign—emblazoned on the side of the bus—came into view. "That's ridiculous," he exclaimed, gesticulating with his open hands at the rainbow-colored papyrus font subtitling the photo of a blonde-haired, blue-eyed child spread across the side of the vehicle. "I used to work for those guys. They told me they were going bankrupt and let me go without paying me two months' salary. I guess I know where the money went."

Eniola's example is far from unique and reflects how many African students in Beijing face the somewhat paradoxical situation of being subjects of an alternative educational globalization—Sino-South rather than Euro-American—yet have to depend on the signs of English cultural capital to supplement university scholarships that often fall short of their financial expectations as newly "cosmopolitanized" international students.[3]

A number of western-based scholars have demonstrated how China is rapidly adopting an escalating horizon of expectation, aspiration, and desire.[4] The forms that this adoption might take have been vividly described in ethnographies of conspicuous consumption, the commodification of desire, the curbing of urban migrancy, and the branding of lifestyle, respectively. However, the English subtitles that accompany the reformulation of Chinese postsocialist modernity through many of these adoptions are less emphasized. Such adoptions include everything from the appropriations of English language as an auxiliary lingua franca for Chinese engagements with virtually all outsiders to English's textual rhetoric in a wide array of artistic and protest mediums. No doubt, China scholars will—and in some cases do—hold the opinion that the presence of signs of English and Englishness in China are superficial trappings with little ideological content—provincial even—in the context of a simultaneously "rising" and "deeply ancient" Sinosphere.[5]

Such a view betrays an unfortunate recruitment of Sino-exceptionalism that has become a feature of western China studies as well as several anthropologies of China that contextualize themselves within its intellectual tradition (an orientation formerly understood as Sinology). This Sino-exceptionalism can further be observed in a discursive double movement between Sino-exceptionalism and what Chinese anthropologist Mingming Wang (2014) has criticized as "Sinified" and "internal" Orientalisms in the context of the anthropology of China:

> Western anthropologists who study China have "Sinified" Orientalism. In the anthropology of China, the concept of "internal Orientalism" has become popular. Anthropologists who focus on studying the interrelationship between ethnic groups and the Han in China have begun investigating how popular discourses shape— e.g., feminize—the image of ethnic groups with romantic technologies of domination. They have taken important notes of certain "social facts" of representation, and argued for the critique of "internal othering." This kind of research is surely not trivial, but it does have certain obvious shortcomings. It, for instance, fails to acknowledge that Chinese "internal Orientalism" has always been derived from the conflation of the internal and external. (16)

Here, Sino-exceptionalism—as the dialectical shadow of Wang's broader discussion of Occidentalism—presupposes a bounded, inscrutable space-time within which an ideological Chineseness will easily and unproblematically encompass outside or foreign semiotic formations that enter it. The efficacy of Sino-exceptionalism within the matrix of western Sinology and area studies more generally depends on the selective canonization and recruitment of Chinese scholarship that perpetuates this exceptionalism. Such ethnographic materials then, as Wang suggests, adopt—while masquerading as evidence for—the western Orientalist gaze by both projecting it onto and confirming it within the Chinese academic context. Among many other problems, this discursive double movement depends on a "dilution" model of cultural/ semiotic interaction, as well as the maintenance of a world consisting of hermetically sealed, exceptional space-times, that remain inscrutable until rendered translatable within the "universal" archive of Sinology and area studies—something that cannot happen without the consent and ratification of "local" scholars seeking recognition in the elite journals of the academic Anglosphere.

In embracing China as a space of historical as well as contemporary contiguity and dynamic interaction with the Global South, what follows opposes Sino-exceptionalism and aligns with Wang's critique of the construction of China as a bounded territory and disciplinary exception. Wang suggests that this boundedness and exceptionalism is complicit in perpetuating rigid Occidental/Oriental divides that become impasses to accounts of historical and cultural interaction that fall outside of Eurocentric east-west binarisms: of which China-Africa encounters represent but one example. Thinking China in terms of its non-western others, however, requires taking seriously the mutual dependency on shared (or overlapping) discourses and broader contexts that might seem to undermine the very proposition of a genuinely postcolonial, non-western, condition of personhood promised by a Sino-South encounter.

TRANSLATING BEYOND POLITICAL MONOLINGUALISM

In the previous vignette, Eniola—like many other African educational migrants in Beijing—is compelled to teach English (in many cases illegally) in order to support a newly acquired, self-reportedly "cosmopolitan" lifestyle in China. This is a pattern for many African students studying in the Chinese capital. Thus, both the exploitation he described earlier as well as the political economy of language at play is far from unique among the increasing numbers of African students in Beijing and other major academic centers. In the first instance, teaching English to supplement studying Chinese in China has become a paradoxical feature of Sino-South educational globalization. In the second, having the capacity to speak English is often the only form of social currency that black African students in China have, as it becomes the means to both attain income—teaching in the English as a Foreign Language (EFL) market—as well as build friendships with cosmopolitan Chinese teachers, students, and other foreigners. Here, English is prevalent even in Chinese university settings, where increasing numbers of classes are being taught to African students who have been a more common presence on Chinese campuses since the first ministerial conference of the Forum on China Africa Cooperation (FOCAC) in 2000 (Bodomo 2012; King 2013). Even Francophone and Lusophone interviewees claimed that their English improved far more dramatically than their Chinese after becoming university students in Beijing. According to another informant—a French-speaking Malagasy economics major named Rousseau Bakoly—committing to English more than Chinese reaps benefits because "knowing English and some Chinese offers more opportunities for friendship than being really good at Chinese." According to him, having good English and some Chinese had the benefit of improving one's romantic prospects, as "many foreign girls only speak English [other than their native tongue], and many Chinese girls want to practice their English."

Beyond the common-sense assertion of Anglo-American soft power hegemony, we must ask: How does English persist as a currency mediating Sino-South encounters where the imbricated signs of English language-ness, cosmopolitanism, and whiteness become the favored forms of social capital among actors who have been historical others to the Anglosphere's racio-linguistic worlds? In exploring this question, we must reconsider literatures that have underlined the limits and pragmatics of postcolonial translation (Spivak 1993; Bhabha 1994, 1995; Bassnett and Trivedi 1999) particularly when the so-called neutrality of English becomes compromised by the ideological vectors of whiteness and cosmopolitan desire. In this genealogy of postcolonial theory, translation can be understood as an analogical shorthand for getting at the interested and unequal contingencies of postsocialist and postcolonial encounters that imbricate a double temporal consciousness. Because of the unequal situatedness of postcolonial subjects in relation to the historical and material afterlife of colonialism, translation—in this metaphorical sense—is not only a capacity that arises out of having to inhabit double-, or indeed multiple kinds of, consciousness. It arises from the constant burden of both postcolonial and still-colonized subjects to have to reconcile temporalities of history, language, and subjectivity to their still colonial audience.

Monolingualism, as a feature of the imagined audience of translation, (as in Benedict Anderson's [1983] literary public) places the burden of a disjunctive, lived counterpoint on the multilingual, usually colonized, translator. Ironically, however, it turns out to be the monolingual voyeur who then judges the translator's work, work that becomes simultaneously exploited and negated to present the smooth surfaces of a politically monolingual world. This is a point that has been compellingly raised by Daniel Vukovich in his *Illiberal China* (2019). Hence, the metaphor of translation does not fetishize language once we understand that the use of language is already at issue in making the very arguments for translation—the reflexivity that is immanent to translation is the reflexivity that is immanent in language itself. No forms of representation or reception—especially those reflexively about representation and reception (like this sentence)—can unfold without mediation. The point that any abstract formulation depends on fetishistic, sensorially perceivable materializations—like sign-able, audible, or entextualized language—to talk about abstractions or fetishes, was already explicit in Karl Marx's (1972) own insistence on immanent critique. Instead, the metaphor of translation—in postcolonial theory—draws attention not only to the double burden of translating and translational personhood on the part of the colonized, but also the double burden of time travel—or living in a counterpoint between unequal social histories—that remains a feature of the persistent historical precarity of postcolonial subjectivity.

To think that postcolonial concerns are absent in the context of contemporary Afro-Chinese interactions would be both intellectually naïve and historically ignorant. At the same time, to take China as a simplistic proxy for a historical trend set in motion by Euro-American colonialism would also be to reduce colonialism to a game of leveraging power and extracting resources, without asking what conditions of value and imagined subjectivity drive these historical-material and discursive processes: be they explicit power grabs or the more insidious effects of endless accumulation. As English-teaching fuels African students' attempts at attaining cosmopolitan dreams in China, Chinese development bank personnel and government officials overseeing Global South investments in Africa, Asia, and Latin America are increasingly recruited out of the law and business schools of Oxbridge and the Ivy Leagues. Just as archetypes of cosmopolitan personhood are less hospitable to black bodies as a result of decades of American soft power, Beijing's attempts to place Chinese soft power on an equal footing frequently fail due to English and Mandarin Chinese occupying radically different international positions of influence. China, unlike its Anglosphere counterparts, must often work through English translation when engaging other non-western interlocutors. In light of this situation, and in relation to what will follow, the perspective that languages and the conditions of possibility for any translation are populated by the people who maintain them will become evident to the reader if it is not so already. Yet most of us seldom have this immediate intuition due to the fact that language, history, conditions of mass-mediation, as well as our available forms of personhood are always experienced as prior to or above us (Inoue 2006; Agha 2007a; Carr 2011).

To analytically demonstrate the contingencies of personhood and space-time in the contemporary dialectics of postcolonial translation, it is imperative to give an account of the ways in which certain kinds of marginal subjects—non-white, second-language English speakers—are unequally burdened by having to undertake multiple and transtemporal participant roles. The designers of the *China Exploratorium* must not only motivate China's relevance in the world, but must do so for a default English-literate audience. The pragmatic effects of historically plural subjectivity and its unequally distributed burden should not be undermined by positing the "facticity" of linear historical experience: as in a historical chain-of-being argument where China can unproblematically supplant Euro-American colonialism while conveniently eliding its own prior emplacement as civilizationally inferior to "the modern west."[6] This is especially the case in situations where different sets of interlocutors become stratified in relation to mediums of participation and their imbricated, transnational framing: for instance, Chinese and African subjects mediating their mutual encounters through English, and in relation to divergent and unequal space-times of racialized historical colonialism as well as the fantastic utopic imaginary of unmarked cosmopolitan futurity.

CHRONOTOPE AND ANGLOSCENE

It is this articulated relationship between English and its associated signs of race, cosmopolitanism, and mobility that I wish to term the Angloscene. In unpacking the dimensions of the Angloscene, I find Mikhail Bakhtin's (1981) concept of the chronotope to be useful. In his essay *Forms of Time and of the Chronotope in the Novel*, he emphasized language's capacity to evoke space-time via the reading subject's ability to embody different times and places from those that they inhabited at the moment of reading. For Bakhtin, a genre of language (or mutually intelligible sign system) could act as an intimate teleportation device that allows the reader to access remote fictional or historical worlds. In defining chronotopes, he was attempting to articulate the immersive or teleportational propensity of language-based worlds, existing as entextualized space-times within novels and other text artifacts. Importantly for Bakhtin, the embodied intimacy of the chronotope was also of a publicly shareable and accessible kind, given the fact that chronotopes were intelligible to the very publics they addressed, while being formed and maintained by these self-same publics. This publicly shareable and socially maintained dimension of chronotopic affinities and affordances is often overlooked in literary studies that deploy the chronotope merely as a means of foregrounding the novel and other entextualizable forms of art as social and political artifacts. However, we can go much further. Bakhtin's more neglected concept, heteroglossia, enables an enriched understanding of how chronotopes emerge in institutionalized social settings—like the publishing houses, circles of literary criticism, national broadcasters, and state-regulated curriculums of his day. I encountered two such settings during my own fieldwork: the Hanban headquarters as well as the Central Party School, both of which are in Beijing.

In the case of the Hanban, I was able to visit on my own thanks to the generous introduction and facilitation through a Chinese professor and friend—as well as a former Hanban official—who arranged for me to meet and interview another Hanban official, Hong, who was in charge of curriculum development for Confucius Institute materials. I met Hong Laoshi (Teacher Hong) at the Hanban headquarters in Beijing, accompanied by a Chinese graduate student intern who was meant to facilitate my passage through the massive building. Upon arrival, I was taken directly to Hong Laoshi's office and tea was brought in. It was established that I was a South African graduate student without ties to the United States. Having undertaken this disambiguation ritual a few times, I indicated that my concerns were Afro-China oriented, but coming from an Afro-centric perspective. She emphasized that the Hanban and its CIs prioritized Sino-African and inter-Asian cultural and educational exchange. We talked about whether language education could ever be undertaken without ideological and cultural exchange and agreed that this was impossible. I then asked why she thought that some people believed this—thinking of an example in my home country where the head of a China studies department rumored to be in an adversarial relationship with its Confucius Institute was adamant that there was no conflict given that their department worked on political and economic matters, and the CI worked on linguistic and cultural matters. Responding to the question, Hong Laoshi stated carefully: "I think that would be an incorrect perception." Our meeting concluded once Hong Laoshi had asked me how CIs were received in South Africa, to which I answered honestly: "Quite differently from the US."

I then was taken to a different area where I was shown an archive of materials that CIs were distributing to their centers around the world. There was a collection of language textbooks translated into over a dozen different languages, placed on shelves under a large banner in English and Chinese which read: "Culture / *wenhua*." I was then led to another exhibit space, the China Exploratorium, which has been somewhat succinctly described by Jennifer Hubbert in the following way: "The first stop on the Chinese Bridge program's tour of Beijing was a trip to Hanban headquarters. . . . In the 'Exploratorium' section, an instructional space that resembled US children's museums by offering opportunities for hands-on manipulation of artifacts and computerized lessons on history, students could don Beijing opera costumes, manipulate beads on a massive abacus, make paper and print a book, and view ink-brush paintings, all either common symbols of traditional Chinese culture or recognized examples of historically advanced technological accomplishments" (2019, 85).

As Hubbert suggests, the space was a multisensory exhibit featuring objects, textures, images, and imaginaries of various regions in China. Up until that point, I had not traveled much in China, nor did I have a reference point for the scale of CI activities in different places. Though China is undoubtedly vast and diverse, and CI transnational activities could hardly be accounted for in a single exhibit, both the "culture" room and the Exploratorium are expected to function like chronotopes within which material culture and language can be synthesized under the rubric of a singular state project. In this way, the Hanban shares many similarities with the selective archive of a multinational university, the Goethe Institute curriculum, or the South Korean national museum.

The chronotopic functioning of such institutions is contingent upon their maintenance through language and participation in the institution on the part of a vast number of stakeholders. Hong Laoshi and I are not equal participants in the maintenance of the Hanban participation framework, but the salience of the institution very much depends on our chronotopic calibration through this interaction and many more like it. The feature of language that enables this calibration, Bakhtin reminds us, is heteroglossia, which can be understood as the feature of communication that permits mutual intelligibility: the element of unoriginality and familiarity that underpins every seemingly "new" or "novel" message. The fact that language is already shared, and that all expressive potentials are immanent in it, mean that the poet relies on the unoriginality of language to make their original permutations intelligible. What makes a poetic contribution original then is a combination of unoriginality and the unfolding and nonpermanent universe within which chronotopes cycle through unfolding into flesh and evaporating into oblivion. It is institutionalized intersubjective labor that enables the heteroglossic maintenance of always historical chronotopes against the erasures of "becoming."[7]

This relationship between heteroglossia and chronotopic formation was potently foregrounded in a different context, the Central Party School (CPS). The CPS is the premier educational center for elite cadres of the Communist Party of China and serves as a significant intellectual archive and training ground for members of its Central Committee. The CPS, in collaboration with the Central Compilation and Translation Bureau (CCTB), oversee canonical interpretations of Marxist and Hegelian thought, as well as their ideological calibration with Xi Jinping thought, Dengism, and Maoist reform. As a member of an interdisciplinary and international delegation of mostly American and Chinese social science PhD candidates from US universities, I found myself fortunate enough to enter the CPS campus and meet with some of the faculty and translators from both institutions. Having been screened in advance of the visit, we relinquished our phones, passports, and recording devices before entering a minimally furnished but beautiful seminar room: lacquered wooden surfaces, porcelain cups with old propaganda slogans, and two prominently placed sets of calligraphy on the walls of the seminar room. The professor casually remarked that these were the penmanship of Deng Xiaoping and Mao Zedong. Fragrant Longjing tea was served and we settled in for a long discourse that sutured Hegelian and Xi Jinping thought, reconciling continuous revolutions all the way down to the present—"we are on track with our party's socialist vision" and "[despite many challenges] things are [and have been] getting better." Such seamless suturing and reconciliation is profoundly dependent on the interdiscursive recruitment of the chronotopic potentials of the props in the room and the dramatic staging of the visit. This chronotopic interplay of co-texts permit transhistorical materializations in the present that further presume upon a familiar contextualizing language: modes of speaking and co-textual signification that articulate (in the sense of "gluing") aesthetic and linguistic registers of socialist internationalism for the right kind of receptive listener. Notably, it is not the objects of language that evoke transhistorical or transgeographical breaching of space-time, but rather their embodiments and resonances with already familiar incorporations.

What I call the Angloscene extends this principle of trans-spatiotemporal incorporation, recognizing that chronotopes depend on, while also being depended on, as sites for the production and maintenance of personhood. As such, chronotopes can never be political vacuums. The capacity to produce and depend on them can favor some, while compromising others. This prompts us to understand the Angloscene as itself a meta- or macro-chronotope: a broader or encompassing ideological space-time that constrains the indexicalities (context-defining propensities) of chronotopes emerging within or in relation to it. In this sense, the Angloscene can be understood as recruiting chronotopic capacities, including the desires of subjects, in the service of generating nexuses of alienation and dependency that entail, and are entailed by, the ideological interplay of English, cosmopolitan mobility, and white space-time. The Angloscene is thus a material and ideological affordance for generating certain conditions of personhood, while itself depending on persons for its maintenance.

In understanding the Angloscene through the lens of the chronotope, I hope to suggest the ways in which "English-language-ness" and "cosmopolitan desire"— as contrapuntally converging space-times (simultaneously distinct and mutually convergent)—come to pragmatically entail an ideological landscape that forms the context in relation to which Chinese and African students must generate or discover their affordances for mutual personhood.

To be sure, my use of Angloscene *does* gesture phonetically toward the popular iterations of "-cene" that have come to problematize historicity and contemporaneity within a recent species-oriented paradigmatic shift in Euro-American anthropology. However, I favor "-scene" as a suffix that immanently understands interactions and mediation as constitutive of personhood. The difference between -cene and -scene is one of spatialized, bounded time that is more or less indifferent to people and personhood; versus a more dynamic interplay between the reflexive capacities of personhood and the mutual contingencies of space-time. For there is no personhood without space-time and no space-time without reflexive personhood. In sociologist Erving Goffman's dramaturgical theory of interaction, for instance, we may understand scenes as recruiting personhood and personhood as depending on scenes (1959). Similarly, for Frantz Fanon—a trans-Atlantic contemporary of Goffman's—postcolonial personhood and the space-time of colonial trauma are mutually constitutive within the colonial *socius* (Fanon [1952] 2008, 84–85). What is at stake for myself and these thinkers is not a vulgar human-centrism. In the work of Goffman and Fanon, as well as generations of Durkheimian interlocutors from Marcel Mauss (1985) to Jean and John Comaroff (1999), it emerges fairly emphatically that personhood is not reducible to categories like human and posthuman. Of course, this insight has been a mainstream common sense in legal and juridical settings where institutions like corporations have been afforded the status of persons. Situating this move in an older sociological language, I suggest that a scenic view of personhood suspends the concept of the human as a settled formation; and instead posits that nature and posthumanity are unthinkable propositions without the reflexive capacities that can be identified within the interstices of personhood and space-time. The scenic view I am proposing is one where personhood is simultaneously unsettled as a stable semantic formation, while recognizing personhood's pragmatic efficacy as a project that semantic, ethical, phenomenological, and materialist endeavors as social commitments depend upon. Among African students in China, for instance, the ideal African person that must emerge out of Chinese education is not entirely known. This semantic gap, however, does not paralyze African subjects in their attempts to make personhood in a new context—even if it requires them to pragmatically repurpose or reuse a combination of older and available props to make new persons while citing older scenes. Deconstruction and translational nihilism are not options for subjects who must motivate a pragmatic, intelligible personhood even if it comes at the cost of significant historical and contemporary compromises.

Rather, Anglocentric icons of value and their cosmopolitan co-texts appear to be both the signs through which to achieve some degree of financial and social mobility, as well as the conditions constraining African cultural capital in a Chinese social landscape. The way in which these signs and co-texts of Englishness hang together as evocative of a broadly cosmopolitan personhood are suggestive of a space-time populated by interacting types of persons where these very signs and co-texts have meaning, value, and efficacy. In Afro-Chinese Beijing, the Angloscene emerges as a chronotope of intersubjective personhood that sustains the meanings, values, efficacies of English signs and their co-texts. Here, the Angloscene is not a synonym for English lingua franca as just another form of cultural capital. Rather, it contests the understanding of English as a bounded, arbitrary manifestation of shifting historical power relations indifferent to the ideological particularities of language and its contexts—where the Angloscene is the condition of possibility for English to be understood as more than *langue* and *parole* (Saussure 2011). As a nexus between ideology, personhood, and language, the Angloscene affords English a materiality, spatiotemporality, and social domain, allowing English to not only transcend its taxonomy as a language among languages, but also its range as the disinterested communicative interface among non-western others. It is through the broader domain of the Angloscene that English is able to entail its space-time and particular affordances of subjectivity. In all these senses, the Angloscene emerges as a less benign iteration of what anthropologist Nancy Munn might have once termed an intersubjective space-time (1986). Similarly, however, space-time and personhood are mutually contingent conditions for the valuation and enactment of cultural capital in the case of the Angloscene.

NO ENGLISH, NO WORRIES

In the context of Afro-Chinese encounters in Beijing, the Angloscene's spatiotemporal and intersubjective propensities are particularly pronounced. In addition to allowing Rousseau, Eniola, and many like them to overcome social isolation and access short-term economic opportunities in China, many African students suggested that mastery of English enabled academic access, allowing my informants to take "better courses" from "international scholars" at their Beijing universities. Many complained, however, that the Chinese language classes offered at their universities—at many top-tier institutions in Beijing—were inadequate because of large student numbers and a lack of conversation practice in class (often numbering over thirty students). After sitting in on a few classes with Rousseau, and watching a somewhat harassed-looking female Chinese teacher trying to motivate over seventy African and other foreign students to repeat phrases from a conversation book, I came to understand his apprehension. His teacher, Liu Laoshi, shared apprehensions of her own. She too felt that the mass-education she was providing for the foreign students was ineffective. In an interview, she stated that the "classroom environment [provided] no opportunity for feedback . . . you can't surpass the affective threshold." In using the terms "feedback" and "affective threshold," Liu Laoshi demonstrated a background in teaching English as a Foreign Language (EFL). This is unsurprising since many Chinese teachers who specialize in Chinese Foreign Language (CFL) education also teach English as a Foreign Language, as EFL has been the primary model for CFL training. English grammar and other language terms also make up the default reflexive register for teaching Chinese language points to foreign students of Chinese, which means that every student learning Chinese and every teacher teaching it must work through English as a default pedagogical language. Liu Laoshi would later take a teaching position at a private language education company teaching Chinese to smaller groups of mostly white expat students in the east of Beijing, describing her move as having "been promoted." In retrospect, there was certainly a stark contrast between her new four-person conversation classes, and the lecture hall of her former university job—the intimate, well-equipped "first-world" classroom at the top of a corporate building versus the cold, dusty "third-world dungeon" where she was getting a chorus of students to yell out a cacophony of Chinese tones augmented by the concrete and plastic surfaces of the overcrowded, neon-lit space. As I came to discover, however, it was not only the Chinese classes at Rousseau's and Eniola's universities that presented obstacles to a first-world educational imaginary.

Over three years of ethnographic research as a student, mentor, and colleague among African students and Chinese educational personnel, I came to understand that "better courses" by "international scholars"—at institutions like Dahua University—presented their own contradictions. At this elite university, I sat in on an international relations class (offered in English). The class consisted of around thirty students, the majority of whom were Chinese, with around a third of the class being made up of foreigners—most coming from South Korea and African countries. Eniola was attending this class and attempted to ask the instructor a number of questions about the professor's PowerPoint presentation. After two questions, the instructor—a Chinese male in his late forties—gave Eniola a nonplussed look. He then responded by indulgently replaying the PowerPoint slides that might somehow prompt revelation, much to the exasperated sighs of the rest of the class. After this happened a second time, however, the professor promised to send Eniola and the rest of the class the lecture notes. Eniola stopped asking questions at this point, but approached the professor at the end of the lecture, worried about whether he understood the class, much of which appeared to be explained in Chinese as a supplement to the reading of the English presentation. The teacher, who appeared to be in a hurry, tried to put Eniola at ease by saying in both English and Chinese, "Don't worry, *meiguanxi*," before heading back to his office. In many instances like this, Chinese professors who are not comfortable with English are put in a position where they have to augment their credentials as international scholars to maintain academic positions that are extremely precarious—driven not only by a demand for international education, which they must supply, but also by the unthinkability of an international education without English . . . even when virtually no English is being conveyed or understood. To be sure, many instructors are able to conduct research and read in English, but are uncomfortable fielding questions and verbally engaging students that speak a variety of different "Englishes" with accents and registers that are difficult to contextualize. I noted that this was a problem even for Chinese lecturers who had attained academic English fluency in British and American settings, where anything that deviated from an acquired standard became unintelligible.

Nonetheless, in these interactions, students, teachers, and professors come to rely on English as lending legitimacy to the "international" education that their universities offer, as well as their future cosmopolitan aspirations. Here, the delicate work of promoting an international education rests not only on the mobilization of English as a unit of commensuration, but also on the signs of cosmopolitan aspiration that accrue around English in Sino-African encounters like this. This necessitates an interplay between explicit processes of entextualization and contextualization, where the contextualization of English—what is done with it—simultaneously supersedes and supercharges its entextualization—what is said with it (M. Silverstein 2014). For Mikhail Bakhtin, this simultaneity rests on a curious semiotic phenomenon: the meanings that accrue around signs—always understood to be intersubjective and dialogical—appear to simultaneously recruit and constitute past meanings, "taking on flesh" that appears to be both emergent in the here-and-now, and familiar in the sense of drawing on a shared past. Bakhtin's formalist theory of language further posits that because of this propensity, textual objects, like novels, are just one kind of linguistic artifact that in themselves form a very small part of a semiotic landscape that is contingent on the reception and production practices of a public totality of language speakers. Language, for Bakhtin, becomes a political site of social production and revolution because of its imbricated semiotic co-texts and contexts—or co(n)texts (1981).

Our contemporary moment explicates these political and public contingencies of language: where the simultaneous co-texts of social- or mass-media contiguity and their associated live-stream of discourse and commentary come to both intertwine and amplify public intimacies of social movements like migration, mobility, and expulsion. The co-textual and the contextual portability of the language that connects conditions of mobility and mass-mediation to histories and futures populated by aspirational and traumatized persons, in this way, is very much at issue in understanding global contradictions between public knowledge about alienating forms of social movement, on the one hand, and concrete political action based on that knowledge, on the other.

In this vein, English's relationship to its co(n)texts imbricates ideological forces that appear to both liberate and constrain Chinese and African interlocutors in their contemporary encounters. The co(n)texts of English, in this case, may include cosmopolitanism, international education, as well as imagined white bodies that constitute English's ideal inhabitants. These signs, I suggest, hang together in such a way that their ideological relationships both constitute and are constituted in the interactional here-and-now of Sino-African encounters. But what makes such signs "hang together" in this way? Bakhtin suggests that the condition of possibility for such constitutive and constituting relations between signs to emerge—understood as a socially ubiquitous phenomenon—is an intersubjective capacity to construct and depend on semiotic nexuses of spatiotemporal relations in our meaningful engagements with the material universe. In other words, constitutive and constituting meanings of signs are contingent on a simultaneous semiotic construction of space-time—a kind of ideological gravity for signs to have reinforcing meanings to subjects that depend on them. Through this interplay between signs and their associated personhoods, written and spoken forms of English, as well as nonverbal communicative acts (such as flipping through PowerPoint slides), can be mobilized in a given context to evoke an "international standard" as opposed to the, at times farcical, attempt at mass education purely in Chinese. This is a fraught endeavor that many aspirational cosmopolitan Chinese and African actors remain committed to, regardless of constant failure. Rousseau, Eniola, and their teachers—for better or worse—are in this endeavor together. They are precariously dependent on and are constrained by their commitment to the Angloscene. How does one then understand the seeming contradiction of coming to depend on English and its signs of social currency as a supplement to Chinese soft power in the form of scholarships and aid that initially bring African students to China?

HORIZONS OF ANGLO-AMERICAN MALWARE

The apparent durability of the Angloscene and its associated, necessarily racialized, "cosmopolitanism" explicates a number of the contradictions inherent in recent criticisms of Chinese soft power as they emanate from academic and media contexts in the western Anglosphere (Sahlins 2015). Among African students attending elite Chinese universities, third-world cosmopolitanism—indexing a collective historical "third-world solidarity" struggle—is meant to encompass a broader encounter and aspiration toward an alternative, non-Anglo-global common of the kind that a number of African anti-colonial and postcolonial thinkers have called for (Fanon [1952] 2008, 1963; Baldwin 1963; Biko 1978; Mbembe

2001). At present, the escalating educational migrancy from Africa to China is unprecedented not because of the encounter of African students with the Chinese education system. This has a far older history (Hevi 1963; Snow 1989). Rather, the escalation appears to have generated an unease—arising predominantly in the west—about a perceived counterpoint between China's augmented prominence in global and soft power economies and a rapidly emerging, Chinese-educated African elite public. Disassociating themselves—often dismissively—from their "trader" counterparts in southern China, I have observed how many African students in Beijing attempt to perform or translate their position as members of a China-based, globally oriented Pan-African elite public sphere.

In this light, however, it must be understood that the particular kind of Pan-Africanism one encounters in China arises in the context of vast numbers of African students not only attending classes together but also rooming together in university dorms, often finding themselves in African university communities numbering in the thousands on some campuses. As a result of being segregated from Chinese and often other western students (a common placement policy on Chinese campuses), African students form intercampus networks facilitated by the close proximity between universities in Beijing. This process is further ampli-fied through convenient Chinese social media networking interfaces like WeChat (Weixin), which I will briefly discuss later. As such, a climate of expansive—even at times volatile—Afrocentrism, -culturalism, or -nationalism frequently sub-sumes any interest in Chinese language and educational immersion. Although many students seeking an immersive experience do exist, they often find that the endeavor is a lonely one, requiring a commitment to compartmentalizing their social and solitary identities. In expressing this social dimension, many infor-mants feel intense pressure to exude an English-inflected cosmopolitanism to their Chinese and non-Anglophone African peers, while using Chinese or other African languages among themselves to internally put down or generate complex plays of one-upmanship. Linguistic hierarchies enter into a polyphonic relation-ship with other semiotic vectors, like media genres, political and entertainment icons, nationalism, gender hierarchy, personal histories, and various forms of racism. What regulates, arbitrates, or renders these vectors as translatable is an inter-relationship between discourses of race, language, and mobility. The Anglo-scene emerges immanently—even while it appears to exist prior to, above, or with-out—at the nexus of this inter-relationship: as a space-time of commensuration where a diffuse notion of aspirational mobility becomes the end goal of not only African, but also Chinese educational labor in China. From this standpoint, Chinese and African student life as well as outlook—especially in contexts like Beijing—become impossible to disentangle in moments of interaction where mul-tiple horizons of "cosmopolitanism" appear to converge at once.

While aligning with practice-based (Bourdieu [1986] 2011) and performative (Butler 1999) theories of personhood, the Angloscene strongly emphasizes that the maintenance and historical recruitment of personhood cannot unfold without spatiotemporal contingencies and the pliability of semiotic infrastructures. Such maintenance and recruitment certainly depends on the discursively limited availability of signs—in the case of performativity—and on the limiting contingency of hegemonic forms of cultural capital—in the case of practice. However, I want to get away from the idea that signs and forms of capital in themselves *cause* people and chronotopes. This is not what Bourdieu (1977) or Butler (1999) have argued. The imaginary provocation of signs-cause-people as a counter to an equally imaginary orthodoxy of people-cause-signs is an unfortunate unidirectional folk intuition that goes against reflexive formulations of these thinkers. This is an unfortunate symptom of an emerging intellectual subculture, within which much contemporary academic writing depends on professionally elegant but intellectually truncated expression. Writing against a unidirectional relationship between signs and personhood, I put it to the reader that: on the one hand, signs and forms of cultural capital can only be efficacious within accommodating affordances of space-time and horizons of personhood, while on the other, these very spatiotemporal accommodations and horizons of personhood cannot be dialectically mediated without the signs and forms of cultural capital they also afford. For instance, African imaginaries of Chineseness, and Chinese imaginaries of African-ness are difficult to conceptualize outside of imported imaginaries of orientalism and primitivism that must be recruited from outside the Sino-African encounter so as to be reconstituted within it. And yet, the fact of a Sino-African encounter—and the need for intelligible horizons personhood to populate its past, present, and future—is inescapable.

An important example of this compromised contingency emerges in David Borenstein's recent short documentary on foreigner-renting in China, which appeared in the *New York Times*.[8] It reflected how, in order to add value to property prices in the increasingly prevalent context of ghost cities, Chinese real estate moguls have begun recruiting foreign bodies, which through their copresence are meant to make a property or building seem "more desirable." What is telling in the documentary—and was also confirmed by a Zimbabwean informant who was once hired as a drummer by one of these companies—is how black bodies, while still suggestive of foreignness, nonetheless signify a "less expensive" foreignness than their white counterparts. Here, signs of whiteness and Englishness are fundamentally intertwined, given the now well-documented example of African students pursuing English teaching jobs, where many are overlooked in favor of whiter applicants regardless of their lack of English-speaking ability. These are often white foreigners, who are not English first-language speakers, but come from countries like Russia, Spain, and Germany. Thus, from the perspective of many African learners, Chinese cosmopolitanism's horizon of expectation emerges increasingly in English subtitles with white characteristics. Of course, this observation doesn't detract from, and is certainly experienced in counterpoint with, the daily reality of student life in Beijing.

As African students arrive in the Chinese metropole, to an environment that requires a facility with Chinese that vastly transcends their one or two years of textbook training in their home countries, the only legible categories are the occasional "English" signs of value that protrude like stepping stones on a seemingly fathomless sea of (initially) illegible characters, interactions, and objects. However precarious their footholds might be, they appear like an oasis compared to the often brutal negotiation of infrastructure, bureaucracy, and social media—all predominantly in Chinese, with (in most cases) very little preparation before coming to China. It quickly becomes apparent that these luminous signs of the Angloscene are connected to a vast education industry in China. One thinks here of institutions like New Oriental (Xindongfang) and increasingly prevalent lookalikes, indexing a privileged world of English-language abilities and American universities as the aspirational end-goal of Chinese educational labor. This domain of consumption is evidenced by the relentless emergence of all manner of arcades (online and on every block) that foreground the images of entrepreneurs and celebrities like Yao Ming—in his role as the exemplary subject of English learning—and Kai-Fu Lee, one of a number of figures who have increasingly come to embody American educational aspiration. These individuals, once rendered into archetypes of aspiration through a multifaceted media assemblage, come to merge with popular representations of Steve Jobs and George Clooney, for example, as the iconic distillations of a situated horizon of expectation and personhood. But, how do such associations emerge, and how do African students engage them in China?

Perhaps a clue arises in the ways that emanations of the Angloscene come to predominate in any meaningful interaction between Chinese and African cosmopolitans—where such interactions must be regulated and made legible in English, in relation to the ideological ontology the Anglosphere encomapsses. Rather than through the mere centrality of spoken English in Chinese-African student encounters, or the artifacts of cultural capital that index the Anglosphere's particular flavor of "Europe," the Angloscene is a space-time that orders and gives ideological gravity to such tokens within its orbit of typification. This ordering and typification can be demonstrated through the ways in which African students engage, or perhaps participate in, the maintenance of the Angloscene through their linguistically and technologically mediated practices of spatiotemporal evocation. Paradoxically, the appropriations of chronotopes of the Angloscene—cosmopolitan performances, ways of speaking, and strategic recruitments of an international (white) gaze through combining signs of English and unmarked cosmopolitanism—appear to generate obstacles to African students' self-making labor, while simultaneously becoming prostheses that must be depended upon to, as some informants phrased it: "translate China" or at least make themselves legible within it.

JUSTIN BIEBER'S UNDERPANTS

"I don't get it!" exclaimed Lerato Thulo, a South African accountancy major at Beijing's Daji University. We were having a coffee together at the Sculpting In Time chain in Haidian's EC mall. It's the kind of space that a variety of migrants in Beijing flock to, where their buying power can supplant the "problematic worlds" their accents and appearances might otherwise index. She was following a WeChat feed on her phone where someone had posted an article that condemned China's human rights record in light of a recent execution of a South African expatriate found guilty of drug trafficking. The group chat, which I also had access to, was the Azanian Students in China (ASIC) WeChat group. As we both read the discussion thread, we realized, all of a sudden, that a censor had deleted the student's post after a few minutes. This sparked a debate about censorship among the students, some seeing this as a "violation of free speech," while others regarded it as "an appropriate measure" that "perhaps should be implemented in South Africa." Interestingly, this last comment was referencing a discussion a few days prior about the problematic role the media in South Africa played with regard to African and race politics in general. As we read the comments and laughed at some of the more animated flourishes, Lerato continued, "Why do [the Chinese] have to take shit from America anyway? They make everything, but they have some white guy wearing CK underpants meant for Chinese customers." She was referring here to Justin Bieber's partially nude image in one of Calvin Klein's 2014 advertising campaigns, which we had made fun of earlier for taking up almost forty square meters of a shop window in the mall.

Here, the interaction between two South Africans engaging the media contexts of familiar debates in our home country combined with the familiar, all-commensurating texture of the transglobal mall and its universally cosmopolitan coffee shop evokes another space-time that momentarily displaces that of Beijing. Through our communication-in-context, otherwise "neutral" signs become reconstituted through their recruitment in the interaction. The dulcet tones of "Blue in Green" from Miles Davis's *Kind of Blue* album, the familiar flavors of coffee and cheesecake, the mutual legibility of the tones of our respective South African accents, even the image of Justin Bieber all coalesce to allow us, for a moment, to forget the ten grammar points and forty new characters we had to learn for the following day's quiz, or possibly the inevitable hassle of yet another visa renewal at the Entry and Exit Bureau the following week. No tokens of the Angloscene have an essential character that allows them to be *translated* as such. They come to work in this way through an interaction, and through their received and reconstituted arrangements during the unfolding of intersocial space-time. It is this process of contextualization that allows the experience of a concatenation of total sensory worlds all to be relied upon to temporarily anesthetize—through sensory distraction—the experience of Beijing. The associations together—generating an intersocial chronotope between Lerato and myself—affording the Sculpting In Time cafe a synesthetic time machine–like propensity. Through occasional meetings in such spaces, and the recombination of many of these indexicalities, otherwise mundane coffee shops can be transformed into space-times of recuperation for many beleaguered international or aspirationally cosmopolitan subjects seeking recourse from various hostilities or discomforts experienced in classrooms, offices, and even factories. In many cases, they become anesthetically dependable infrastructure.

But what manner of dependency does this distraction and anesthesia engender exactly? The intelligibility of the signs in question and their personal associations, accumulated through our respective spatiotemporal trajectories up until that moment, relies precisely upon their ubiquity—their postcolonial heteroglossia (Bakhtin 1981). Our very register of mutual interaction is a default first language—the ever-present commonality among postcolonial multilinguals without mother tongues. This spatiotemporal displacement and reconstruction, as a form of anesthesia, makes explicit the Angloscene's entailed compromise. In reducing intensity, it potentially paralyzes awareness. It is here, where the Angloscene emerges, where the nexus of our respective, potentially very different receptions of "common" yet plural spatiotemporal experiences down to the present converge to evoke our partially shared chronotopes of the Angloscene. It is a pluralistic index of our contrapuntal colonial and postcolonial alignments emergent in our interaction and shared experience. For this reason, the mall and all the potentially chronotopic props it contains can never be a nonspace to an African student in Beijing, even if it is a space of temporary forgetting (Augé 1995). However, emerging from this anesthetic dimension of the Angloscene, as I will now show, can be somewhat jarring.

As we were leaving the mall, Lerato and I saw more than twenty young Chinese men and women wearing suits and carrying brochures for Wall Street English, an English education company with branches throughout the world. The brochures were offering GRE and TOEFL preparation in addition to regular English classes. Lerato looked at one of the leaflets being distributed and addressed a young female sales representative in relatively fluent Chinese: "Yīnwèi wǒ shuō Yīngwén fēicháng liúlì, suǒyǐ nǐ juédé wǒ néng qù Měiguó ma?"—"Do you think that, just because I can speak English, I will be able to go to the US [to study]?" This was followed by a rhetorical interrogative: "Huh?" Whether, due to her pronunciation, additional phonemes, somewhat accusatory approach, or possibly even a mixture of confusion and embarrassment on the part of her interlocutor, the Chinese sales representative stared at the South African awkwardly and didn't say anything. At that point Lerato, looking somewhat incensed since reading the pamphlet, turned to me and dismissively stated: "See, even if you speak Chinese to them, they don't want to understand." The exchange was concluded with an exasperated click of the tongue on the part of Lerato—"*Xh!*" (kǁʰ)—accompanied by a "waving-off" gesture.[9]

In a subsequent interview, it emerged that Lerato's frustration stemmed—on the one hand—from what she saw as a misguided commitment to western education on the part of her Chinese interlocutors: "English isn't enough to get you into Oxford, otherwise, why am I here?" On the other, it stemmed from what she perceived as being negated as a "low-quality [black] foreigner" when, from her perspective, she had already mastered a skill—in this case, English—which "[all Chinese] see as a golden ticket," but which hasn't helped her at all. For Lerato, and many other African students in China, it is quite obvious that, while they are embracing the possibility of an alternative Sino-African globalization, their Chinese peers seem to be moving in a different direction by chasing the branded emblems of Harvard, Yale, or Stanford emblazoned on every institution that promises a shortcut to global educational excellence. In leaving an Anglocentric world, particularly in the case of Anglophone African students, they come to encounter one that embraces not only the language, but also the cultural capital of a world within which blackness and African-ness continue to be liabilities (Mbembe 2001; Bodomo 2020). It is here where the commitment to a shared alignment with the Angloscene paradoxically fails to ease discomfort, yet continues to render paralysis.

ENGLISH AS A LIFE RAFT

Toward the latter part of my fieldwork, I received a message that would suggest the existential limits of the Angloscene. Via an anonymous China-Africa student network, I received the following email from a contact traveling around eastern China:

> I thought I would share a little news with you. Currently, I am writing to you from Hangzhou, where I have just arrived by speed train following a "crisis call" from another African student there. He is a gay Senegalese who is unable to go home to renew his visa because he [fears imprisonment] on the basis of his sexuality. The Chinese LGBTQ community has arranged short-term solutions for him but can do very little following recent amendments to Chinese immigration law. Because of these sudden changes in policy, it is virtually impossible for Africans from any country to renew their visas without going back to their home countries. They are forbidden from renewing anywhere else. As a result, he faces Chinese prison if he overstays his visa, and because of his citizenship, he can go to very few other places in the world for longer than two weeks. He is now awaiting a French consular official's evaluation of his case to see if he qualifies for refugee status in France . . . we will know his fate in a few days.

Soon after receiving this, I was introduced to Damien, the subject of this exchange, and we secretly met a few months later near the West Lake in Hangzhou. After a long discussion where he described the ways in which China and a Chinese education were the conditions of possibility for the exploration of his sexuality, and following an elaboration on some of the details in the correspondence, he finally told me what he was doing in Hangzhou. "You have to understand," he explained in a heavy Francophone accent, "English saved my life." Teaching English illegally, it turned out, had kept him afloat for almost a year, but the period for renewing his Chinese visa had arrived and, at the time of writing, a new set of visa laws for Africans were instituted barring those in mainland China from renewing their visas anywhere other than in their home countries. For Damien to return home would mean arrest upon arrival because of the fact that his parents, who were government officials, had already reported him to the authorities there. English teaching had indeed saved his life, but only temporarily. The space-time of the Angloscene he was clinging to was a lifeboat with a hole in it, and it was sinking fast. When, after a few months, the date arrived for his French refugee visa interview, I contacted him to ask how things had gone. He did not qualify for refugee status and was distraught. Soon afterward he was unreachable and up until now I have still heard nothing from him. Whatever the outcome, his commitment to the Angloscene—having "saved his life" by fleetingly keeping him temporarily afloat—ultimately compromised him.

STEVE BIKO IN BEIJING

From the broader perspective of China's educational investments, Lerato's paradox and Damien's dilemma seem to mirror a number of recent debates on Chinese soft power. On the one hand, Sino-African dialogue continues to escalate on political, economic, and educational fronts, evidenced by current FOCAC and BRICS initiatives, and accompanied by a considerable escalation in Chinese-sponsored educational endeavors in both Africa and China (Alden 2007; Brautigam 2009; Bodomo 2012; Li et al. 2012; Chan et al. 2013; King 2013). On the other, all of these initiatives—despite being overwhelmingly China-driven—continue to be made legible and evaluated within an interconnected landscape of predominantly English-language-based media, aesthetic, political, ethical, and economic discourse and its associated signs of cultural capital.[10] Despite a sustained Anglo/western hegemony in social, political, and educational settings worldwide, there has been much nervous hand-wringing over Chinese influence in the media and disciplinary theaters of the Anglosphere, at times followed by "corrective actions," notably in the US academy (Sahlins 2013; Crovitz 2014) and more recently in Sweden (Zhang 2015). What these controversies clearly demonstrated was the limited media landscapes, associated languages, and aesthetic values within which debates over "global" educational initiatives are able to unfold. These politically monolingual media and rhetorical theaters of evaluation—unfolding predominantly within the media Anglosphere, where "lessons were taught [to Beijing]" and "academic freedoms protected [from China's inveigling influence]"—emerge as a clear explication of the ways in which not only English but its associated sensory and media worlds at times foreclose rather than merely "frame" the context of educational and political interaction (Crovitz 2014; Zhang 2015).

For these reasons, media representations of the Chinese educational-political matrix have been less than transparent and far from even-handed, precisely due to the ways in which "China," as an oppositional term to "the west," becomes monolithically fetishized in the western media lens (Vukovich 2019). However, in the case of Lerato and others, it is increasingly apparent for those standing outside of western media Orientalisms, that the perceived dualism between the alterities of yellow peril-ism and the commensurations of unmarked cosmopolitanism globalism are ultimately contextualized via the same English subtitles. Many African students in China have already realized that the superficial rhetoric of this dualism in the Anglo media sphere that elides the less easily demarcated friction between a western media-based horizon of value that, on the one hand, presupposes an iconic equivalence between all participants in a "neutral" value system, while on the other, entails the very asymmetrical alterities this presupposition continues to generate. This is especially true for those encountering the cruel optimism of trying to cultivate an alternative. In defining cruel optimism, critical theorist Lauren Berlant has noted:

> A relation of cruel optimism exists when something you desire is actually an obstacle to your flourishing. It might involve food, or a kind of love; it might be a fantasy of the good life, or a political project. It might rest on something simpler, too, like a new habit that promises to induce in you an improved way of being. These kinds of optimistic relation are not inherently cruel. They become cruel only when the object that draws your attachment actively impedes the aim that brought you to it initially. (2011, 1)

Berlant's framing resonates profoundly for African students like Lerato and Damien, where the expectation that the west is appearing less capable of setting the terms of everyone's representation in the wake of an increasingly legible theater of interactions (between China and Africa, for instance), gives way to a frustration at a persistent hegemony of a western sphere of aspiration. This further engenders perhaps an emergent sense that the implied pluralization of this asymmetry—through an imminent multilingualism—is not so much "arriving too slowly" as not really arriving at all. However, many of their Chinese counterparts—cramming for TOEFLs and GREs—are following the same initial intuition as Damien. Here, recourse to the Angloscene represents something more akin to a life raft than a stepping stone, or at least something to help one survive a swim to shore (which itself is yet to emerge on the horizon). If it is manifestations of power we are after, it is surely in this situated rather than arbitrary theater of postcolonial translation—the absent presence of Anglo-whiteness in Chinese projections of soft power—where it might be excavated with perhaps fewer overtones of yellow peril. For African students in Beijing, what appears to be at stake is an intelligibility that transcends marginality by any available means. This has many parallels with activist and thinker Steve Biko's call for the appropriation of Black Consciousness as a conduit for achieving a "full expression of self" (1978).

As an education activist and icon of anti-imperialist struggle, Biko's legacy—through its citation in and beyond contemporary student struggles back on the continent—animates endeavors of many Africans studying in China. This is clear in the ways he is often quoted in student social media groups to index solidarity or even misalignment with student struggles that are not far from the everyday consciousness of many, particularly Southern African, students living in Beijing. Rather than being a flat-footed racial essentialist, and quickly written-off as such by many superficial readings of his work in western academe, it is worth noting that Biko never made any claims about the intrinsic differences between white or black races in promoting an educational decolonization. Instead, he encouraged young Africans to appropriate the alien, racialized categories of difference within which colonized subjects found themselves to be emplaced. His utopic vision of a nonracial nation-state following revolution is consistent with an argument that underlined the situated and discourse-driven nature of the very categories of race and racism. For Biko, racism—like the Angloscene—emerged out of intersubjectively translated signs of difference and sameness (or alterity and iconicity), where sameness and difference were far from arbitrary possibilities. Racism thus requires a space-time to perpetuate its stratifying force where the chronotopic capacities of signs were exploited within a racist ideology to continually reinforce the meanings of blackness in relation to whiteness, and not in relation to the "arbitrary" signifier of race. For this reason, Biko encouraged young Africans—constrained by conditions of apartheid and its colonial precursors—to appropriate, rather than provincialize racialized signs that were doing racist work. His was a move that assumed the immanent categories of a hegemonic context (blackness and whiteness as opposed to "race") and sought to overturn them from within, or at least reveal the internal contradictions of their appropriation. This is a strategy that itself emerged from the limited possibilities of expression with which previously colonized subjects had to make do. For African students in Beijing, their cosmopolitan dreams must unfold in the absence of previous success stories of Africans who "made it" in China or through Chinese education. At the same time, their Chinese interlocutors are themselves in pursuit of a horizon of aspiration located in an elusive, but certainly English-speaking, metropole. For Chinese and African subjects imbricated in this economy of desire, such contradictions indicate the limits of cosmopolitan commensuration in provincializing the perpetual present of a still far from decolonized world. The chronotopic propensities of the Angloscene disrupt projects of decolonization in precisely the ways Fanon once suggested, where without an idea of what "having-been-translated" might look like, a "being-in-translation" must unfold within the limited confines of other worlds, in others' words.

2

The Purple Cow Paradox

A group of fifteen or so Chinese women, ranging in age from about sixteen to thirty-five, are standing in a line along Da Jie Road in the Haidian district. They are offering both document counterfeiting and daycare services for other migrant families, who are mostly working in service industry jobs and are unable to take care of their children at work. From early morning until early evening, these women walk up and down the road with babies in their arms, advertising their services to passers-by. As dusk arrives in a cloud of urban mist, a complex mixture of smoke from the streetside lamb kebab grills (*yangrou chuanr*) mingles with the smog from the afternoon traffic and a white fog of pollution that has drifted into the city from the south. At this moment, when the sun is either engulfed by these layers of human substance or given a beautifully muted orange hue, the women with other people's infants return to their makeshift residences and workshops to complete the orders they received that day, or to prepare for a second occupation. As they do so, many distribute name cards advertising services for romantic or erotic companionship, offered either by themselves or others.

All of them are Chinese migrants from a rural village in northeastern China. They are all without *hukou*, residence permits that allow Chinese citizens to "own" property or live legally within a designated place—in this case Beijing. Not having a local *hukou* is a common situation for the swelling population of migrants in urban centers throughout the country (Carillo Garcia 2004; Jacka 2015). As a result, many non-Beijing working-class residents find themselves increasingly vulnerable to exploitation from employers, property owners, and low-tier government offi-cials. If one of the women in question were to be arrested for engaging in the illegal activities mentioned earlier—counterfeiting or prostitution—she would either be jailed or sent home to her province, having lost any profit she'd gained in the city through fines or bribes. The babies these women carry for others are an arrest-prevention "insurance" measure, given that police officers in Beijing are reluctant to arrest anyone carrying the infant of another person, because of the complexity involved in finding the child's mother. The Haidian police are fully aware of this and the women also know that the police are aware of their activities. This uneasy tension between their precarious position and their reliance on it appears to be the cumulative result of the simultaneously unenforced yet exploitable illegality of practices like prostitution and non-*hukou* labor migrancy. As a result of these precarities—not only of employment status, but also of living conditions and constrained mobility—the erotic services offered by some of the counterfeiters may be the only opportunity to have a place to sleep for the night: whether arranged by a customer, pimp, or "provider-lover" (Hunter 2010). Such "opportunities" make explicit not only the fundamental differences in access to capacities for mobility compared to elite, aspirationally cosmopolitan Chinese subjects, they also reveal how rural Chinese women must inhabit urban space, and often sustain their own mobility in a zone of liminal, yet functional, illegality compared to the large numbers of rural men who undertake contract labor in large Chinese urban centers.

Trotsky Tsvangirai, a Zimbabwean student at Da Hua University, became such a provider-lover to one urban migrant, Meimei. He came to know her through decoding one of the name cards she regularly dropped on the street in front of his university. Through the use of his Pleco Chinese-language app on his iPhone, he translated the services offered on her name card and called the number. Following the exchange, much of which (by his own admission) he was unable to follow, they met one evening in the back of a massage parlor "behind a secret door that looked like a cupboard," as he explained in one interview. After a number of visits as a regular customer—partially funded through Trotsky's English-teaching pocket money and following his improved Chinese-language abilities—Meimei came to spend additional evenings in his dorm room and received dining hall lunches with a counterfeit student card in exchange for a companion-like living arrangement. This relationship resembles what Mark Hunter (2010) has referred to as "provider love," which is differentiated from prostitution as the impersonal exchange of an erotic commodity. In a more transnational setting, Jennifer Cole (2010) has explored these themes in the context of Malagasy-French sexual economies. Meimei and Trotsky's relationship, though irreducible to a paper caricature of the sexual and erotic dynamics at play in their interactions, can certainly be approached in the ways Cole's and Hunter's work suggests. In terms of my own limited access, I came to know a lot about their relationship and was even introduced to Meimei because of the fact that Trotsky and I often played music together in his dorm room—we were both guitarists and fans of Zimbabwean Chimurenga music—where Trotsky was something of a Zimbabwean hipster.

Meimei and his relationship can be understood as a meeting of two migrancies—hers from rural Sichuan and his from Zimbabwe—where both of them regard Beijing as a space of cosmopolitan, urban opportunity despite the possible threat of terminal immobility or simply "getting stuck," which might result from the discovery of their interaction—the looming precarities of imprisonment or deportation. However, the difference between them is that the futurity of Meimei's migrancy is simultaneously certain and chronic, in the sense that working-class sex workers like Meimei—with no educational background or *hukou*—face considerable intersectional obstacles. Here, constraining economic conditions in rural China bring larger numbers of *hukou*-less and exploitable migrants into Beijing (Gaetano 2004; K. Yang 2008). Trotsky's future position, by contrast, is both uncertain and temporary, since—as suggested in chapter 1— the result of his educational mobility generates the expectation that he is to be transformed. Of course, this kind of mobility has its limits: In the first instance, it does not give him the capacity to perform the same kind of mobile personhood as the city's growing white expat population. In the second, if he were caught with Meimei, his possibilities of travel—not only to and within China—would potentially become curtailed.

Eventually, Meimei and Trotsky's arrangement came to an end when the groups of women began to disappear from the university entrances in Haidian. One day, Meimei simply stopped coming to his dorm. At the time of writing, the group outside of Trotsky's university had diminished from around thirty to just one or two advertising their counterfeit services once or twice a week.

INTERSECTIONALITIES

Many contemporary arguments concerning ideological stratification of gender and sexuality have treated language, mobility, and race as discreet "intersectional" domains. Bridging these domains, however, remains elusive as can be seen in much canonical work within each of these realms.[1] This perhaps results from ethnographic difficulties in identifying or empirically grounding an overlap between ever-changing semiotic and linguistic practices; the unfolding hierarchies of race, class, sexuality, and gender; as well as the always emergent intersection between identity and value distinctions as integrated social phenomena within a political economy of mobility. Seeing how Trotsky and Meimei's relationship is explicitly situated at a nexus point between these vectors—rather than involving each discreetly—remains an obstacle to critically theorizing intersectionality beyond Eurocentric settler colonial contexts, even if a persistently implicit stratifying relationship between language, race, and mobility remains evidentially intelligible. Perhaps this is an "epistemic" problem as Michel Foucault ([1966] 2002) has suggested, but how are epistemes sustained both in the micro-interactional present while being contingent upon historical micro-interactions?[2] This analytical contradiction remanifests when the analyst considers the effects of intersectional stratification as not only palpable in English-speaking, elite disciplinary theaters interested in marginal people; but that they are, in fact, experienced by the very marginal people being talked about. In what follows I will show how the attempted realization of aspirational archetypes of cosmopolitan personhood among two groups of elite women—one Chinese and the other black African—generates further compromised conditions for these already marginal, intersectionally vulnerable subjects.

In doing so, I hope to demonstrate how linguistic anthropological framings of spatiotemporally contingent personhood—particularly those expounding on the ideas of Mikhail Bakhtin—have profound methodological affinities with analyses of micro-interactional poetics and their politics in the humanistic social sciences.[3] Additionally, I will demonstrate how some of these affinities are foregrounded in a few different contexts and modes of interaction within Beijing's Afro-Chinese Angloscene: how an intersectional relationship emerges between mobility, language, and race in this context. Finally, I suggest that critical engagement with intersectionality—in precisely such settings—allows for analytical opportunities to map the contours of white space-time as a horizon of stratification that persists and mutates precisely within the "equal opportunity" logics of globalization.

INTERSECTIONAL MOBILITIES

In the summer of 2014, Palesa Ntsoaki and I arrived at her residence after one of her classes at Pingguo University. Palesa was a black female MBA student from Botswana who shared an on-campus apartment with two other women—also MBA graduate students in her program. One was from Sweden, the other from Indonesia. International student residences are usually separate from Chinese residences in Chinese universities. Before we sat down for our interview in her cramped but cozy apartment, Palesa offered to brew a pot of rooibos tea—a popular beverage in its place of origin, Southern Africa. As Palesa poured two steaming cups of tea, I returned to the topic of a conversation we were having on the way to her apartment and asked about her next step in getting a job in Beijing. She sighed, took a sip from her mug of tea, and said in a prim English accent—acquired while attending a private girls' high school in South Africa—"I am going to be the best Purple Cow I can be."

The Purple Cow in question was drawn from a book by Seth Godin, an American marketing guru. Titled *Purple Cow: Transform Your Business by Being Remarkable* (2009) this text has become a prominent discourse object among one group of aspirational African elites in Beijing. For many in this community, it mediates attempts to generate students' own icons of achievable cosmopolitan futurity via Beijing. This is attempted in the absence of present role models of African excellence that stand as ideal and attainable futures facilitated through a commitment to Chinese education. The Purple Cow is also the inspiration for the appropriated nickname that this small group of African students use cynically among themselves and forms a part of a tension this chapter explores: for the majority of the female members of this in-group, the very raceless, genderless cosmopolitanism that the Purple Cow epitomizes comes to compromise, stratify, and ultimately reinforce the asymmetries that these students aim to provincialize through their commitment to an all-commensurating "cosmopolitan" horizon of aspiration.

As many like Palesa attempted to embrace the Purple Cow in pursuit of their educational goals in Beijing, their female Chinese student peers were attempting similar (neo)liberal projects through their own literary genealogies. Caihong Qiao ("Rainbow Bridge") is one of many small Chinese feminist organizations in Beijing and is co-run by Vivian Xu—the organization's American-educated founder. Rainbow Bridge forms part of a network of similar LGBTQ organizations in China, which at the time of writing continued to organize annual intensive courses (or boot camps) in feminist theory. These boot camps and seminars are promoted with a view to recruiting elite Chinese students with profeminist politics into American institutions like Harvard, Princeton, and Yale. For many of them, and for this group in particular, Sheryl Sandberg's *Lean In: Women, Work, and the Will to Lead* (2013) has become an important discourse object—in English and Chinese—around which to promote an elite public sphere of feminist Chinese who embrace the "equal opportunity" promise of free-market capitalism as a path to personal empowerment and gender equality.

In the activities of the Purple Cow and Rainbow Bridge communities in Beijing, a contradiction emerges—one that arises in the cruel optimism of aspiring to Godin's and Sandberg's respective promises of universal personal transformation. This contradiction gave impetus to the formation of Chinese and African cosmopolitan spheres, as well as consolidating their compromised relationship to the Angloscene. Compromise and contradiction in matters of social transformation and revolutionary politics have been an enduring concern for critical feminist scholars. Audre Lorde ([1984] 2007) and Judith Butler (1999) have in their respective projects converged on the problem of the master's tools' Hegelian affordances: their retooling for liberation inevitably recapitulates the dynamics of oppression. In her early framing of intersectionality, Kimberlé Crenshaw (1991) identified the ways in which universal implementation of legal reforms frequently discriminated against the very marginal subjects such reforms were meant to assist or to protect. In what follows, I will explore a common analytical thread between the very different empirical contexts within which these incredible thinkers identified the political stakes of compromise and contradiction. This common thread lies in some of the paradoxes of language generally, and, more particularly, within a domain of language and social interaction called enregisterment.[4]

In the same way in which the "newness" of a commodity obscures the primordial and cultural relations of respective natural forces and chains of organized human activity that produced it, the contemporary meanings, circulations, and associations of "words," signs, and languages obscure the social labor of history that has engendered the semiotic and value systems they mediate. Just as the work of assigning economic value for objects has little relationship to their intrinsic or use value (Marx 1972), so too the attributions of meanings to language signs (at various scales) unfold and transform through time, having no intrinsic meanings in themselves (de Saussure 2011). In fact, the very attempt to fix, standardize, or regulate meaning and value in both cases necessitates constant tinkering and semiotic transformations precisely so as to stabilize the mutual endeavor of value maintenance. This is because the constantly changing material conditions of history and space-time that encompass such stabilizing acts necessarily render the fixing of meaning and value an unstable enterprise that entails persistent curation and the establishment of elaborate institutions tasked with such complex divisions of social labor (Manning 2001; Lee 2018). No singular economic model can stand the test of time. Similarly, no grammatical system can endure without adaptation and change. Neither operate in the vacuum of a "special theory" of controlled value. Rather, both must operate in the more general realm of interaction-based meaning-making. These paradoxical dynamics of meaning and value were foregrounded within the interactions of Chinese and African students in Beijing—where commitments to the "equal opportunity" language and associated theories of personal value transformation of Purple Cow and Lean In ultimately came to remake a familiar stratified hierarchy that these respective projects were meant to undo. In unpacking the ways in which language and value seem to be fundamental to the persistent dynamics of intersectional stratifications in any combination of race, mobility, gender, sexuality, and class, I have found Asif Agha's explorations of enregisterment (2003) and mass-mediated chronotopes (2007a, 2007b) extremely valuable.

HOW TO BECOME REMARKABLE

In 2014 I had attended a number of Purple Cow events with Palesa in Beijing. These were arranged by Purple Cow members who wanted to host "seminars" specifically meant to feature and discuss the implications of Seth Godin's book for African students in China. As a student about to graduate in China, Palesa was looking for a job in Beijing, where she had been living for nine years as the daughter of a diplomat. At the time, this process was proving difficult. This, I naïvely thought, seemed surprising given her political buy-in. Her parents had considerable government connections; what's more, she had acquired complete Chinese colloquial and technical fluency after completing both a bachelor's and master's degree at top Beijing-based institutions. This was a remarkable and difficult achievement among African students in China. The majority of African students in Beijing don't see any reason to become fluent in Chinese since most of them graduate after taking their main subjects in English—meeting the baseline language requirement for graduation from a Chinese university.

Some, like Palesa, have also had to build relationships with Chinese patrons who have sustained their residence or endorsed their continued studies in Beijing. Such "elite" students have all benefitted from Chinese and government support from their home countries, as well as political and economic relationships that are often reinforced through kinship ties to ministers, diplomats, or heads of state. For example, a considerable number of Zimbabwean students whose parents have close ties with the ruling ZANU-PF party attend and have scholarships to the same university where President Robert Mugabe's wife attained her degree in Chinese studies.

Large numbers of elite African students in China (many in Beijing) represent an important outcome of Chinese soft power and Sino-African educational and governmental cooperation. As such, many new arrivals have become persons of interest to an earlier wave of African elites who have situated themselves as Sino-African brokers trying to motivate the market value of both a Chinese-educated African subject, as well as a climate of south-to-east exchange where Sino-African relations cut out western middlemen. Miriam Bakgatla is one of these first-wave brokers. She styles herself as an entrepreneur, talent scout, and Sino-African expert, and is one of the few long-term members of Beijing's Sino-African community—a position acquired through both business and political acumen (as someone who worked for the government of an African country and came from a political family background). Through her organization, Azanian Achievers China (AAC), she generated opportunities and organized projects—like the Purple Cow initiative—that attempted to promote China-Africa relationships and broker opportunities for African students as well as Chinese business and government personnel. Through this process, she has become a formidable gatekeeper for her young African male and female apprentices—a guardian of their interests through events and workshops meant to "promote and mobilize African talent in China." At one event, she opened our discussion with a quote from Seth Godin's text: "If a product's future is unlikely to be remarkable—if you can't imagine a future in which people are once again fascinated by your product—it's time to realize that the game has changed. Instead of investing in a dying product, take profits and reinvest them in building something new" (2009, 27).

Suggesting that African students in China are like this product and, in particular, should "embrace [their] inner Purple Cow," Miriam emphasized a mode of conduct where her apprentices should carry themselves as "self-made," and create narratives of professional excellence, where one has achieved "success through one's own endeavors." In one-to-one interactions with many Purple Cow members, Miriam also often emphasized that remarkability was measured according to an "international standard" where "the game has changed." How the game has changed, however, was less important than Miriam's overall message: "In marketing your Purple Cow . . . every second and every contact counts." Later on, when I was able to interview Miriam, she explained further: "We have to make the most of our opportunities as African students in China by finding a way of profiting from our very unique, but not yet marketable brand . . . the Chinese underestimate us because we are blacks, but we don't see them as colonizing us since we are here to take their country one little piece at a time." Voiced in a dialectic of black consciousness (Biko 2002, 48–53) and neoliberal "common sense," this was a position she and other Purple Cows maintained as a matter of course.

Seth Godin's Purple Cow concept becomes a conduit for this self-expression, framing an ideal subjecthood that attains personal or financial realization by understanding a universal set of laws governing human interactions; in essence, it is a how-to guide for making oneself marketable to others, where the reception of others is more or less taken for granted. Given this co(n)textual a priori, Seth Godin's text emphasizes an approach to making what is unique about your brand desirable to others—a recipe for self-fashioning an all-commensurating person-as-commodity (M. Silverstein and Urban 1996, 1–20). This particular aspect certainly resonated with several subjects, who, like Miriam, were trying to tailor philosophies like the Purple Cow not only to the context of African students' aspirations in China but to cosmopolitan translations in a variety of subaltern space-times.[5] Miriam's particular angle, however, equates the Chinese-educated African subject of excellence with the Purple Cow as a product that is "truly remarkable." Of course, *translating*—and thus motivating—a "sameness" between the African educational migrant in China and the efficacious neoliberal subject necessitates an erasure of the possibility that her product's future "is unlikely to be remarkable." It also requires a constant vigilance about the fact that the future of her product depends on others' imaginative labor and conditions of felicity (Austin 1975; Appadurai 1996, 2016): "If you can't imagine a future in which people are once again fascinated by your product, it's time to realize that the game has changed" (Godin 2009, 27).

In arguing for the remarkability of her apprentices' expertise, Miriam often demonstrated her knowledge of dominant China-Africa narrations of history, by equating the Purple Cow with historical giraffes brought as gifts from Africa to China during the early Ming dynasty. This serves as a popular historical reference—in the Chinese context—of Admiral Zheng He's gift to the emperor after returning from his expedition of Africa during the early fifteenth century (1405–1433) (Yamashita 2006; Dreyer 2007). When I later asked why she compared the Purple Cow to the giraffe, she answered: "Because everybody only remembers the fucking giraffes and none of the other gifts . . . giraffes are remarkable."

It is worth noting that Miriam's Purple Cow is an un-actualized potential in the sense that it is retrospectively *anticipated to* emerge through the strategies laid out by Seth Godin's Purple Cow. As Palesa suggested before, she *aims to become* the best Purple Cow she *can be*, hinting at the ultimate unattainability of the Purple Cow's "ideal type"[6]—where one form of cosmopolitanism sets the horizon for its Afro-Chinese "third world" analog. The relationship between these two cosmopolitanisms is further complicated by African and Chinese students' electronic and social propinquity with those beyond Beijing via social media landscapes in multiple international space-times. This Beijing-and-beyond connectivity generates a pluralistic but highly stratified cosmopolitan diasporic chronotope. Following WeChat, Twitter, and WhatsApp feeds on their newly acquired smartphones—commonly during a stopover in Hong Kong—African students and Chinese students try to calibrate these increasingly divergent chronotopes.[7]

From the perspective of many well-connected Beijing-based African students, it is also clear that recent mass-mediated decolonial narratives, like #RhodesMustFall, #FeesMustFall, "decolonizing the University," and "Africa Rising," heavily inform Miriam's appeal to an empowered, postcolonial, yet very Anglophone, elite "Afropolitan" ethnoscape (Appadurai 1996; Mbembe and Nuttall 2008).[8] As suggested so far, this has more than a little to do with English as a former language of command to many African students (particularly in the context of the internet age). In this setting, English's perceived role in brokering an "international" cosmopolitanism for their Chinese postsocialist interlocutors counts for somewhat less. However, a counterpoint between English as a neutral lingua franca and hegemonic discourse appears to unfold in the space-time of subjects like Palesa and Miriam adopting the Purple Cow register—where aspirational horizons and their compromises are immediately entangled in hierarchies of race and mobility that constitute a supposedly neutral ideal subject. To be sure, this desire for a neutral means of leveraging more desirable futures out of constrained contemporaneity is by no means specific to the African students in Beijing.

MOTIVATING LEAN IN

Vivian Xu met me in her apartment close to the Lama Temple in central Beijing. She had worked in China for a number of years, moving between China and the United States since childhood. She later studied at one of the most prominent Ivy League colleges and went on to found the organization Rainbow Bridge. At the time of our interview, Vivian was a graduate student at another prestigious American university and was also running an English-language editing business in Beijing (alongside her Rainbow Bridge activities). This was because she needed to sustain her income while deciding on a project for her PhD dissertation. In addition to establishing a lucrative side-profession assisting Chinese students' undergraduate applications to prestigious US universities, Vivian was an LGBTQ activist. Working for Rainbow Bridge was one way of bringing together entrepreneurship and liberal activism. The workshops or boot camps her organization arranged brought US academics from top-tier institutions into expensive Beijing hotel conference rooms, where young Chinese women (mostly high-school students and undergraduates) paid a considerable fee to participate in seminars that taught a combination of western feminism and US college application strategies. All of this was taught in an environment where English-language immersion and the possibility of a reference letter from a white American professor was part of the workshop's package deal.

My short-term role at Rainbow Bridge, and other organizations like it, was to work as teaching assistant, editor, and facilitator, but mostly as a token white face providing international flavor (or color) to educational activities that fundamentally did not require either my presence or expertise beyond the horizon of cosmopolitan aspiration that my whiteness indexed. This was apparent to both Vivian and the other facilitators working for Rainbow Bridge. Vivian would likely agree that I was useful not because they believed in my competence, but rather because they believed in others' belief in it: this mirrors Slavoj Žižek's (1989) argument for the persistence of ideology despite actors' reflexive awareness of the ways in which they are stratified by it. Vivian later stated in an interview that "the parents paying for the workshop want to see authentic [white] foreigners." In this capacity, I helped to organize seminars, grade written work, and provide mentorship on how to approach US college and university applications. During a boot camp held by Rainbow Bridge in the summer of 2016, I was able to observe classes taught by Vivian and an American Ivy League professor (another authentic white foreigner) who had been invited especially to participate in some of Rainbow Bridge's workshops.

During one of Vivian's classes, titled "How to approach your college admissions essay," another narrative of marketable remarkability emerged. Drawing on a book titled *50 Successful Harvard Application Essays: What Worked for Them Can Help You Get into the College of Your Choice*, Vivian emphasized the need to "make your application stand out," that a US institution like Harvard "does not value the typical profile of a nerdy, modest, female, Asian student." She underlined the fact that applications essays "need to make their authors look remarkable . . . even if you don't really feel you are." Vivian's presentation immediately provoked a discussion, during which one college student, Ally, put her hand up and asked Vivian if saying she was a lesbian from China was likely to make her application stand out in Harvard medical school's application pool? Ally was also the leader of a *Lean In* reading group at her elite university in Beijing and a strong advocate for Chinese women seeking elite education abroad, particularly in the United States. To this end, Ally's parents had invested a considerable fortune in providing her with an "international" education and long-term immersive classes in English, which she spoke with a perfect (possibly Californian) American accent, even though she had never left China. Her occasional interjections in class, punctuating discussions on feminist revolution or heteronormativity with phrases like "totally awesome!" or "that shit cray" respectively conjured a sense of having-already-arrived in a place she was always meant to be. Ally, like the other workshop participants, was completely enamored with Vivian's "professional" presentation, with her and many of her classmates consciously copying Vivian's semiformal attire following her introductory seminar, saying, "I want to look as professional as her."

Responding to Ally's question, Vivian hesitated for a moment, then looked down to her right where I was pretending to prepare the next PowerPoint slide for the presentation, and continued honestly: "Yes, saying that you are a lesbian and how that has given you diverse and unique experiences may definitely benefit your college application." For the remainder of the seminar, Vivian emphasized the need for remarkability, citing the archetype of the cowboy as a social-value icon in American society, where you have to be the "hero of your own narrative." When I later asked Ally what she thought of the seminar and what prompted her question to Vivian, she cited Sheryl Sandberg, saying that "she shows how women can pursue their rights in China." I asked if anyone in class could really be anything like Sheryl Sandberg. I was drawing on bell hooks's critique of the author of *Lean In*, which had been taught by their Ivy League professor that morning. Ally responded without hesitation: "Yes, Sheryl expects all women to be more remarkable." Indeed, *Lean In* does emphasize that the achievement of remarkability depends on courageous actions of individual women contesting society as members of an oppressed class: "We hold ourselves back in ways both big and small, by lacking self-confidence, by not raising our hands, and by pulling back when we should be leaning in" (Sandberg 2013, 8).

These descriptions raise important questions regarding both Vivian's and Miriam's charges: Is Sheryl Sanders the cowboy of Ally's narrative, just like the Purple Cow becomes the placeholder for Palesa's cosmopolitan future? To what degree are Miriam and Vivian able serve as actualized manifestations of, and conduits for, these respective projects of Purple Cow and Lean In? Drawing on a western philosophical genealogy of thought concerning the relationship between personhood and property, Ilana Gershon (2017) theorizes contemporary logics of mobility and the cultivation of subjecthood as having a contingent relationship within neoliberal logics. She reveals how "branding a self" as competitively remarkable—in the ways similarly voiced by Vivian and Miriam—has become integral to this process. Taking a more historical-ethnographic approach, Timothy Burke has discussed the social histories of two hygiene commodities—Lifebuoy and Lux—in Zimbabwe (1996). Similar to Gershon, Burke explores the ways in which archetypes of personhood mediate the relationship between persons and an encompassing capitalist political economy, but situates this process within a longer historical durée. What the specific examples of Azanian Achievers and Rainbow Bridge more generally reveal is that such neoliberal logics (old and new) are underpinned by other far-from-neutral, encompassing cultural currencies. English, whiteness, and heteronormativity are dense formations of social capital constituting a web of intersectional vectors that refract neoliberal as well as older capitalist ideologies of value that underpin the commensurations of personhood. As Cedric Robinson (1983) powerfully revealed in his political economy masterpiece: capitalism precisely operates through the recruitment of categories of value—like race—that appear to transcend or precede capitalism itself. This should be apparent to anyone paying attention to the relatively recent Euro-American trend toward identity branding.

CANONIC POETICS

While Vivian's "success" served as an aspirational beacon for many of Rainbow Bridge's participants, her own relationship to the aspirational horizon she represented for others was more complex. Although Vivian had received a considerable amount of grant money in the United States (for her research project in Beijing), she had always been involved in entrepreneurial activities, given that her parents had largely cut her off, as they did not approve of her being a lesbian. Thus, she was required to be financially independent. After she received grant money and left to begin fieldwork in Beijing, her white male project advisor discovered that she was running what he called "a side business in the field." He reported her to the grant-awarding organization, who revoked her funding. All this came after humiliating her among faculty members and her peers at her own university. As a result, Vivian had to intensify her entrepreneurial activities to compensate for the loss and the labor needed to *motivate* the efficacious elite, Anglo-Chinese cosmopolitan personhood she had worked so hard to cultivate. Yet, the very aspirational horizon she pursued always situated her, and many like her, as in-between cosmopolitan chronotopes. In one chronotope, she was the Ivy League–educated educational professional in "truly cosmopolitan" Beijing; in the other "third-world" chronotope, she was the precarious, cheating Chinese graduate student who is perpetually "almost-but-not-quite Harvard," despite having checked all the boxes to achieve that status. The way in which Vivian becomes systemically marginalized in one context while valorized as an aspirational icon in another extends the geographical and analytical terrain upon which racialized, gendered, and queered intersectionalities might be mapped (Crenshaw 1991; Butler 1999; Lorde [1984] 2007).

Through her own rigorous and empirically directed research into the stratifying social effects of blanket forms of legislation on the very subjects the US legal system often aimed to "protect," Kimberlé Crenshaw demonstrated the ways in which women of color find themselves doubly stratified in terms of race and gender in American multicultural contexts. At the same time, she reflected the ways in which an equal-opportunity assumption of identity politics could ultimately come to compound the racial and gender asymmetries they elide. Vivian's case extends Crenshaw's argument given that Vivian both became the receiver of almost-unmarked privilege in one national context (China) while becoming precariously marked in another (the United States), revealing both intersectionality's analytical purchase beyond singular, bounded, national polities and also the ways in which whiteness emerges as a problem beyond the bodies that may normally be understood to inhabit it.

One critique to the intersectional analysis at play here is the argument that Vivian's professor was not intentionally prejudicing her in this instance, but was rather meeting his obligation to the relevant funding institution. This would be an excruciatingly wrong-headed observation, fundamentally missing the point of an interasectional analysis given: (a) that intersectional violence is not about individual intentions, but rather persistent structural outcomes; and (b) I encountered dozens of young non-Chinese social science scholars undertaking explicit entrepreneurial activities while doing NSF, SSRC, or Fullbright grant-funded research in China who had never had this experience. Perhaps there is something wrong with the funding or selection structures of these organizations? In either case, the professor knew that her work was an extension of her involvement in LGBTQ organizations, yet reported her "cheating" as purely self-serving entrepreneurial endeavors.

The fact of Vivian's queer identity as a marginalizing factor in her own life, despite promoting the value of its "remarkability" to Ally, underscores the performative, yet far from arbitrarily relative, dimensions of intersectionality. In providing a dialectical frame for conceptualizing the ways in which intersectionalities emerge performatively, Judith Butler (1999) defines performativity as where "one who waits for the law, sits before the door of the law, attributes a certain force to the law for which one waits." Performativity thus becomes the "anticipation of an authoritative disclosure of meaning" as "the means by which that authority is attributed and installed." It is thus through this dialectical temporality that "anticipation conjures its object" (xiv). Here, performativity's range is limited by the degree to which subjects like Vivian can gain their footing in different ideological contexts of interaction.[9] The fact that this horizon of aspiration—which she promotes to Ally and others—is one that marginalizes Vivian, certainly does not make her a charlatan. It indicates the limited range of aspirational potentials available to her and those she mentors, whose only choice is to operate in a performative mode until alternative ideological gaps arise. While Crenshaw provides a historical and case-based account of how the fact of intersectionality is visible through its effects, and while Butler provides a compelling argument for its dialectical emergence performatively, this stratification can also be studied in real-time interactions.

As Judith Butler shows, observing language performativity requires both attentiveness to language as fundamental to the emergence of intersectional stratification as well as an understanding of language as both mediating and inextricable from that context. Here, linguistic anthropologists' concern with a phenomenon called enregisterment opens up analytical terrain for revealing intersectionality's interactional manifestations (Gal 1991) as well as performativity's dialectical manifestation in mass-mediated ethnographic contexts (Nakassis 2012). In his work, Asif Agha reveals enregisterment as a process emerging between actors encountering one another within an interactional space-time or chronotope (2003, 2005, 2007a). He does this through a rigorous synthesis of Bakhtinian and Goffmanian views on language and co(n)textual phenomena as providing the semiotic means and categories for social stratification. In his discussion of *voicing* (Bakhtin 1981, 1984) and *footing* (Goffman 1979) as analytics informing enregisterment, Agha proposes an attentiveness to the figures of personhood and stereotypes these dual processes animate. In Agha's work these appear to be dynamically socially motivated archetypes appearing to simultaneously emerge out of—and yet are motivated to presuppose—the space-time of semiotic interaction. As a starting point, Asif Agha defines registers as "contrastive patterns of register use [that] index distinct speaking personae in events of performance." Furthermore, "the social existence of registers depends on the semiotic activities of language users, particularly those characterized . . . as matters of alignment" (2005, 38).

In the following analysis of an interaction between several members of a Southern African community of students in Beijing, I try to capture a complex play of alignment and disalignment that animates multiple intersectional tensions through the ways in which different voices in a conversation become stratified. The following interactional text is drawn from an interaction among members of Purple Cow in 2014. The interaction took place at the corporate headquarters of an elite Southern African students' organization in China called the Azanian Achievers Group in the affluent district of San Li Tun in eastern Beijing. The participants were: CK, a black male Botswana MA student in China; JP, a white male English-speaking South African on a short-term study exchange in China; Gabriel, a younger male Zimbabwean student studying business in China; as well as Miriam and Palesa. Here, both Miriam and Palesa are the most elite Purple Cow members participating in the interaction.

The transcription method I use here is informed by Bakhtin's metaphor of "voicing" to depict the ways in which language's diachronic emergence always presupposes a dialogical, intersubjective ideological space-time.[10] For Bakhtin, the primary metaphors of language were aural, tactile, and emergent between moving parts, much like the experience of listening to contrapuntal voices converging in real-time—not as linear, stratified melodies, or vertical, synchronic harmonies that essentialize meanings to the sum of their parts. Drawing inspiration from Bakhtin's understanding of language as a musical metaphor (as opposed to the inverse) my analysis aims to give a sense of contrapuntal alignment and disalignment voiced between different actors participating in an interaction. In doing so, I will focus on moments in the course of this contrapuntal voicing, where attentiveness to a *canonic* poetics reveals both implicitly enregistered interactional orders (Goffman 1983) as well as their potential recruitment in service of overturning initially presumed upon interactional orders among the participants.

In making use of a western musical metaphor, the canon, I identify moments where actors repeat or anticipate words or phrases uttered by a conversational protagonist (as a means of emphasizing alignment and disalignment) during this dynamic encounter. By way of this metaphor, I am trying to capture the staggered aural effect—mirroring those of choral canons—as a way of emphasizing an affective alignment to a "head voice" by taking on a subordinate, rather than protagonistic role—for instance, the example of the backing singer in American popular music. Such moments, I suggest, distill or reveal implicit interactional orders that may contradict those that are explicitly assumed. In the case of the following interaction, Miriam and Palesa are recognized as leaders of Azanian Achievers. However, through the unfolding interaction, the stability of this hierarchy is rendered somewhat more precarious.

Once everyone had arrived for the session, and the door to the boardroom we were occupying was closed, I opened with the general question as to how everyone had initially found adapting the life in China. CK spoke first, emphasizing how jarring the transition from Gaborone (Botswana) to Beijing was:

1 CK: Now it's good I'm enjoying it,
2 but at first the language barrier was
3 there.
4   **[JP then enters the interaction once CK pauses]**
5   JP: Ja, but it's a bit of a challenge
6   this language thing, eh? When I
7   got here, my initial thought was
8   that, you know, there'd be more
9   people that understand English or
10   basic English, but none of that eh.

Here, CK leads, explicitly contextualizing his initial arrival in China in terms of a language barrier. His delivery is relaxed at this point in the interaction. JP, the only white person in the focus group apart from myself, quickly interjects, trying to build rapport with the Azanian Achievers by using "Ja" and "eh" as South African English shibboleths to signal potential alignments with South Africans in the room generally, but with myself in particular. He, like CK, keeps his delivery relaxed, maintaining or perhaps emphasizing a South African accent, using "Ja" to index agreement with what had just been said, and "eh" seeking confirmation of his participation. Both CK and JP indicate obstacles and disappointments with their experiences of the absence of English in China.

Speaking to JP, before the focus group, he appeared to embrace the discourse of post-apartheid reconstruction and reconciliation: "It's a whole new world, eh, we can all sit around the same table and just talk about China." JP was referring to other black people sharing the same corporate setting overlooking one of the wealthiest parts of Beijing, imagining an equal postracial interaction unburdened by less-privileged interlocutors who still constitute an economic, mostly black, majority in his home country. In his conciliatory hubris, JP further sought to indigenize himself by recruiting me to his aid, drawing attention to the fact that, like me, he too was "a real dutchman like Jannie . . . we are from the same tribe"—deliberately using both the diminutive form of my Afrikaans name, *Jannie*, and the derogatory ethnic slur, *dutchman*, as both a self-deprecating strategy and a way to suggest both that he was on equal footing with his other African interlocutors, and that he had "pale native" solidarity with me.

Picking up on (what he perceived to be) the elite makeup of the group, JP often invoked the rhetorical phrase "we all want the same thing, right?" both prior to this meeting and in later interactions with Azanian Achievers whom he hoped were his peers. Through this, he appeared to suggest that they are equals in the interaction, in so far as they were all English-speaking, educated "global leaders." The reception of JP's position within the group, however, was another matter altogether. CK responded to JP's "language gap" observation, attempting to expound on his own analysis:

1 CK: Yeah, because a lot of people . . .
2   JP: [**starts talking over CK**]
3   until you get in a
4 CK: [**directs himself at**
5 **Gabriel**] People in other
6 cities say "in Beijing
7   JP: cab, you're like oh shit.
8   [**stops talking**]
9   Gabriel: [**immediately leans in**
10   **To listen, nodding visibly and**
11   **intently at CK**]

In this exchange, CK begins by addressing himself to JP, who then cuts him off and starts addressing the group as a whole. CK, however, reasserts himself by speaking to Gabriel, who is seated next to him. Meanwhile, JP's imposition has not gone unnoticed and an alignment with CK begins to form where everyone in the group turns to direct themselves toward CK. This is picked up on by JP, who tails off and stops talking. It is more or less at this moment that CK begins to slow down and enunciate, almost in a burlesque, using a posh British accent. The group uptake of the switch from a Tswana- to posh English accent—with its measured phrasing—is marked in what follows:

1	JP: [. . . Looks offended and keeps quiet]
2	
3 CK: **and Shanghai . . . you'll be**	
4 **okay," but when you get here**	
5 **no . . . 'cause**	
6	Gabriel: **you'll be okay . . .**
7 CK: **from the airport**	
8 **it's like the first**	
9 **person you see**	
10	Miriam: **doesn't speak**
11	Palesa: **doesn't speak**
12 CK: **and it's difficult.**	
13	Miriam: **English**
14	Palesa: **English!**

Facilitated by CK's change of rhythm and emphasis, the black members of group intensify their alignment by anticipating what he will say next, endorsing him through a chorus-like voicing of the phrases "you'll be okay" and "doesn't speak English." The result of this interaction is that JP is effectively excluded from the participation framework from this point onward. CK as the oldest black male in the group quickly establishes his seniority through the assistance of Gabriel (at twenty-five, the youngest person in the focus group). Meanwhile, Miriam and Palesa participate in the conversation having been demoted to attentive praise singers of CK's performance.

Not only should this interaction be taken as an exemplar of a discourse pattern that pervaded the interactional gender dynamics of elite Anglophone African students in Beijing, it was also an interactional dynamic within which Miriam and other black women in this community were acutely aware of. Miriam and I discussed the problems of patriarchy fairly regularly—as an almost mundane topic of discussion among younger African female students as well as older women (like Miriam) with a certain English educational status and background. On one occasion, I asked how she dealt with it as a leader in this community. She explained that her status as a black woman in China already placed her on the back foot outside of the African community, and that dealing with "strong" African men who ultimately needed her network to survive, was comparatively easier to manage "because it's familiar." When I asked about other younger black women and the obstacles of patriarchy, she noted that they would have to find their own way like she did: "It's not easy, but if you can make yourself indispensable, and make it so that others need to depend on you, then you're in with a chance."

I ventured: "Make yourself the best Purple Cow you can be?"

"That's it," Miriam noted with a sagely nod, but then realizing that I was perhaps not being entirely sincere, added: "*I'm* not joking."

Among men in the community, there was a similar degree of awareness, but significantly different responses to it. While some felt that it was a pervasive social problem that needed to be addressed and that there should be greater gender equality among Africans, as I note in the following chapter, there was also an outright hostility against young women who were critical of patriarchy. One unusual response emerged in an interview of a former Azanian Achiever— Zakes Mbuli—who seethed at his frequent exclusion from this group, holding Miriam accountable for being ostracized: "That woman is a *sangoma* ['witch' or 'witch doctor']. She pretends like she wants to help you to your face and then sends a *tokoloshe* ['witch's familiar' or 'demon pet'] to get you later . . . she likes to keep everyone close and under control but doesn't like it if you talk too much. I just had enough of the mind games and decided to make my own *guanxi*."

Here, Zakes, who still had many friends in Azanian Achievers, felt that he had not only been excluded but had to become part of an out-group and no longer had access to Miriam's network or resources. Marking her as a *sangoma*—an initiated woman or man constituting a supernatural threat through the wielding of occult power—Zakes suggested that Miriam was able to capriciously enact unseen retribution against her victims and blessings upon her acolytes. In exiting the patronage network, Zakes imagined himself to be immune to the intersubjective witchcraft she might otherwise be able to enact upon him through mutually contingent and dependent social relations, or *guanxi*. Thus, from Zakes's perspective, Miriam transcended the usual bonds of patriarchy that governed mere mortals, something Miriam did not seem as convinced of—however, I might have been more naïve than Zakes about Miriam's powers.

The tension between the "equal opportunity" aspiration Miriam and Palesa endorsed before, and gender hierarchy in the conversation cited here, emerges not simply because the actors' internalized ideologies of white heteronormative patriarchy—ultimately obviating actors' motivation of an equal opportunity cosmopolitanism mediated through the seemingly neutral register of English. Rather, I suggest that closer attention must be paid to the social space-time of unmarked aspiration that subjects like Vivian and Miriam attempt to partially inhabit and are constantly thwarted by. Doing so necessitates attending to the intersectional horizons that unmarked English enregisters through their interactions. Here, I suggest reading the limitations of the dream of the Purple Cow from within a raciolinguistic *space* and *time* (Fanon [1952] 2008) that reveals the failure of its motivation.

DECOLONIZING THE CHRONOTOPE

In his own formulation of Mikhail Bakhtin's chronotope, Asif Agha discusses the contingencies between the intersubjective emergence of personhood and the mass-mediated space-times they depend on. Here, Agha reconfigures the chronotope as a formation "of place-time-and-personhood to which social interactants orient when they engage each other through discursive signs of any kind" (2007a, 320). In aligning themselves respectively to the text-worlds and reading publics of Lean In and Purple Cow, Vivian and Miriam's students forge and participate in chronotopes that are dialectically both of their own making, and yet must also transcend them as part of an aspirational space-time that is yet to be achieved. For Agha, time "is a semiotic isolate," thus impossible to unmoor from its dynamic contextualization in articulated assemblages of co(n)text and personhood as different, but none-the-less mass-mediated archetypes—like the interactions in which the Purple Cow and Sheryl Sandberg presuppose an articulated cosmopolitan contemporaneity and associated personages. This kind of space-time, however, must be mediated. As Agha suggests, time "is textually diagrammed and ideologically grasped in relation to, and through the activities of, locatable selves"—in this case, Miriam and Vivian's presence as those who index, but who do not fully inhabit, the space-times of the text objects they mediate (2007a, 320). Thus, in the motivation of any icon, and recognition of any sign, *a receiver and a space-time of reception are entailed, even if both appear to be absent.* Here, three points—a legible sign, a spatiotemporal context of reception, and a point of reception (a subject)—form a mutually contingent triangle of reception. Describing the chronotope as being "peopled by social types," Agha aligns himself with Bakhtin's view that media reception—print or otherwise—constitutes a socially contingent subject formation like that of personhood. Of course, such social types can be chimeric in their construction. In Purple Cow and Rainbow Bridge communities, implicit social types—like the white English-speaking American cosmopolitan—can become obscured by the explicit motivation of multicultural nonracial subject inhabiting the "neutral" register of English as *the* global language. Such plural, but far from equal, possibilities can be understood in relation to Bakhtin's insistence on the unfinalizability of persons and personhood. This perspective is grounded in the assumption of an indeterminacy of identity as constituted intersocially rather than autonomously and individually out of voices that can never be located or rooted fully in only one body (Bakhtin and Holquist 1993). This is articulately framed in Bakhtin's elaboration what he calls the "act of understanding": "In order to understand, it is immensely important for the person who understands to be located outside the object of his or her creative understanding—in time, in space, in culture. For one cannot even really see one's own exterior and comprehend it as a whole, and no mirrors or photographs can help; our real exterior can be seen and understood only by other people, because they are located outside us in space, and because they are others" (Bakhtin 2004, 7).

Thus, chronotopes and the persons they diagram into being, and vice-versa, form mutually dependent dialogically emergent formations. This is the case because a dialogical outlook points to reception as the emergent site of a sign's meaning, value, and material efficacy. This suggests a fundamentally distributed account of meaning-making, complicating easy readings of flat-footed identity politics on the one hand, and supposedly radical anti-identity and anti-political claims on the other. Instead, emerging asymmetries arise multidirectionally—simultaneously bottom-up, top-down, and perhaps even sideways in the case of the sign configuration, "third world" in its original sense. However, they are far from relative or absent formations.

This insight was not lost on Frantz Fanon, another thinker who pointed to a similar relationship between space-time and personhood. For him, the political stakes of these intersectional asymmetries mattered profoundly. In his *Black Skins, White Masks* ([1952] 2008) Fanon explicitly notes the role of spatiotemporal contextualization in providing the weight that grounds signifiers and allows for a distillation of their resulting essentialisms. In his critique of Octave Mannoni's (1950) *Prospero and Caliban: The Psychology of Colonization*, Fanon provokes the analyst—of dreams or political economy—to attend to the material conditions within which the signs of memory and alienation unfold. Decrying Mannoni's misinterpretation of the traumatic dreams of Malagasies, Fanon writes: "We must put the dream *in its time*, and this time is the period during which 80,000 natives were killed, i.e., one inhabitant out of fifty; and *in its place*, and the place is an island with a population of 4 million among whom no real relationship can be established, where clashes break out on all sides, where lies and demagoguery are the sole masters. In some circumstances, we must recall, the *socius* is more important than the individual" (Fanon [1952] 2008, 84–85 emphasis in original).

Fanon's spatiotemporalized "socius" emerges as a trans-historical chronotope that persistently materializes the colonial consciousness in the decolonizing present. It is not the repetition of history, but the reiteration of it in a dynamic dialectical historicity that continues to animate the intersocial space-time of the still colonized postcolonial subject. The implication here is that chronotopes are both not equal and emerge relationally vis-à-vis other chronotopes. To be sure, Lean In and Purple Cow may, on one level, imbricate very different reading publics or chronotopes, and here every reader co-constitutes their fractal Lean In or Purple Cow chronotope within it. On another level, Purple Cow and Lean In also diagram a cosmopolitan, English-speaking horizon of aspiration to Miriam and Vivian's social projects. The seemingly equivalent, and relative, potentialities of all of these chronotopes, however, are quickly unsettled when it emerges that African and Chinese subjects are less easily able to inhabit such space-times of personhood compared to the white English subjects these chronotopes implicitly presuppose. This becomes particularly apparent when the seeming persistence of a colonial chronotope burdens postcolonial subjects in ways that white subjects do not appear to experience beyond narcissistic guilt or denial. In Miriam and Palesa's compromised relationship with the Purple Cow, and to a certain extent in the limits of Ally's projection of Sheryl Sandberg onto Vivian, important challenges to any claim of language arbitrariness emerges, thus making chronotopic construction and imagination a consistently politicized domain. In the case of Azanian Achievers and Rainbow Bridge, this is particularly explicit in the ways their attempts at legibility unfold within the unmarked (perhaps white), still-Anglocentric space-time in which the Purple Cow and Sheryl Sandberg are mere tokens.

This space-time thus suggests a contradiction between constraint and liberation, but from and in relation to what? In the following section, I will conclude with a transhistorical contextualization of the hierarchies of mobility that complicate the emergence of postintersectional personhood. In doing so, I will propose that the compromised commitment to Purple Cow imbricates a dialectical history of race and gender relations that are very much part of a legacy of apartheid and colonial political economy of labor migrancy in the interactional reiteration of a third-world space-time.

INTERSECTIONAL (IM)MOBILITIES

In viewing the deferment of Vivian and Miriam's *motivated* aspirational horizons, it might appear that the gender-emancipatory possibilities of a cosmopolitan space-time are being short-circuited by a patriarchal backlash: on the part of the male members of Purple Cow or the white male professors in liberal American universities. Instead, I propose that the history being drawn from and the ideological context that sustains the elusive aspiration toward the Purple Cow are suggestive of another intersectional tension, one that concerns the postcolonial politics of (im)mobility.

Anthropologist Julie Chu (2010) has evocatively captured a contemporary tension between mobility and immobility as equally traumatic conditions in the lives of Fuzhounese subjects in China, among whom she identifies a complex, intergenerational mobile imaginary. Not only do contemporary Fuzhounese migrants value mobility as a capacity that stratifies different mobile or immobile subjects, the same anxieties also animate and sustain relationships between the living and the dead. Crucial in mediating these various kinds of mobility are two forms of currency that appear fairly prominently among her informants. The first is paper money that looks suspiciously like American dollars, the second is debt converted into a form of Maussean gift, where the capacity to pay off debt after having been in debt becomes a mode of sustaining intersocial ties—what will be discussed in chapter 5 as *renqing*. Both of these forms of currency ultimately come to commensurate the same "compulsion" toward mobility and index "America" as almost metaphysical destination: where subjects have always been arriving even if they've never left Fuzhou. Perhaps this dialectical contradiction emerges precisely in relation to the ideological backdrop that imbricates late capitalist mobilities, manifesting in the infrastructural projects Chu's subjects are witnessing in Fuzhou.

There is a difference between the mobility desire described in the Lean In and Purple Cow discussions earlier and the compulsion to mobility that emerges in Chu's discussion. Here, I do not feel this difference arises purely out of the (so-called) subjective nature of ethnographic observation and various ethnographers' emplacements. Instead, I suggest that the difference reveals an important distinction between educational and other forms of migrancy—Chinese traders in Africa or African traders in China, for instance. In my work, as has also been explored in Lisa Rofel's (2007) work, desire is animated by the imagined capacity to transform into a more ideal or cosmopolitan subject. If one travels for education, there is a guaranteed transformation that those both abroad and at home come to count on. In less desire-driven forms of migrancy, one must travel in the hope of a transformation (of social or economic status) that is far from guaranteed. In the first case, mobility is a desirable and transformative capacity. In the second, a compulsion to move—whether desired or achieved—is one's only option. Neither subject, however, is necessarily more precarious than the other, and in both cases, failure to maintain mobility may result in (a perhaps terminal) stasis—as demonstrated in Damien's example in the preceding chapter. Describing similar precarities in the context of white racist uptake of non-white immigrant mobility in contemporary Australia, Ghassan Hage uses the term "stuckedness" to get at this failure.

For Hage, stuckedness emerges precisely out of a sense of existential mobility as a basic human pursuit shared by many of his respective Australian informants: particularly between white racists and perceived-to-be non-white immigrants:

> Existential mobility is this type of imagined/felt movement. . . . This differs from the physical movement of tourists, for instance, whose physical mobility (travel) is part of their accumulation of existential mobility. In a sense, we can say that people migrate because they are looking for a space that constitutes a suitable launching pad for their social and existential self. They are looking for a space and a life where they feel they are going somewhere as opposed to nowhere, or at least, a space where the quality of their "going-ness" is better than what it is in the space they are leaving behind. (Hage 2009, 2)

As non-white elites with a lot to lose, we can also see something like Hage's existential mobility at play in *motivating* actors like Miriam's and Vivian's respective cosmopolitan projects. However, in their case it is the pursuit of existential mobility that comes to generate the intersectional stratifications that sustain their very own conditions of stuckedness. Additionally, we can understand icons of personhood—like Sheryl Sandberg, cowboys, giraffes, or Purple Cows that orient the "remarkable selves" under construction here—as generating omissions that (perhaps fetishistically) occlude the possibilities of inverted, dystopian chronotopes of stuckedness interrupting the smooth textures of the cosmopolitan lives being pursued—regardless of their compromises. Such dystopian archetypes might be spatiotemporally proximate and yet negated. For instance, contemporary migrant women, like Meimei, whom Vivian and Ally certainly do not want to be. They can also be historically remote, and yet painfully present—the conditions of industrial colonialism and apartheid that exploited the limited choices of Miriam's and Palesa's mothers and grandmothers up until a few decades ago.

HISTORICAL (IM)MOBILITIES, COLONIAL MODERNITIES

Once again, my invocation of history does not suggest a linear, deterministic relationship between past and present. Instead, what is at play is reiteration rather than recursion of the dynamics of a colonial-capitalist past in the context of contemporary Sino-African Beijing. The demand for labor in industrializing African urban centers in this region during the nineteenth and early twentieth centuries was predominantly fueled by mining booms in gold, copper, and diamonds, leading to the development of cities like Johannesburg, which due to its size and continued prosperity became a quintessential African metropole. In the work of sociologists and historians Christopher Ballantine (2000), Charles van Onselen (1982), and Laura Longmore (1966), a number of important features about labor migrancy and its social transformations around Johannesburg become apparent. It created a disconnect between men coming to labor in urban areas and women who were expected to manage rural homesteads that white farmers and the colonial state were increasingly expropriating. In both cases, Black South African men and women were transformed from land-owning-collectives—mediated through complex "cattle bridewealth" and kinship-based hierarchical systems—to bare labor. Black South African subjects were either struggling to maintain household and kinship relations on shrinking land where neither cattle nor grazing was sufficient to do so, or were selling their domestic, mining, and industrial labor in urban centers, unable to afford to participate in the kinship-property system. Many men became inscribed in what van Onselen (1982) calls the prison-mine complex, where African men finding themselves in colonial-commercial centers like Johannesburg were either interpolated into the industrial labor system—which was dangerous and exploitative, but ultimately more economically viable than a shrinking homestead or a white farm—or forced to find alternatives at the margins of a predominantly male, urban world. The alternatives were certainly criminal given the ways in which the black African males' movements and capacities to live near urban areas were severely curtailed by a set of laws that simultaneously forced and curtailed their mobility. These were called pass-laws and were a kind of domestic passport offered to African migrant laborers allowing them to travel to find work. At the same time pass-laws allowed very limited movement for black men and women, whereby curfews were placed on those working within white urban areas. A property could not be owned, and only certain kinds of residences adjacent to urban areas could be maintained. These adjacent areas were called "locations" and their existence along with the other pass-law constraints aided the "compartmentalization" (Fanon [1952] 2008) of white and black chronotopes within the same urban areas.

The worlds that opened up in the obvious cracks within this overtly constraining system took on a variety of forms. In van Onselen's (1982) work, such constraints were the condition of possibility for the emergence of an elaborate criminal class and urban culture in Johannesburg, while for Ballantine (2000), the resulting condition of labor migrancy resulted in a highly gendered music and media landscape that, in its gritty glamorization of urban life, set the tone for cosmopolitan aspirations of not only black South Africans, but black migrant labor coming from Zimbabwe and Botswana to work in or around the goldfields of the Witwatersrand. Such transbordering subjects came to see Johannesburg as a regional nexus point for their aspirations—a stepping-stone metropolis. For Longmore (1966), Hunter (2010), and to some extent Ballantine, this "cosmopolitan" urban domain emerged as an appealing "opportunity" to many African women, many of whom were no longer content with trying to maintain homesteads, where often they were at the mercy of fairly repressive in-laws. Add to this the rapidly deteriorating conditions on the homestead as a result of land expropriation and the power vacuums left by a mass male exodus to the mines, and one can understand the fairly strong motivations to leave for cities like Johannesburg. Upon coming to the city, many found niches—legally or illegally—taking up domestic labor in white residences, opening taverns that would serve beer and food as well as provide entertainment for laboring black men, or engage in various forms of compensated male companionship ranging from "romantic" or "provider-love" (Hunter 2010) to prostitution (Longmore 1966; Ballantine 2000). Ballantine, in particular, emphasizes the ways in which black labor migrancy—while providing new theaters for female labor—ultimately exacerbated or engendered less-equal relationships between black men and women in Southern Africa. In all these discussions, male roles were reduced to activities motivating the circulation of colonial-commodity forms—through mining, industrial, and even musical labor. Female roles, by contrast, had to further conform to the fulfillment of male desire, be it as maintainers of the homesteads and family affairs, or as the providers of companion labor in the urban centers as sexually commoditized subjects.

"WE'RE STILL GETTING FUCKED"

The resonance between this historical description of colonial labor migrancy in Southern Africa with female migrants in Beijing is deliberate. In the Chinese capital, Palesa and other female Purple Cows find themselves under pressure to conform to similar limiting possibilities between sexual objectification and the expectation to "return home and take care of the homestead"—preferably with a comfortable job and a pension. While the next chapter will go into detail as to how such expectations are contested with equally limiting results, I will suggest that many female Azanian Achievers who quietly embrace the "equal opportunity" logic of the Purple Cow do not, in fact, express this through public "sexual freedom," which is treated skeptically. As Lindiwe, another black South African informant, put it in an interview: "Freedom from what? We're still the ones *getting fucked.*" Here, Lindiwe was drawing attention to both the persistence of patriarchal power dynamics as reflected in the focus-group discussion mentioned earlier, as well as the limited numbers of female African students compared to their male counterparts in Beijing. This situation leaves female Purple Cow members both outnumbered and vulnerable to power dynamics that are largely out of their control, even if their leaders are women (as seen in an earlier interaction). Instead, many commit to the Purple Cow in two ways. In the case of Palesa, they resist relationships in Beijing in the service of having a successful career "back home," or, in the case of Miriam, represent themselves as "strictly professional" cosmopolitan subjects within Azanian Achievers, choosing to have relationships with men mostly outside of an African peer community.

Compared to Miriam and Palesa, Vivian and Ally experience vastly different kinds of limits. Indeed, most of the participants in Rainbow Bridge's boot camp found the concept of intersectionality troubling to fathom, claiming that "all women in China experience equal discrimination," a perspective once voiced by Ally and which drew unanimous approval from the other class participants. This confused their visiting professor, who was trying to teach them bell hooks's (2013) critique of Sheryl Sandberg's *Lean In*—the two opening texts of the workshop. Indeed, the relatively privileged position of many of the workshop participants may have precluded any kind of critical engagement with black and ethnic minority women in China. However, the cracks of Beijing's migrant underworld require little excavation to uncover intersectional strata, not unlike those of the industrial-prison complex that the Africanist historians evocatively described.

In this chapter, the constrained translation of mass icons of "personhood" revealed intersectional orders emerging in the absence of ideal "Sino-Afropolitan" cosmopolitan precedents. This contributes an important extension to both discussions of gendered enregisterment as well as theories around race-gender-sexuality intersectionalities, given the fact that the majority of these prior analyses have been staged in the context of bounded societies, nations, or language communities that have shared a long-term proximity. In a Sino-African encounter, the more spatiotemporally complex, dialectical dimensions of register formation and intersectional stratification can be observed in an interaction that is less obviously overdetermined by overt structuring processes like the nation-state and language standardization policies. To be sure, my analysis suggests that elements of these structures are still far from absent, however, in less expected modes of ordering.

Furthermore, the intersectional ordering I have identified here is contingent on an overarching spatiotemporal contextualization of meanings and associated values that engender their own dependencies—where signs of language, mobility, and race generate the space-time for the reiteration of "common sense" gender asymmetries.[11] In support of my discussion, I additionally provided an example of interactional analysis where the identification of "canonic poetics" empirically reveals many of the implicit participatory hierarchies that more conventional discussions of intersectionality (Crenshaw 1991) often effectively demonstrate in more rhetorical settings (Flores 2018). In the following chapter, I will expand on these themes, showing how the relationship between English and its associated, racialized signs of cosmopolitanism—as a kind of virtual gravity for Sino-African interactions—provides often constraining rather than liberating possibilities for a genuinely decolonized subjecthood.

3

Who Can Be a Racist?

Or, How to Do Things with Personhood

The previous chapter demonstrated two contexts in which unmarked cosmopolitan horizons, mediated through unmarked English, ultimately engendered stratifying intersectional propensities for Rainbow Bridge and Azanian Achievers. As to how this relationship between the ideological infrastructure of intersectionality and the semiotics of interaction unfolds, a key insight can be drawn from the work of pragmatist philosopher and semiotician, Charles Sanders Peirce (1955). He suggests that relations of iconicity or sameness are always *motivated* (Carr 2011). That is, the indispensable "iconicities" or relations of sameness that constitute both our personal intuitions and public institutions are subject to the intersubjective belief, performativity, and maintenance of meanings and values that nonetheless come to be perceived as durable, transcendent, and enduring even, or especially, to those subjects tasked with the labor of belief, performance, and maintenance. The feelings of one's stigmatization and stereotypification in a given situation are seldom not experienced as a compounding effect of personal and public modes of "being seen." For those with experience of race, gender, sexual, or class discrimination, the potential collapse of public institutions and private intuitions around seemingly arbitrary propositions of sameness and difference can engender crushing anxiety. Stereotypes around "who one is" are necessarily inflected by possibilities of "who one could be" in the perceptions and recognitions of others. Thus, as questions of racialized discrimination necessarily entail concerns of iconicity and alterity; so concerns of racism—as the sociopolitical motivation of racial difference—necessarily entail questions of personhood. This chapter attempts to engage the broader pragmatic question haunting current inquiries into the (im)possibility of Chinese racism: Who can be racist?

RACIALIZED INFRASTRUCTURES
AND TRANSLATIONAL LABOR

During the Ebola virus outbreak in 2014, students from a number of different African countries were quarantined in "Ebola residences"—as students referred to them—across campuses in Beijing. The policies were not enforced in a way that took account of different African countries' relationships to the Ebola outbreak. One South African student reportedly protested saying the American international students were being preferentially treated, as the United States had more outbreaks of Ebola than South Africa. She accused the administrators of a racist decision. The administrators were perplexed, arguing that more African countries had Ebola than North American ones. Hearing this response, many Chinese students agreed with the African students, suggesting that the university administration was shifting goalposts on the issue. However, the administration stood firm on its decision as a statistically and thus scientifically informed set of measures directed toward the greater good. Testing and quarantine, however, rapidly concluded once widespread dissatisfaction was apparent. For black students from African countries, obvious forms of racism persist in China, even when they are denied through geographical and demographic recalibrations as a particularly pernicious, though seemingly objectivist, form of gaslighting—mostly because such denials and recalibrations seem so hurtfully reflexive to black African students in China. Furthermore, the very fact that forms of discrimination have taken on a nuance since 2010 does not erase fairly recent memories of racialization (Sautman 1994). In reckoning with these experiences, however, it is unfortunate that the interpersonal textures a dynamics of these interactions are left out while focusing on the outcomes of victim and perpetrator—as though both positions can be taken for granted in the absence of ideological and institutional frameworks. To put it directly, this focus risks attributing essential agency to gender and racial phenotype in the ways Barbara and Karen Fields have criticized (2012). Here, I want to explore an interaction that demonstrates how institutional and ideological scales of racialization can manifest within interpersonal encounters in fairly explicit ways, and importantly, that this convergence is facilitated by a discourse of racialization that is neither essential nor quintessentially local.

Chimai and Hondo were two Zimbabweans whom I befriended in the later stage of my fieldwork in Beijing. Chimai was something of a virtuoso on the *mbira*—an instrument with a close association with Zimbabwe, even though it travels through many musical contexts in Southern Africa. Like me, Hondo played guitar. The three of us got together relatively frequently to play. We were short on rehearsal space as our respective residences had understandable noise restrictions. At the time, I was fortunate to have access to a working space in one of the

American university research and outreach centers in Beijing, so we would meet there in the evenings to practice. On one occasion, Hondo left the rehearsal to go to the bathroom and exited into the seminar rooms adjoining hallway. I then heard a loud, anxious back-and-forth in the hallway, through the door that Hondo left ajar: "Why are you here?" and "Who let you in?" I got up to investigate and found Hondo confronted by one of the center's visiting faculty, Professor Xu—a prominent scholar at an American university who split his time between China (his home country) and the United States—where he taught and lived. As both were looking at me with awkward hesitation, I spoke first and explained that Hondo was my guest and then asked what was going on. Professor Xu, visibly unsettled, dropped his voice and explained haltingly that he was concerned with the center's security and just needed to establish what was going on. I had seen many foreign guests enter and leave the center, none of them encountering this reaction.

It is obvious that the surface power dynamics of such an encounter heavily favor Professor Xu. It is also apparent that Professor Xu was recruiting an uncannily familiar American mode of urban racial profiling during his late-night encounter with Hondo. What is perhaps less evident is the effect of my walking in on the interaction and the immediate framing effects of my entry into the scene—as a white, English-speaking body. Hondo, up until that point, admitted to being confused by a Chinese civilian questioning him like a police or security official in English. My arrival and Professor Xu's response triggered a different appraisal of the situation. Later, trying to make light of the situation as we were walking back to his dorm, he joked: "For a moment there, I felt like I had just stolen fruit from a [white] farmer." To be sure, this kind of encounter is less frequent in contemporary Zimbabwe (to say the least). However, socio-linguistic memory reaches back to times when such interactions were encompassed by cruelly racist ideological machinery that heavily favored the white farmer.

When I returned to the center he following day, Professor Liu—a different, locally affiliated Chinese faculty member—stopped me in the hallway and noted: "I heard about Professor Xu and your friend." This set up a confidential discussion during which she assured me that Professor Xu was not being racist, indicating that he had told her about the interaction and that I might have likely "gotten the wrong idea." My witnessing apparently generated potentially problematic iconic equivalencies with settler colonial racism. More importantly, these equivalencies not only seemed intelligible to my Chinese and Zimbabwean interlocutors. They also constituted as source of considerable anxiety and a need for effacement in light of their name-ability through my walking in. *For whom* one is racist appears at least as important a consideration as asking: "Who can be racist?"

What Hondo and Professor Xu's encounter demonstrates is that racism and intersectional violence depend on the intersubjective maintenance of forms of iconicity—this constitutes a division of *translational labor* that is operationalized through *motivating* a constant tension between whiteness and its unmarked mediations. Notice the subtle behind-the-scenes work between a number of actors in managing, on the one hand, the recognition of racial ordering via whiteness, and, on the other, whiteness's effacement through claims of misrecognizing "realities" that were actually unmarked. In the double-movement of recognition and effacement, race becomes stratified not only in relation to subjects' capacities for mobility, but also in relation to the dimensions of language that accompany mobile subjects like Hondo and Professor Xu. We can observe this more generally where both explicit racism, in the form of racial essentialism, and liberal racism, as a relativistic denial of race, require and necessitate consensus and co(n)texts for racism to do their ideological work.

How *a race* as a token becomes "iconic" of a horizon of excellence or dysfunction, or how *race* as a type becomes obviated by making it arbitrary both depend on *translational labor* of sameness and difference—or iconicity and alterity. Such *translations* of iconicity and alterity in relation to token and type are necessarily mediated through practices like alignment, reception, and consensus around how *a race* is "like" or "unlike" another, or how *race* stands as an arbitrary category rendering races as equal tokens of the same deferred type. It is this simultaneous dependency on consensus (explicit or implicit) and context that I am trying to evoke in understanding the pragmatics of race, its contingency on the reception of whiteness, and how "racism" uncannily emerges among non-white subjects in a non-western context.

While Peirce himself does not use the metaphor of *translation* in framing his definitions of symbol, icon, and index, linguistic anthropologists and many pragmatists have taken up his identification of iconic and indexical semiotic processes as suggestive of fundamentally nonagentive dimensions of social mediation (M. Silverstein 1976; Carr 2011; Wirtz 2014). In this regard, linguistic and other semiotic practices make meaning by receiving meaning, which in turn remake meaning and so forth. This being the case, iconic or iconizing processes—making things stand as "different" or "same"; and indexical processes, where meaning only emerges co(n)textually—in "context" and in relation to other signs or "co-texts"— are fundamentally intersocial and intersubjective (M. Silverstein and Urban 1996). Thus, translation as an *intersubjective* as well as iconicity/alterity-motivating process does not imply causal volitionality or a commitment to rational, individual intent. Translation thus presupposes a more interactional, reception-based conception of meaning-making as emerging through encounters, yet always located within the historical and material conditions that dialectically constitute, and are constituted by, their motivational space-time. In this way "I" and "you" are perspectival signs—or deictics (M. Silverstein 1976)—that occur to their users to be simultaneously preceding the interaction yet in a dynamic relationship with their context of utterance, where their translation can never be felt as "arbitrary" in the ways Ferdinand de Saussure once suggested (2011). In another critique of arbitrariness, Frantz Fanon reveals another dimension of this *translational* sensibility, where translation manifests itself in the violence of decolonization. In *Wretched of the Earth*, he writes: "Decolonization, which sets out to change the order of the world, is, obviously, a program of complete disorder. But it cannot come as a result of magical practices, nor of a natural shock, nor of a friendly understanding. Decolonization, as we know, is a historical process: that is to say that it cannot be understood, it cannot become intelligible nor clear to itself except in the exact measure that we can discern the movements which gave it historical form and content" (Fanon 1963, 36).

Decolonization, an always as-yet-incomplete project, is a semantic translational process—given the ways in which the meaningful relations in one spatio-temporal context must be "incompletely" reconfigured in another. However, as Fanon demonstrates, decolonization is also a *pragmatic* translational process, in the sense that transformation from colonization to decolonization is troubled by an ideological context that does not allow for a seamless shift in relations and reappropriations of power. For thinkers of decolonization, there is an obstruction to the simple *translation* of supposedly arbitrary signs. As English is not merely a language among other languages—something Ngũgĩ wa Thiong'o (1994) continues to tirelessly demonstrate—so, too, whiteness is not just a race among races. The reiteration of these signs, their co(n)textualization, and the way they stratify as much as commensurate their co-signs reveals both the ideological nature of translation, as well as the inescapability of translation as simultaneous social fact and stratifying reality. This is a reality within which "red," "brown," "black," and "yellow" people have come to inhabit or appropriate positions subordinate or adjacent to "whites," and where English becomes necessary social currency for all global migrants even though their capacity to enunciate its phonemes or inhabit its default white subjectivity is fundamentally unequal. These positions, for Fanon, are not arbitrary, because whiteness and other signs of the (post)colonial present never can be.

In this regard Fanon's insights concerning the relationship between race, language, and capacities for mobility among subjects of decolonization stand in an important historical dialogue with thinkers of postcolonial translation like Gayatri Spivak ([1988] 2010) and Edward Said ([1977] 2003)—a genealogy that has influenced a rich lineage of scholars particularly in fields like English and literature studies, as well as history.

In their introduction to the edited collection *Postcolonial Translation: Theory and Practice*, Susan Bassnett and Harish Trivedi note that translation "does not occur in a vacuum, but in a continuum . . . an ongoing process of intellectual transfer," that it is "not an innocent, transparent activity . . . it rarely, if ever, involves a relationship of equality between texts, authors or systems" (1999, 2). The authors' main object of critique, however—and the primary concern of much early literary and historical engagements with the analytic of translation—is whether or not translation emerged as a process that detracted from, or diminished, the "original" historical, literary, or social text being translated. This mirrors a persistent, but currently more depoliticized, anthropological debate around representation as translational practice in anthropology—one which perhaps is most iconically represented by (but certainly not limited to) the methodological tension that emerged between the translational approach explicated in the work of Clifford Geertz (1973, 1977) and the critiques of James Clifford and George Marcus in their edited collection *Writing Culture* (1986). All of these debates are important and ongoing critiques, but only insofar as one is preoccupied with the question: "What is being translated into what?" The following engagement with translation departs from this strictly semantic approach.

Instead, following Frantz Fanon's imperative, explicated at length in the first chapter of his *Black Skin, White Masks*, an important translational insight emerges. Fixation on the question of what is being translated comes at the cost of considering the more pragmatic condition of possibility for translation of any kind: the units (linguistic and other signs) and space-times (material and historical contexts) of commensuration. "To speak means being able to use a certain syntax and possessing the morphology of such and such a language, but it means above all assuming a culture and bearing the weight of a civilization" ([1952] 2008, 1–2). Here, Fanon was fundamentally concerned with a French colonial context in which blacks were not only stratified in relation to whites through their capacity for "good French," but that they were also similarly stratified among one another: the Antilleans' "good French" vis-à-vis their Senegalese subordinates, the elite cosmopolitan bilingual Martinican vis-à-vis the sedentary peasant who has only mastered creole. For Fanon, the colonial world produces limited means for motivating one's subjectivity, value, and conditions of being—commensurations of value under the sign of capital, commensurations of meaning under the signs of a standardized language of command and its co(n)texts.

Given these limited means, colonial and decolonizing subjects ultimately come to rely on the very signs of commensuration that compromise them. The fractal stratifications that emerge as many of Fanon's subjects translate alternatives to their own oppression do not arise because colonial subjects believe in their capacities to overthrow whiteness and French as signs of commensuration. This is clear in Fanon's identification of the unthinkability of black creoles displacing French whites—the subject of Michel-Rolph Trouillot's masterful but severely undercelebrated work (1995, 2003). Instead, the stratifications Fanon observes emerge precisely because of his subjects' maintenance of French and whiteness as units of commensuration in the absence of unthinkable alternatives—a condition that, in turn, dialectically reinforces the very stratifications his subjects are trying to escape. In Fanon's argument, the target of translation—the as-yet-unimaginable future subjectivity of decolonization—is both obscured by and becomes transformed into its means: French and whiteness.

A recent example of a similar stratification emerges in the work of anthropologist Norma Mendoza-Denton (2008), where the ideological recruitment of the racialized cultural capital of English and Spanish respectively become markers of extreme differentiation between two groups of female street gangs within a relatively ethnically homogenous Latina community in Northern California. She depicts how a north-south hemispheric localism emerges between two rival gangs, the Norteñas and Sureñas, and that this hemispheric localism is distilled through an interlinked process of linguistic and racial hyper-differentiation. Her book is a fundamentally important ethnographic contribution and its intervention is very much directed toward informing a public debate around the recognition of racial and linguistic differentiation as social facts within minority communities within the United States. Beyond fundamental regional and political contrasts, my own argument differs from hers in another important sense. Rather than interpreting "language" and "race" as categories of differentiation, I treat "whiteness" and "English" as categories of alignment and disalignment, in relation to which subjects become stratified. Thus, while I am generally concerned with the overall relationship between racialization and raciolinguistics (Alim et al. 2016), I am—as suggested earlier—specifically preoccupied with raciolinguistic horizons of whiteness as an ideological gravity that enregisters racialization. In line with linguistic anthropologists Jonathan Rosa (2016a, 2016b, 2016c) and Mary Bucholtz (2010, 2016), I am interested in the relationships between whiteness, English, and their others, where markedness and unmarkedness, of either English or whiteness, constitutes a constantly negotiated ethnographic tension, between or among subjects, that both inhabit, and perceive themselves to be inhabiting, this very tension.

In doing so, I also want to break with the idea that critiques of whiteness are somehow less analytically sophisticated than critiques of race—a blatantly false and fundamentally paralyzing position that ultimately makes the person articulating the argument into an anti-white racist pariah. It also generates a theoretical disposition that enshrines relativistic inquiry—around race and language—at the cost of recognizing the historically and ideologically situated conditions of possibility for posing ethnographic questions, which are neither equal between ethnographer and informant, nor among ethnographers themselves. I think this matter imbricates something wider than the discipline of anthropology and concerns a climate of consent for exploring certain genealogies of thought while marginalizing others.

It is worth momentarily exploring resistance against, and in some cases hostility toward, attempts at sustaining a postcolonial critique within an elite Euro-American academic sphere. Beyond my own traumatic (but ultimately subjective) experiences in trying to advocate for the merits of postcolonial theory, it is apparent that such a hostility *does* exist, considering the decline of intellectual spaces engaging postcolonial thought, despite the seemingly unproblematic escalation of academic defenses of empire and historical imperialism in recent times. Bruce Gilley's recent article (2017) in *Third World Quarterly*—titled "The Case for Colonialism"—serves as a symptomatic example. After undergoing a double-blind peer review in a journal that has in the past been sympathetic to authors engaging postcolonial thought, the article was published, and to the horror of many of these authors, Gilley noted that it was "high time" the British empire received its due as an agent of development. Among those offended were several members of the journal's own editorial board who threatened to resign unless the article was retracted. This set in motion debates around free speech and censorship over an article many felt should not have seen the light of day unless there was a climate of consent that was unconcerned with its proposition. It is this climate of consent—and the complicity of a default liberal intellectualism—that continues to enable white supremacy under the auspices of open debate.

Opposing this, what I have argued—and continue to argue—seeks recourse to the intellectual legacy of black consciousness thinker, Steve Biko, who noted that intellectual propositions that propose a continuity of white imperialism decades after so-called decolonization ultimately threaten a liberal intellectual sphere that constantly recruits itself as an ally, while benefitting from racial stratifications that it criticizes.

Biko's (1978) revealing critique of white liberal participation in black liberation movements contains a crucial insight for aspiring intellectuals seeking new liberal utopias in out-of-the-way places: that liberal nonracialist arguments for racial liberation are always based on the assumption that categories of race are arbitrary, that racism is illogical, and that therefore all races are equal. Biko observed that this easy relativism obscured the fact that races were already unequal in relation to the racial capital of whiteness, and that liberals were simultaneously complicit in it as the beneficiaries of systematic structures of racial oppression that they could criticize at their leisure. For Biko, the capacity to inhabit this privileged "activist" stance made the "default white" liberal subject the apex predator of a pervasive *liberal-racism complex*—discussed in greater detail in chapter 6.

Reading this classic black consciousness critique from Beijing, it became clear that the dynamics of stratification Biko once identified have neither disappeared nor can they be hermetically sealed within the apartheid matrix. The historical material conditions that informed the world within which Biko's arguments were embedded continue to be at play in the cosmopolitan aspirations of African and Chinese students in Beijing, because the wider context of the Anglo-scene still encompasses both space-times. However, discerning a transhistorical Angloscene's matrix necessitates an approach to translation that operates bottom up, and does not slip into the kinds of semantic subterfuge that converts every proposition of iconicity and alterity into a representational hall of mirrors. To be sure, the *target* of translation is no less obscured: What indeed is the end goal of African students' educational transformations? What are the stakes of their fulfillment through contemporary experiments in Chinese soft power? And, in turn, what icons of "success" inform Chinese students' own experiments in cosmopolitanism as they encounter or pass by their African peers? Following Fanon, I believe that this question, and my account of its theater of interaction, foregrounds whiteness's persistent gravity over a diffuse, equal opportunity replicability of "power."

In what now follows, I would like to contextualize my opening question—who can be a racist?—within the interactionally *translating* and *translated* encounters of Chinese and Africans in Beijing. In this theater of interaction, the performance, adoption, and rejection of various manifestations of "politically correct" personhood—indexed and iconized through mass-mediated persons like Trevor Noah and Oprah Winfrey—becomes the mode through which Chinese and African subjects (to differing degrees) raciolinguistically stratify one another.

ENREGISTERING PC

One summer night in 2014, my informant Adam—a black, Zimbabwean political science student—and I went to a costume party in San Li Tun. With its bars, shops, and restaurants often frequented by large groups of foreigners, as well as many Chinese shoppers and partygoers, San Li Tun has also recently become a place where many young African students started going in order to "make contacts" and enjoy romantic liaisons. When we arrived, a Chinese woman at the party called Lili approached Adam excitedly and introduced him to her partner. Lili was Adam's ex-girlfriend, and had come to the event with her current white American boyfriend, Tim. During the introductions, she said jokingly, "Wow, I guess you don't need a costume." "How's that?" Adam replied. "You know, since you can say you're here as an Ebola patient," she said laughing at what, in the past, may have been a shared form of rough banter between them. Adam's smile dropped and was replaced by an uncomfortable frown. After a moment of hesitation, Adam turned to address Tim, whose jaw-dropped face expressed liberal horror, and said in a sotto, patient voice: "You really must explain to her why that is offensive." Adam and I left the party after a while and went for dinner, during which Adam vented about what happened. I asked him what he would have said to Lili if Tim had not been there. "Well, I guess I wouldn't have been that offended," he said. "I probably would have made a joke about SARS or Chinese people not being able to tell the difference between kitchens and toilets."

In Beijing, many interactions between Chinese and African interlocutors like Lili and Adam are mediated through a complex intersectional relationship between whiteness, English, and cosmopolitan aspiration. Building on the relationship between intersectionality and enregisterment discussed up until now, I will demonstrate how considerations of racially unmarked political correctness— often reflexively referred to by informants as PC—become mediated through ideal language registers. The mobilizations of such registers, like Model C English or the "standard" American Midwest dialect, ultimately engender a highly marked stratification along intersectional lines.

MAFAN FOR WHOM?

Adam's interaction with Lili reveals a number of factors that play a complementary role in framing the racial and gendered vectors of their encounter. His example also diagrams a fairly common genre of flirtatious interaction between many African male students in Beijing and certain female Chinese counterparts. Sexual relationships between them are fairly common, but these are somewhat short term because the African students, like many other foreign male and Chinese students, are in Beijing only for the duration of their studies. Unlike their Chinese counterparts, they are open to—and able to have—relationships with white, Chinese, and African female students. Another and equally important reason for the short-term nature of these liaisons is that their Chinese and white female student counterparts rarely conceive of African male subjects as marriageable, but rather as conduits for sexual experimentation (Rofel 2007).

This context of interaction very much animates Adam and Lili's exchange. Lili would later confide that she and Adam had previously had a relationship before things became *mafan*—"troubled," "messy," "complicated," or "inconvenient." We became acquainted after this event when she learned that I was both a South African student in Beijing as well as a graduate student in the United States. She was keen on attending university in the United States and wanted to know whether I, as a fellow "third-world subject," would help to edit her application materials. This is something I did as an acknowledgment of her clear but possibly ironic invocation of "third-world solidarity" (*disanshijie datuanjie*). However, admittedly, I was keen to find out more about her relationship and awkward interaction with Adam at the party. After learning that I was a South African, she became keen to talk about "Africa things," given her own regional focus as an international relations major. This, however, was only on the occasions we met to talk about her applications, and where she liked to speak about Africans' "closeness to nature":

> Lili: [Africans] are so innocent, like forest animals.
>
> Me: Is that a good thing, don't animals get hunted?
>
> Lili: No, don't think I'm a racist. It's a good thing because they are everything [Chinese] have lost. Chinese are now just robots with giant brains.

In conversations with myself and other Africans, Lili would contrast "African natural" essence with "robotic Chinese society" while simultaneously being quite reflexive about what constitutes politically correct nonracist language to a hypothetical western listener with the caveat, "No, don't think I'm a racist."

When, on a few occasions, we met in a group with her boyfriend's American English teacher friends, she would not discuss "African things" and would emphasize that I was a graduate student in the United States. The present nonpresence, as well as nonpresent presence of her white American boyfriend—in both Adam and my interactions with Lili—is important here, given the way deviations from a normative center can still be seen to constitute that very normativity as the regulating principle that makes the deviation legible in the first place (Bakhtin 1981; Schmidt 1996). However, what ideological gravity imbricating their interactional space-time allowed Tim to haunt encounters without being physically present?

It seemed that since her "faux pas" at the costume party, Lili came to adopt a register of political correctness whenever her boyfriend was around, but which was almost completely abandoned in his absence. This seemed to emerge over the time I observed Adam and Lili's respective interactions. The switching between abandonments and adoption of PC constituted a fairly extreme form of code-switching, indexing Lili's compartmentalization of dual personas and perhaps suggestive of Lili's gradual coming to awareness of a transnational, raciolinguistic double-consciousness—if not her own, then certainly one she perceived in her interlocutors. Thus, Lili's abandonment of PC, in its reflexive transgression, further reaffirmed Tim's absent-presence. Likewise, references to Africa, Africans, and African relations—her university specialization—were only cursorily referenced around her boyfriend, while his absence activated revelry in all manner of "African" oddities and inquiries—with qualifications like "I'm not racist or anything but . . . " again suggesting a persistent awareness of PC even when—or perhaps especially when—it was being transgressed. Whether this was due to her reluctance to let her boyfriend know about the fact that she had had a relationship with a black African, or her attempt to live up to the cultural expectations of western liberal political correctness's essentialism paranoias, is not clear. In both cases, however, the effect still constitutes an encompassing whiteness, English, and cosmopolitanism, as an imbricated horizon of aspiration of which Adam could never be a part of. Adam's role in her life was that of a concealable conduit. After hours of English lessons, academic paper editing, and the delineation of cultural references to the world of the Anglosphere and its others, Adam became a stepping stone to co-presence it. However, it appeared that now, this "stepping stone" had to be elided as a matter of self-preservation. But self-preservation from what?

To Lili's parents and grandparents, America, English, and whiteness are appropriate civilizational aspirations. At the same time, they continue to exchange her details (picture, age, and credentials) with those of potential Chinese male suitors among kinship, friendship, and professional networks in her hometown. An African from Africa (particularly a black person or *heiren*) within these aspirational hierarchies simply does not compute. Adam, who has been in China for almost six years, is aware of this situation and these parameters, which by this time have the effect of eliciting more cynicism than outrage in our conversations and interviews. It is also his awareness of the order of things that allows him not only to recruit her boyfriend to the role of "placing her in the world of her choosing," as he would later remark, but also to demonstrate to his former "lover-apprentice" how he understood the Anglosphere's regime of political correctness and its limitations better than she did. In doing so, he imagines that he has made her white American boyfriend the custodian of her further civilization, as he put it, "she's now his problem . . . I'm handing over the reins."

Here, the veil of white political correctness quickly allows the patriarchal machinery of civilization to do its work. This machinery—mastered initially by Adam, given his own historical colonial emplacements, and then later transmitted to Lili—not only delineates what can be said but also the language in which speech has potency. Adam and Lili could always have continued their exchanges in Chinese, the initial common language through which the two of them first met in their university classes. This is due to Adam's Chinese abilities, which—like Palesa's—are considerable compared to many of his fellow African peers. English, however, gradually became Adam and Lili's mode of exchange due to Adam's initial role as Lili's English tutor, augmented by his own facility with the language as an English private-school-educated Zimbabwean. But this was also driven by Lili's own desire to rapidly improve her English. Here, her motivation stemmed from her parents' own considerable expectations that she attend a foreign university, and their investment of millions of renminbi (RMB or Chinese yuan) toward her attendance of additional English classes at private institutes like Xindongfang (New Oriental). Such investments—in the case of Lili's parents and grandparents—for families from small Chinese towns in northeastern China, must be contextualized in terms of the ways in which English ability and its associated "cosmopolitan" world might allow for a leapfrogging or at least temporary displacement of brutal regional Chinese classism that a small town northeastern accent might otherwise engender.[1]

From the perspective of many multilingual, postcolonial subjects like Lili and Adam, English and its associated "rational" political correctness—usually in "un-accented" and "civil" tones—appears to explicitly disavow institutional racism and classism of any kind (cf. Hill 2009). Compared to the discussion of white political correctness as a mode of institutionalized othering, as has been discussed in the United States and other western academic and media theaters (Hill 2009; Jackson 2010; Gupta 2014), the Sino-African reception and deployment of PC draws attention to the resilience of white Anglocentrism's regulatory emergence, even in a context where it is supposed to be explicitly absent. Here, PC seemingly even provides a gender- and class-neutral refuge from patriarchal bullying and regional classism for African and Chinese women in their respective contexts. However, as reflected by Lili and Adam's catch-22, this landscape of political correctness—and the racial-linguistic complex it elides—implicitly generates limited possibilities of expression for those who are simultaneously its subalterns, and who themselves have no real stake in the deployment of the asymmetries that white PC-ness (in its often-sanctimonious invocations) supposedly protects them from.

RACE AND ENREGISTERMENT

The way in which PC-ness becomes linguistically mediated between Lili and Adam, thus racially stratifying them in terms of the presence/nonpresence of Tim, can be understood as an extended example of enregisterment as introduced in the previous chapter. Here, Asif Agha's general definition of enregisterment must be considered and then extended:

> Language users often employ labels like "polite language," "informal speech," "upper-class speech," "women's speech," "literary usage," "scientific term," "religious language," "slang," and others to describe differences among speech forms. Meta-linguistic labels of this kind link speech repertoires to enactable pragmatic effects, including images of the person speaking (woman, upper-class person), the relationship of speaker to interlocutor (formality, politeness), the conduct of social practices (religious, literary, or scientific activity). They hint at the existence of cultural models of speech—a metapragmatic classification of discourse types—linking speech repertoires to typifications of actor, relationship and conduct. This is the space of register variation conceived in intuitive terms. (Agha 2007b, 145)

Most examples of enregisterment diagram various forms of social stratification along lines of gender, class, and other modes of hierarchy. In their work, Susan Frekko (2009) and Kathryn Woolard et al. (2014) have provided canonical examples of enregisterment among Catalan speakers in Catalonia. Rarely, however, do studies of enregisterment engage the question of racial stratification in contexts of encounter that transcend conventionally defined speech communities in an engagement with the west or western modernity. Additionally, race—in a non-western setting, among non-whites, and through its mediation via English—is indeed an unusual case for examining enregisterment. The exploration of enregisterment in such a context, however, has important implications for demonstrating key conceptual interventions of black feminist theories of race and gender intersectionality beyond the English-speaking settler colonial realm.[2] Up until now, canonical case studies of intersectionality have been made primarily in western contexts or interactions more overtly framed within the rubric of "the west and its others." Enregisterment—in this way—becomes a way of expanding the range of intersectional critique into the discourse of third-world histories and the contemporary encounters they mediate and are mediated through. Unlike gendered and classed terms, like those presented by Agha, racialized non-western, non-white encounters do not imbricate conventionalized modes of address between variously raced people in English-speaking societies where white subjectivity mediates racism. Everyday gendered and classed terms of address can be conventionalized through (nonetheless contradictory) arguments that posit the simultaneous "reality" of differences, while at the same time suggesting that they are "canceled-out" by the equal opportunity promise of long-term social reform where "things are always getting better" for women and the working class.

Race, in contrast, begins with its nonrecognition, given the ways in which English-speaking, "liberal" societies tend to treat nonracialism as their politically correct default (Erkens and Kane-Berman 2000; Mills 2017)—where race is problematically argued to be logically arbitrary, and therefore ontologically nonexistent. Thus, the experience of racism for those who have it (non-whites), becomes an absurdity or illogical tragedy to those that don't have a race (whites). For this reason, conversations where different societies and language communities can be enregistered according to different gender norms cannot be broached in terms of the enregisterment of different societies' racialization norms. This is why non-whites, in making use of the English language, could never invoke the hierarchies of white racism toward whites, anywhere.

This raises a second enregisterment concern—its emergence among non-whites in a non-western encounter. Why do global, multilingual non-whites play by the rules (or feel they are expected to) of English PC? If Lili racially insults Adam, he can—within limits—return the insult with equal and possibly more devastating effect. Neither of them, however, could ever really turn the racism tables on Tim, who occupies an unassailable higher ground on the aspirational landscape of the white, cosmopolitan Anglosphere. Their best chance of offense, although landing with little effect as long as Tim plays by the same PC rules, is to name him a racist. Here, I propose that Adam and Lili's encounter—and indeed other Sino-African interactions in Beijing—certainly fall beyond the conventional sites of enregisterment, but in ways that suggest a more flexible conception of the "boundedness" of speech communities. Analyzing interrelated, but not parallel, racialized and gendered stratifications beyond nation-state or monolingual speech community necessitates an approach that both situates their intersectionality through the encounter, while simultaneously attending to intersectionality's contextualizing historical and material conditions. Here, Frantz Fanon and other postcolonial thinkers' transnational and transhistorical analyses of intersectional stratification become an important theoretical resource.

As suggested so far, the *translation* of difference (or sameness)—in this case, the contradictions manifested in the related racial and gender stratification of a non-western encounter—must account for an intersubjective space-time or chronotope within which this ordering can unfold: an intersectional order. In contextualizing interactions like those of Adam and Lili, Frantz Fanon—in his *Black Skins, White Masks* (2008)—drew attention to two chronotopes of stratification: "The Woman of Color and the White Man," and "The Man of Color and the White Woman."

These two figures are key psychoanalytic protagonists in Fanon's analysis of the colonial encounter and its postcolonial reiteration. As ambiguous formations that problematize simplistic colonial binaries, they become ideal examples to depict latent postcolonial asymmetries even where these seem to be occluded by the appearance of the "progressive" multiracial couple. Adam, Tim, and Lili's interactions take this latency a step further in providing a contradictory insight concerning the relationship between the raced signs of whiteness and non-whiteness in the Sino-African encounter. In the first instance, we can understand Adam as linguistically adopting a kind of whiteness both by playing a civilizing role in Lili's life at the beginning of her educational life in Beijing, as well as retrospectively through her later co-presence with Tim. Ironically, this co-presence also blackens Adam by virtue of him initially being rejected, and later voicing jealousy at the position occupied by Tim at the party. Lili, in contrast, appears to become Fanon's woman of color at different points during her move from the relationship with Adam to one with Tim. Paradoxically, her co-presence with Tim also retrospectively whitens her in relation to Adam through her negation of their prior relationship, and simultaneously remakes Adam into Fanon's dialectical black man to the white(ned) woman. From this perspective, it may even be possible to construe Adam's act of revenge at the party as a way to recapture his now retrospectively lost whiteness by underlining Lili's incapacity to live up to it.

These interactionally emergent potentials reveal a key contradiction. Adam and Lili, by virtue of Tim's presence, seem to oscillate in their capacity to occupy racialized positions vis-à-vis one another. This occurs through their transforming temporal trajectories and social alignments as Lili ascends an ideological updraft while Adam plunges down into the turbulence left in its wake. Tim's position of whiteness, by contrast, seems firmly entrenched. Their fluid versus his entrenched relations are strangely at odds with the marked versus unmarked positions they respectively occupy in American or British Commonwealth racial imaginaries (Frankenberg 2001; Gilroy 1992; Hage 2000). Whiteness, masked as political correctness, emerges again as unassailable, leaving its others in a precarious and perspectival position: Lili, like Fanon's Mayotte, aspires to drink the milk that will make her and her children whiter (Fanon [1952] 2008, 29). But how might whiteness emerge when Tim is not present?

In 2016, a Chinese detergent commercial went viral in and beyond China. The American news network CNN was one of the first to pick up on the story. Their online US edition concisely depicted the commercial with an abbreviated vignette: "A black man and a Chinese woman are flirting, as he leans in for a kiss she thrusts a detergent capsule in his mouth and bundles him into a laundry machine. She sits atop the washing machine as the man screams inside until, to her apparent delight, out pops a Chinese man dressed in a clean, white t-shirt."[3] The commercial was for a Chinese detergent brand, Qiaobi, and was released near the conclusion of my fieldwork. At the time, I did not realize that its circulation and subsequent discussion would become a key impetus for the concerns discussed in this book.

Almost immediately after the ad hit, I noted how my African informants and compatriots in China, as well as many Chinese classmates and colleagues, followed and shared the ad on Chinese social media platforms like Weibo and WeChat. They, along with many others, were in agreement that the reason for the commercial's controversy and related virality lay in its apparent racist content.

However—and for reasons that will become clear—not all of my informants believed that the Chinese ad producers were racist. The authors of the CNN article, James Griffith and Shen Lu, described the content of the commercial as "staggeringly racist," but also noted that: "The ad isn't even original. . . . It seemingly rips-off a similar, also offensive, Italian advert, in which a slim Italian man is washed with 'color' detergent and emerges as a muscular black man with the slogan 'color is better.'"

Indeed, Qiaobi was referencing an Italian commercial for another detergent, Coloreria Italiana, which had aired ten years before (in 2006)—complete with the same soundtrack—although, at the time, with far less western media outrage over its content. The outraged virality over the Qiaobi ad appeared to retrospectively infect Coloreria Italiana in almost a parody of Walter Benjamin's (2007a, 2007b, 2007c) famous argument that "copies" of aesthetic objects constitute their "originality." Italians and Chinese were not only equally racist, Chinese racism was an "inauthentic" copy of its Italian original. For instance, in the days following the airing of the Qiaobi commercial, the UK-based online newspaper, *Daily Mail,* ran the headline: "You thought the Chinese advert was racist . . . wait until you see the Italian ad that inspired it," along with its own terse vignette: "The advertisement starts with a wife loading up the laundry before her skinny white husband walks in wearing only socks and his underwear. She beckons him over with a smile before shoving him into the washing machine. Trapping the man inside she sits on top of the device until the cycle is complete. At the end of the wash, her husband has been completely transformed. A large burly black man is unveiled and rises up to flex his muscles, the [white] woman looking mighty impressed."[4]

Contemporary media representations of black subjects in China certainly do not celebrate the comradeship of a nonaligned, third-world solidary past. However, the prevalence of references to blackness, like those in the Qiaobi commercial, continue to generate an important question among internationally aware African and Chinese students in China: "Can Chinese be racist?" While most of my African and Chinese interlocutors answered in the affirmative during numerous debates in Chinese and African social media circles, a few had critical reservations concerning the capacity to return insult: "Can Africans be racist back?" For this minority of Chinese and African students, racism had a more ideological, meta-semiotic function. For them, and indeed many thinkers of the critical race theory canon, racism generates an unassailable inequality and a unidirectional communicability: "How could you ever racially insult a real flesh-and-blood white man, other than calling him a racist?" This question was voiced by various Chinese and African informants. "As for Chinese, you can always laugh at them, even when they think they are white," noted others (also both African and Chinese students). For these informants, racism produces an impossibility of insulting the inhabitant of whiteness, which stands as the only genuine position from which racism matters. One informant, Daniel Masuka, who first introduced himself by telling me that I would only remember his English name, rhetorically asked: "If we can all be racist to each other, then why would racism matter?" Some informants like Daniel were former victims of inter-African xenophobia in countries like South Africa. For them, genocide and other forms of identity-based violence were certainly violent and terrifying, but they were not the same as racism, which belonged to a very different cultural, historical, and ideological order of experience.

In fact, for some, structural and other forms of racism were either inevitable or, in the case of Daniel, "acceptable" compared to the trauma of xenophobic violence. His reference point, as a Zimbabwean, was the memory of his time as a student in Johannesburg, South Africa, and the ongoing experiences of his working-class compatriots who were still there. This was by no means a valorization of racism, far from it, but rather a testament to an enduring, transnational ideological condition that is so compromised that even in recognizing its contours there is no way out of its stratifying grip. In this reading of racism, whiteness stood as a condition of value that non-white Beijing informants found themselves marked in relation to, even when no white bodies were physically present. This was because unmarked whiteness, as I will argue, was still the privileged category of cosmopolitan mobility and the assumed point of articulation for standard English or its received pronunciation (RP)—what I will reveal to be the motivating factors of mobility and educational desire.

Perhaps in China, as the Qiaobi commercial suggests, Chinese men might become white enough one day, but that destiny still appears to be very much deferred for educated, aspirationally cosmopolitan black subjects like Adam. For he—unlike Fanon's recruitment of the fictional character Jean Veneuse—*does* know his race and has a pragmatic understanding of how whites (and aspiring Chinese) understand him (Fanon [1952] 2008: 46).

There are, however, varying registers of whiteness that might play a role in stratifications beyond Lili and Adam's encounter. In what follows, I will reveal how a similarly complex enregisterment around English and whiteness can occur fractally among Beijing's South African community of students. Here, whiteness still emerges as the apex of stratification, but with social and historical co(n)texts particular to one community of students—where the South African historical relationship to a linguistic register termed Model C English facilitates a more general intersectional stratification in relation to PC English, reiterating the relationship between signs of whiteness and English PC depicted in Lili and Adam's encounter. I would like to qualify that Model C enregisterment—while being specific to the context of South Africa and South African students—does have its analogs among other African students in Beijing. Due to my close familiarity with the particular context of Model C, being a product of the educational horizon it imbricates, I will focus on explicating the relationship between Model C and the wider context of English's raciolinguistic stratification in Sino-African encounters. In future analyses, by myself or others, I am certain that analogs of this enregistered stratification of whiteness, at different scales and within different communities, can be excavated.

ENREGISTERING MODEL C AND PC

For Lerato (see chapter 2) and many other South African students in Beijing, there is an opposition between black vernacular Englishes and elite Model C English. In her analysis of the cultural capital of certain English accents in a South African educational context, Kerryn Dixon provides a fairly standard definition of the Model C accent as follows: "Speaking with a 'White' [South African] English accent is seen to be ideal—and the students who speak fluent English without the intonations of African languages are often referred to as having a 'Model C accent'" (2011, 81). Animating the notion of Model C is an unmarked, hierarchical, standard version of English, which comes to mark black African bodies who speak with it. In the context of certain encounters, it is difficult to separate Model C from the figure of the coconut—"someone who is dark on the outside but white on the inside"—as an icon of personhood (Carr 2011) that is the inhabitant of the Model C accent. This co-presence is key since a white subject can't have a Model C accent, even if they had acquired it in the same place. In the past, it has often been used as an insult to distinguish between elite, compromised blackness with its co-presence to, and reliance on, whiteness, and authentic blackness marked by a vernacular accent. In recent times, however, coconut has been positively appropriated by many black elite South African media commentators and academics like Eusebius McKaiser and Panashe Chigumadzi. In articulating this choice Chigumadzi states:

> I've chosen to appropriate the term and self-identify as a coconut because I believe it offers an opportunity for refusal. It's an act of problematizing myself—and others—within the landscape of South Africa as part of the black middle class that is supposed to be the buffer against more "radical elements." Instead of becoming the trusted mediators between black and white, we are now turning to conceptions of blackness and mobilizing anger at the very concept of the rainbow nation. The fantasy of a color-blind, post-racial South Africa has been projected onto us coconuts, but our lived experiences are far from free of racism. (2015)

McKaiser, reflecting a similar political alignment, but with a close attention to the language-based dimensions of the lived experience of being a coconut in post-apartheid South Africa, writes the following in an article titled *The Unbearable Whiteness of Being*:

> Hi. My name is Eusebius. And I am fluent in the grammar of whiteness. I am such a clever black that as a scrawny little boy—hey wena, no one is born with an mkhaba! I really was scrawny once—I quickly learnt the grammar of whiteness. I remember practising "bru" in a sentence, followed by other gems such as "sarmie," "dos" and "oke." If you don't know these words, I pity you. You are doomed. Kiss upward

mobility goodbye, baba. The grammar of whiteness is key to doing well in corporate South Africa. You must sound like the chief executive's son, not the chief executive's maid's son. You catch my coconut drift? I am multilingual like that—Afrikaans, English, a wee bit of Xhosa (on a good day), and a whole whack of whiteness. That is why I, how do they put it, "fit in everywhere." (2013)

White grammar, as McKaiser terms it, is the condition of possibility—among elite non-white, non-Anglo South Africans—for "fitting in anywhere." In part, the article was widely understood and cited—even on Anglophone African social media in Beijing—as an attempt at provincializing whiteness. McKaiser textually attempts to do this not only through his use of Zulu expressions like *mkhaba*—contextually denoting the acquisition of a "beer belly" or "bloated stomach"—as a moment of self-deprecation directed toward mostly black, specifically Xhosa-speaking readers familiar with the term. He also does so through his disparaging contextualizations of white South African English terms like *bru* ("buddy"), *oke* ("dude"), *sarmie* ("sandwich"), and *dos* ("to take a nap"). McKaiser simultaneously does this through linguistic inclusion—of a black-aligned audience—and exclusion of a white audience ignorant of *mkhaba*. However, McKaiser also points to the limits of this provincialization in that the white South African English terms require no translation for their black interlocutors, while the inverse is not the case when it comes to a term like *mkhaba*.

For elites like Chigumadzi and McKaiser, Model C has an additional function within the communities that would otherwise undermine a so-called coconut's lack of black authenticity and capacity to speak. Within communities and interactions where a white space-time is assumed to be absent, and where McKaiser and Chigumadzi's arguments are cited—like that of the elite Southern African student community in Beijing—the emergence of Model C can often become a gendered talisman against such discrimination by virtue of its association with an inter-social chronotope of de-racialized or rational political correctness (Bakhtin 1981; Agha 2007a). In contestation of encounters where black authenticity is brought into conflict with an adherence to white normativity—often under the guise of a "modernity versus tradition" dispute—such a chronotope of rational political correctness can quickly become activated through the invocation of a Model C register. In what now follows, I will show how one such encounter plays out when decontextualized from a "typically South African" theater of media reception.

THE SOCIAL LIFE OF A MEME

Given many South African students' access to a black social media sphere in Beijing, popular memes that emerge in the South African media context—which certainly do not end at the nation-state's borders—are quickly circulated among African students from a number of different African countries. One such popular meme was Ziright iGirls. As with most social media memes, Ziright iGirls began its life prior to its mass-circulation, but through that circulation came to transform its meanings. It is commonly pronounced and spelled "ziright iighels" by a number of South African Xhosa speakers, although the spelling "ziRight iGals" has also become a popular alternative, following the wide circulation of a South African house music track by the same name—performed by Euphonik and Bekzin Terris, featuring author Khaya Dlanga.[5] One informant and South African black social media expert, Z, explained its prior contextualization as a term usually used when "young, or older, [Xhosa] men will go enquire if the women still have enough alcohol to drink by asking *ziright iighels*, which means: 'are the girls alright?'"

As a meme, however, Ziright iGirls began going viral when fast-food chain Nando's picked up on the expression as it was being used on South African social media and referenced it in an advertising campaign under the slogan *Zisela ntoni igirls?* or "What would the girls like?" This sparked a mass appropriation of both expressions in situations outside of the Xhosa-specific contextualization within a matrilineal kinship and gendered-language world. As a result, its appropriation often came to be denounced as patriarchal, patronizing, and sexist among many (including many South Africans) who were unaware of its Xhosa-specific contextualization. This, however, did not hinder its popularity and further circulation among a Pan-African student community—like that in Beijing—attuned to the South African "Twittersphere." The absurdity of this circulation came to a head during a casual soccer game in Beijing between two groups of African students.

Azania United is a group of soccer players from Zimbabwe, South Africa, Botswana, Madagascar, and other Southern African countries. During my fieldwork, I was a regular member of the team, and played on defense, most likely because of my poor footwork, although—according to one of the senior players—my selection was based on an ethnic stereotype: "I like the aggression of you rugby-playing Boers." On one particular occasion, we were playing against a combined team of predominantly African students from Senegal and Côte d'Ivoire (including two Koreans and one Fijian to make up their numbers). One or two of our opponents were classmates who had regular interaction with the Southern Africans and thus there was a good deal of friendly banter between the two teams, despite a fierce competition within Beijing's African University Student League. A group of Azania United's female supporters—mostly from South Africa—were standing behind our goalposts. Early in the game, one of our opponents broke through the middle and scored a spectacular goal in the top left-hand corner of Azania United's goal posts (this may or may not have been partly my fault). The goal scorer, however, rushed toward the group of girls in celebration yelling *Ziright iGirls?* in what was clearly an abrasively French accent. The addressees of this inquiry were at first dumbstruck, but confusion quickly gave way to hilarity as the addressor's intent became apparent. Following the laughter, the latter sheepishly rejoined his team for a more collective celebration. Not all invocations of *Ziright iGirls*, however, are met with the same hilarity.

During an argument on the social media forum Azanian Students in China (ASIC), *Ziright iGirls* reared its head once more. One black female member—Comrade Y—was making a politically charged argument about the #RhodesMustFall protests taking place in South Africa: "We must oppose violent means of protest at all cost. . . . It plays into the hands of our oppressors." This was endorsed by two other female students on the forum. At that moment, another black male participant—Comrade X—entered the fray stating *"Ziright iGirls?"* The female members immediately turned on him in English, accusing him of being "patronizing" as well as "sexist." Seeing this exchange, I privately contacted Comrade X—who was one of my teammates—and asked whether he thought he was guilty of the charges laid against him. His response—stated in a heavy Zulu accent—was that "This Oprah [Winfrey], PC thing is a problem. Take away the Model C shine and the story is very different." Here, Comrade X not only draws a link between PC—as a very general, English discursive *type*—and Model C—as a specific *token* of phonolexical speech. He also suggests that these discursive formations—as sign sets—work together in blocking him from getting his meaning across. Thus, by way of unifying these sign sets, he invokes the figure of Oprah Winfrey as a distilled archetype—or icon of personhood—transferrable across the potentially divergent chronotopes that PC and Model C might otherwise index. In doing so, Comrade X generates a third space-time (with Oprah Winfrey as a mediator) within which PC and Model C operate very much like Weberian elective affinities—in that they reinforce and constitute Oprah Winfrey as the ideal type of modern, cosmopolitan black femininity.

Here, and in other instances that will follow, we see Oprah Winfrey emerge as an unwanted (or perhaps even dystopian) icon under which a particular brand of metadiscursive encoding (Urban 1996) is perceived as regulating appropriate PC behavior in the register of Model C, which has now become unmoored from its South African context. In this sense, Comrade X is modeling one of Slavoj Žižek's (1989) observations concerning the nature of ideology: that ideology operates less because we believe it than because we believe others do. Comrade X judges himself as being critical of the relationship between PC and Model C in regulating the signs of value available to Africans in the world. However, he is also fully aware that knowing this and recognizing its conduits—in this case, Oprah Winfrey—does nothing to change the ideological gravity of the world within which black Africans stake out a legibility even among one another. In light of this observation, the question emerges: Does Oprah Winfrey have any challengers?

OPRAH GIRLS AND TREVOR NOAH BOYS

After Adam and Lili's fallout (discussed at the beginning of the chapter), Adam and I chatted over a small pile of Portuguese egg tarts that can be bought for a bargain at any Chinese KFC. The topic of discussion predictably centered around racism in China, after which Adam—washing down a final egg tart with a gulp of Pepsi Cola—concluded in mock melodrama: "Ah, you know, sometimes, you want to explain to [Chinese] people why things are racist, but then, *you look into their eyes and you realize . . . there's no hope.*" The last phrase was a direct quote from South African comedian Trevor Noah's portrayal of an encounter with a white American Californian girl who had asked Noah if he "had ever had AIDS" in his 2012 stand-up show, *That's Racist.*[6]

It is frustration at the inescapable inevitability of race that perhaps prompts Adam to invoke Trevor Noah's figure at the KFC that night. Voicing Trevor Noah as an icon of personhood appears to momentarily provide an escape from the space-time of dead-end inevitabilities masked by the language of "rational," "nongendered," "nonracialized" egalitarianism. Here, mirroring Noah indexes a streetwise worldliness that can quickly transform both universalizing political correctness and Beijing's more predictable street racisms into the kind of farce that the sassy anti–politically correct, stoic male Afropolitan can always rise above. However, as will become apparent, committing explicitly to Trevor Noah as a mass-mediated icon of personhood, and implicitly to what Noah is not, engenders its own limitations.

"*These fucking Oprah girls*, they come to Beijing, only hang out among themselves, then they get all pissed off when their boyfriends want to date other girls. Then, when they get ditched, they go and sleep with their ex-boyfriend's best friends. It's lame, bro." South African student Edlulayo "Ed" Zuma said this to me when commenting on African girls in Beijing's student community and their incapacity to move—romantically speaking—beyond relationships with African men. The "Oprah girls" comment was provoked by an ex-girlfriend "bombing" him with messages on WeChat accusing him—in English rather than Zulu which they both speak—of "male insecurity," "internalizing his problems," and "not sharing his feelings." As we sat in his shabby dorm room eating *pap* (a South African maize porridge) while he continued to engage with his ex's WeChat messages, his roommate walked in, stole a glance at Edlulayo's exasperated texting, and commented in his French accent: "How is Oprah Winfrey?"

The person referred to as Oprah Winfrey in this conversation is one of the members of Azanian Achievers (from the previous chapter), who herself began to feel socially alienated and made a choice to withdraw from community gatherings—soccer matches, parties, and cultural days organized among African students in Beijing—to focus her energies on projects like Purple Cow and Miriam Bakgatla's organization. She was about to graduate and return to her country to take up a government job. Hers is a prominent pattern among talented black female students in Beijing, who—with exceptions like their mentor, Miriam—find the environment fairly hostile and usually end up returning to their home countries to try and take up government or private sector posts with little possibility of travel, and seldom recognizing their China-Africa expertise. While in Beijing, once they commit to styling themselves "professionally"—that is, with Model C English accents and formal "business language"—male students like Edlulayo refer to them as Oprah Winfrey girls. "They constantly want to go Doctor Phil on you . . . *how's that working out for you?"* (voiced in a mock American accent). To be sure, this is not the Oprah Winfrey of black, everyday female empowerment as has been both invoked and critiqued in the media context of the United States (Epstein and Steinberg 1995; Wallace 1992). Rather, it emerges in its Anglophone African guise as a negative figure of personhood that stands for a naïve commitment to western-centric white political correctness, which for many of my informants is at best idealistic, and more commonly, out of kilter with the jaded expectations of many aspirational black postcolonial subjects. This perception certainly has much to do with Oprah's bad press in South Africa, following the media scandals around her leadership academy in Soweto (Hughes 2011; Stephey 2011). However, this is also part of a more complex denigration of the Oprah brand by a number of prominent African media personalities—notably, Trevor Noah. In what follows, I aim to analyze the process by which Oprah Winfrey becomes a negative icon of personhood via her recruitment into an oppositional role to the Trevor Noah icon of personhood.

Media historian Jim Pines (1992), and subsequently others (Torres 1998; Leonard and Guerrero 2013), have noted how—like in the United States—black experience in Britain was initially constituted from the perspective of a white media context of reception. The picture Pines describes is one in which "the stridently liberal position vis-à-vis white responses to black presence in Britain" becomes increasingly assumed in media representations of racial relations. As Pines unsurprisingly notes, this white liberal position "had precious little impact on overall institutional thinking and practice" within the mass-mediated default of white Britain, in spite of its diversity (1992, 10). This observation in the British mass-media context mirrors the arguments of a genealogy of critical race theorists like Paul Gilroy (1993), Anthony Kwame Appiah (1992), Charles Mills (1998), Frantz Fanon (2008 [1952]), and notably Steve Biko (2002); the latter was quite explicit in denouncing this liberal white position prior to his death in 1977:

> A game at which the liberals have become masters is that of deliberate evasiveness. The question often comes up "what can you do?" If you ask him to do something like stopping to use segregated facilities or dropping out of varsity to work at menial jobs like all blacks or defying and denouncing all provisions that make him privileged, you always get the answer—"but that's unrealistic!" While this may be true, it only serves to illustrate the fact that no matter what a white man does, the colour of his skin—his passport to privilege—will always put him miles ahead of the black men. Thus, in the ultimate analysis, no white person can escape being part of the oppressor camp. (Biko 2002, 22)

Making clear that implicit white liberalism always entails an explicit compromise, Biko mirrors Fanon (2008 [1952]), and subsequently Achille Mbembe's (2001) critiques, in reflecting how there is no "outside" to the black-white dynamic that stages and restages the colonial-apartheid complex. It is through the vortex-like force of this regulating chronotope, that—these thinkers have suggested—black Africans are "blackened" even among one another. Oprah Winfrey, for comedians like Trevor Noah, embodies this compromise, not through the color of her skin, but through the color of her language and the space-time of utopian, politically correct privilege it activates. This interplay of language and race, however, arises in a curious relationship to the gender asymmetries it diagrams, and through it, Oprah Winfrey becomes a disdained archetype among African students in Beijing. By contrast, the performed figure of Trevor Noah—for African male students— emerges as a more relatable alternative to the icons of personhood represented by the world of the Purple Cow and its not-yet-emerged Purple Giraffe. However, even this commitment has slim hopes of escaping the orbit of the Angloscene.

EVERYBODY'S GETTING A BEATING

Noah's world, or at least the version of it that emerges among many of my informants, is filled with materials that students in Beijing can make use of to dynamically figurate internal divisions and asymmetries.[7] As suggested earlier, male Sino-Afropolitans quote Trevor Noah far more frequently than their female peers, with men usually voicing themselves as the "Noah-ing" subject in the moment of citation. As such, Noah represents an archetype or icon of personhood that men can far more easily slip into than their female peers. Furthermore, many of these citations are both *directed at* as well as *about* other female African students, or they become resources to depict and conceptualize relationships with Chinese and white foreign students. Here, many of my male African informants used Trevor Noah's own depictions of his "equal opportunity" sexual exploits to depict their own African, Chinese, and other "cosmopolitan romances"—as one informant put it. Whether these were "fictitious" or otherwise "genuine" depictions of transnational eros, the citation of Trevor Noah's English-language sound bites seem directed toward verbally cosplaying a desired "efficacy"—in mobile or racial terms—which their "success" in achieving it appears to entail. In what follows, I aim to analyze the citation of one of Trevor Noah's well-circulated comedy routines, and how its invocation diagrams the contours of a key dimension of the Sino-Afropolitan ethnoscape and its limited contextualization within the Angloscene.

The footballers of Azania United, including myself, stood in a tiny patch of shade next to Lei Feng University's soccer pitch, gingerly warming up as the searing sun refracted off Beijing's hazy, polluted summer air. The team—made up mostly of students from Southern African Development Community (SADC) countries—were preparing to face their next opponents in the Beijing inter-African league. As each player for Azania United was given their kit, they donned their yellow shirt and blue pants, rolled-on their white socks, and strapped on their boots. As if magically protected by their Nike and Adidas talismans, the tough talk soon began in spite of the weather and air quality that promised a harrowing ninety minutes. As I did my best to muster enough energy just to participate in the heat-exhausted banter, I overheard this exchange:

> Comrade B: "Eish, we are going to give those Senegalese boys a spanking."
> Comrade C: "No, no, bra . . . we spank the monkey, we are going to beat them."

Hearing this, I continued: "And because this is the Oprah show, EVERYBODY GETS A BEATING." At this, the entire group sitting under the tree laughed loudly at what was a direct quote from a widely shared Trevor Noah comedy skit.[8] I could complete the punch line only because all of us had intimate knowledge of Noah's comedy routines and social commentary, which are extremely popular among young Africans throughout the world—even more so since Noah became the host of *The Daily Show*. His prominence was apparent among my informants, precisely because his observations, recontextualized in a concentrated African student community in Beijing, capture the absurd—and often satirical—ways in which already complex miscommunications between Africans become even further distorted when resituated more globally. Noah's routines were constantly shared by Beijing-based African community members who verbally cited, or digitally cut and pasted his YouTube links, if they had access to a VPN (Virtual Private Network) to get around the Chinese firewall. Sometimes his clips were downloaded, copied, and circulated via flash drives or portable hard drives that are exchanged when students gather at social events. It was a common practice, for instance, to bring a media object or shareable data to a sport, music, or drinking event organized among the students. Collective screenings of such materials, some hosted by myself, were also common and reciprocally expected at social gatherings. Trevor Noah features prominently at these events, either explicitly—in the case of viewing one of his routines—or implicitly, where many one-liners from his endlessly circulated skits become ventriloquized. Virtuosic performances become social currency with which to banter about other media materials being shared, or, more commonly, to depict relationships between African students as well as their everyday interactions with Chinese and other foreign interlocutors within Beijing's increasingly hybrid student community. Such videos are media artifacts that play a key role in imagining "cosmopolitan" identities that are simultaneously "Afrocentric" and "global," "grassroots" and "cosmopolitan"—self-descriptive keywords and combinations of phrases that are ubiquitously juxtaposed in gatherings among African students. It is important to note, however, that the "global" and the "Afrocentric" only seem to become translatable in measured Model C English. This combination of register and deixis, mediated through tone, vocabulary, and accent, engenders the simultaneous stratification and articulation of relationships between languages, racialized identities, and classes of mobility emergent in Noah's humor. Furthermore, the ideal signifying subject of this imagining—the figure of personhood inhabiting Model C English and its associated hierarchies—is far from neutral.

In the exchange between Comrade B, Comrade C, and myself, the Noah joke referenced was from a sketch on Oprah Winfrey's Soweto-based leadership academy, which was established in 2007. At the time, the school had come under heavy criticism in the South African and international media when reports surfaced, exposing the extreme abuse and implementation of corporal punishment that female students attending Winfrey's "50-million-dollar" institution had to endure.[9] Noah noted that the disjuncture between "state-of-the-art facilities" and not state-of-the-art teachers was the result of the fact that Oprah "was not dealing with Brad Pitt" when she was interviewing her school's prospective teachers. Through an improvised dialogue between Oprah Winfrey and the school's imagined principal, Noah imagines the dynamics of a hypothetical interview, mimicking Oprah's accent in contrast with an impersonation of a Soweto-style stereotyping of township English. He exaggerates the latter in particular, most likely because of the predominantly South African audience for *The Daywalker*.

> Oprah: You're not going to spank them are you?
>
> Principal: No, nevah, nevah, no, we can nevah spank a child.
>
> [Noah mimes Winfrey's departure on an airplane while cheerfully waving goodbye]
>
> Principal: [Speaking township slang and English] *Oprah is right*. No, us, spanking a child? Nevah. We BEAT them. Ja, we BEAT children. Don't spank a child heh, eh . . . spanking is for playing, you can spank a monkey, spankey, spankey . . . spankey, spankey, monkey, spankey, spankey, ja . . . You can spank a monkey, you don't spank a child. We BEAT.

Here, Noah contextualizes the expectations of a western liberal education within the setting of a township school with a very different disciplinary outlook. The reception of "spanking" is very different on the parts of Oprah and the school principal—not in terms of what spanking is or whether it is necessary or not, for they both seem to settle on the idea that "you must never spank a child." Their contextualization, however, makes explicit that their reasons for agreement arise from very different assumptions regarding spanking's inappropriateness. In creating such scenarios, Noah generates a potential to restage "progressive" globalism within a context that talks back by juxtaposing Oprah's chronotope with that of the township. For Africans who are abroad—men in particular—Trevor Noah has become a resource for coping with their own contextual challenges by spatio-temporally opening up the possibility of translating a difficult encounter in their own imagined Trevor's terms. In the same comedy routine, he goes a step further by drawing attention to the way in which this contextualization and recontextualization is a far from even process. He does this by reflecting how, even when

Oprah's liberal educational outlook is resisted by the school principal's alternative interpretation, this resistance nonetheless takes place with and in relation to a theater of evaluation that valorizes the horizon of expectation represented by Oprah's world. In the sequence following the principal's earlier monologue on the distinction between beating and spanking, Noah transports us to an imagined encounter between a student and teacher in Oprah's school:

Teacher: Mavis, did you do your homework?

Mavis: No, Ma'am.

Teacher: Then you are going to get a BEATING . . .

At this moment Noah switches from a township accent to an impersonation of Oprah Winfrey, which suggests that in some way Mavis's teacher has transformed into (or perhaps become possessed by) the ghost of Oprah:

Teacher: . . . but because it's Oprah's school, EVERYBODY'S GETTING ONE. YOU'RE GETTING A BEATING, YOU'RE GETTING A BEATING, YOU'RE GETTING A BEATING . . . EVERYBODY'S GETTING A BEATING . . . LOOK UNDER YOUR SEAT, YOU'RE GETTING A BEATING.

By transforming the time-space from that of a Soweto classroom to a more sinister iteration of Oprah's Chicago West Loop studio—facilitated through his shift in accent—Noah indicates that even the beatings take place within the logics of Oprah's world, imbricating both its horizon of expectation as well as the exclusions facilitated by her brand. Noah himself is only able to momentarily subvert this hierarchy, by himself adopting his default, meta-commentary accent, which is always in well-delivered, Model C English. The invocation of English as a rationalizing register places him—if somewhat precariously—as a translator between Oprah's world and the Soweto school. Here, he is only able to get away with this move because of his self-identification with the category *coloured*.[10] Noah, however, emerges as coloured-but-not-quite through his routines, because even *coloureds*—whom he frequently parodies—come across as a stereotype that he would struggle to "authentically" identify with. As the child of a relationship between a Xhosa woman and Swiss-German man, Noah always situates himself in his comedy as both "born a crime"—given the illegality of interracial relations under the conditions of apartheid during his formative years—and "daywalker"—drawing on the popular culture figure of a black half-human, half-vampire character in the Hollywood franchise *Blade*. This serves to deictically situate him in a familiar, constantly deferred "not-quite" hybrid, and thus an unassailable position from which to deliver his particular brand of comedy. But it is from this position, tellingly, that he is able to rely on a neutral English accent for delivering reflexive punch lines and meta-commentary to the multivoice, multiracial, polyglot scenarios and interactions he depicts. It is also this neutral meta-voice that utters "madness!" in every skit where the concatenation of speech genres and their worlds climax in a kind of semiotic excess—for it is within the politically correct space-time of the Angloscene that madness's comedic possibilities can reflexively emerge in rational, commonsensical Model C English.

For different African subjects in Beijing, "being Oprah" and "being Trevor Noah" are not only gendered archetypes. They also become foils for mediating the tension between two chronotopes: one the one hand, an unmarked PC—thus, white—space-time, and on the other, a reflexive, sassy, third-world cosmopolitan space-time. Oprah was not a subject position any African female subject would want to inhabit, given its derisive invocation by many of their male peers. Trevor Noah, in contrast, appeared—at times—to be an available, third-world cosmopolitan type—one that allowed for a dignified disalignment from the ironically racializing propensity of English's PC space-time. I say "at times" because Trevor Noah's position as third-world cosmopolitan hero is both highly perspectival and situationally precarious. This is not only given the highly gendered and sexist exclusions this alignment perpetuates, where only male African subjects could aspire to be Trevor. It is also because Trevor Noah's own sassiness is completely contingent on the adoption of a highly rarified English register as the simultaneously rational and rationalizing meta-voice of anti-PC, anti-imperialism, symbolized by the caricatured archetype of Oprah Winfrey in this particular comedy routine.

I would argue that neither Trevor Noah nor Oprah could be racists even if they were to hold racist views and engage in racial essentialism, because—as generations of critical race theorists have argued—racism is not an equal-opportunity proposition. This does not mean, however, that the gendered and raced invocations of Oprah or Noah—as archetypes—do not enregister racism and racist effects. Similarly, Qiaobi and Lili's racism, discussed at the outset of the chapter, is not commensurate with the racisms of white supremacists in Britain, Europe, or other white settler societies—that is, until Chinese become white enough to be colonial agents. Instead, I have suggested that racist encounters—viewed through the lens of a Fanonian translation—are not only about what is said between interlocutors, nor purely about who those interlocutors are, but—equally importantly—what space-times they are both able to recruit, and are excluded from recruiting, to their interactions. In Sino-African encounters, the question of what racism can be, and who can be racist, remains constrained by its still Anglo-centric medium of translation and English's associated PC theater of evaluation. For this reason, "who can be racist?" remains—at least for now—imbricated in a dialectical interaction that both recruits and constitutes white space-time as its ideological gravity.

Compromise

4
_____

How Paper Tigers Kill

The expression "America is just a paper tiger" has remained a common platitude in China ever since its first invocation in Mao Zedong thought. Historian-activist Judith Balso has noted: "Like many other statements of Mao Zedong, the description of imperialists—or even all reactionaries—as 'paper tigers' (*zhi laohu*) became famous beyond China through [Lin Biao's compilation of] the *Little Red Book*, where paper tigers feature in the title of its sixth chapter" (2019, 161). Here, Balso crucially draws attention to the ways in which the paper tiger—as an ideological metaphor—stands in a dialogical relationship with metaphors like "lifting a rock only to drop it on one's own feet," "nooses round the neck of US imperialism," and "the East Wind is prevailing over the West Wind," which are juxtaposed throughout the text. Of this juxtaposition, Balso further notes: "the paper tiger, far from being a *trompe l'oeil* in which the fragility of the enemy would be masked by a belief in its appearance of ferocity, reveals the double nature of any class enemy" (2019, 161). Mao Zedong himself was dialectically reflexive about this double nature:

> Here I should like to answer the question of whether imperialism and all reactionaries are real tigers. The answer is that they are at once real tigers and paper tigers, they are in the process of being changed from real into paper tigers. Change means transformation. Real tigers are transformed into paper tigers, into their opposite. This is true of all things, and not just social phenomena. But why take full account of [the enemy] if he is not a real tiger? . . . Just as there is not a single thing in the world without a dual nature (this is the law of the unity of opposites), so imperialism and all reactionaries have a dual nature—they are at the same time real tigers and paper tigers.[1]

Additionally, we can understand paper tigers, in their popular metaphorical uptake, as ultimately human-made media artifacts that do not represent the same danger as their real others existing within the realm of a primal, chthonic nature. In recent times, however, nature has also emerged as a countertrope to China's postsocialist rush toward the terraformation of an alienating, nature-destroying Anthropocenic modernity—where nature is invoked as a utopic, more Apollonian space-time of harmonious existence between human and nonhuman worlds (Paglia 1990). Nature—in this Eurocentric and dualist (but nonetheless persistent) folk ideology—imbricates a tension between utopic and dystopic potentials. This chapter discusses the mass and socially mediated recruitment of nature as metaphor and translational technology in Afro-Chinese encounters. In doing so, I propose an account of dangerous mediation and translational attunement in Afro-Chinese encounters.

MASS-MEDIATED TIGERS

On July 23, 2016, at Badaling Wildlife World, near the Great Wall in suburban Beijing's Yanqing district, a family of three became victims of a tiger attack. The event received wide coverage in both the Chinese and international media. Following the release of a short clip of surveillance video footage broadcast by mainland media, the *South China Morning Post* provided the following account to an English audience two days after the attack:

> [The video] shows a woman exiting the front passenger door of a white sedan and walking to the driver's door, where she stands talking to the driver, later confirmed to be her husband. A tiger appears from behind her and drags her off. The driver gives chase and all three disappear off camera, before he returns to the car where he is joined by another woman from the back seat, and they run in the direction the tiger dragged the first woman. The second woman was confirmed by relatives to be the 57-year-old mother of the woman who was dragged away.[2]

All subsequent news reports of the event in the week following the attack based their accounts on the Yanqing district government press statement, which noted that the mother was tragically killed by the tiger, and that the daughter was raced to a hospital where she had to undergo surgery. A government spokesperson for the district also indicated that the woman had ignored danger warnings from nearby personnel before the attack, and emphasized that the wildlife park had multiple signs telling tourists to stay in their cars, with warnings being repeatedly broadcast via loudspeakers. The event sparked major debates among Chinese netizens, followed by reams of meta-commentary by journalists following the case as a human-interest story. Debates among Chinese netizens, mirrored in journalistic analyses and investigations, appeared to follow two major themes: victim accountability and modernity critique.

In the first scenario, netizens debated whether the daughter was to blame for leaving the vehicle, or whether the husband caused her to leave the car, and whether the victim should receive compensation. One Sina poll of over 310,000 netizens indicated that only 2.3 percent of respondents thought that the zoo should be punished for the attack.

On Chinese social media platforms like Weibo, commentators made statements like: "The zoo should be asking the family for compensation, they should be compensated for their losses after being forced to temporarily shut down," or "Refund her the ticket fee and nothing more." The second theme of critique, however, emerged more tacitly: that despite the provision of an array of signs that danger was present, the victims were somehow oblivious to, or ignorant of, the immediacy of a tiger threat. This tacit media discourse suggested that there was an emerging panic around the possibilities of semiotic failure, which were revealed in the subsequent legal case around reparations, as well as the institutional responses that followed.

These institutional and legal responses focused on the presence of "clear" signs of danger on the one hand, but also emphasized the need for more innovative signs of danger for future visiting tourists on the other. Thus, a contradiction emerged: the media infrastructure of danger was revealed to be paradoxically both adequate and in need of an upgrade due to its presupposed inadequacy. Here, however, an important question emerges: Could the mediation of danger itself have been the very obstacle to experiencing the immediacy of a tiger threat in the first place? One report discussing the victim-blaming that followed the attack insisted on a common saying: "People's words are perhaps more scary than the mouth of a tiger." In the case of warning signs that demarcate the semiotic infrastructure of danger, could it be that perhaps the translations of metallic, digital, and paper tigers are out of synch with the unpredictable, and thus dangerous, alterity represented by the tiger itself?

These questions mirror an older but persistent media and semiotic anthropological tension—between the interplay of alterity and its translation, where translation has been understood as a general trope of mediation for generations of media theorists. This contrasts with its "purely" language-metaphorical interpretation and implementations in mainstream anthropology (Geertz 1977; Asad 1986). To be sure, this translational concern with alterity has also been demonstrated, with perhaps more explicit, broader anti-colonial stakes in the equally ethnographic work of many literary and postcolonial theorists (Spivak 1993; Bhabha 1994; Sakai 1997). In alignment with critical media and postcolonial concerns, many linguistic anthropologists and semioticians have pointed out that eliding the particularities of language, media, and alterity as a densely imbricated and convergent social-semiotic interface risks occluding its existence as a total set of historical material conditions as well as the sign relations that operate and are given resonance within them (M. Silverstein 1976; Gal 2015; Nakassis 2016b). From such a perspective, language—as a media infrastructure in itself—dialectically precedes and is maintained through *langue, parole,* and an array of communicative and embodied practices and phenomena. Here, it is precisely the dialogical nature of these maintenance processes that many ethnographers might often inadvertently misconstrue as "non-linguistic" or "unmediated"—where communication nests itself in the "differences that make a difference" within a total semiotic domain, as Gregory Bateson once suggested (1972).

Beyond the obvious point that many analysts who are critical of translation as analytic must themselves ultimately commit to a highly mediated set of methods and technologies in order to write about media objects, sites, and informants— including the language—it is clear that the pragmatic indispensability of translation in undertaking research, writing, and analysis becomes nonetheless inevitable. This is because the interpersonal encounters that co(n)textualize media objects and their mediation invariably must presume upon epistemologies of universalism as "structures of aspiration" (Li 2021, 234). For those engaged in the endeavor of translation—like Chinese netizens mediating social hierarchies through media meta-commentary around a tiger attack—the achievement of a translation exists as an unquestionable horizon of possibility, even while its contours seem to ever-recede from one's semantic grasp.

Tigers and their associated natures have led a vibrant life through metaphor in China. Though continually framed as representing a mysterious alterity—a hidden, merciless threat—tigers are nonetheless tirelessly recruited to folktales, analogies, and tropes of compassion, fidelity, and power throughout the Chinese and broader Asian literary context. Similarly, Chinese language and civilization has led a vibrant life through metaphor in the Orientalist west, despite being reduced to a frequently racist "inscrutability" or Herderian "providential" foil for Aryan-Semitic linguistic chauvinisms (Olender 2009). Inscrutability and alterity, thus, represent no obstacles to our capacities for reflexivity about subjects designated as such, nor the ability of so-designated inscrutable or alter subjects to inhabit the intelligible, ethical, and politically recruitable forms of personhood they have been recruited to. Furthermore, metaphors and the reflexive, intersubjective processes through which they are generated are in fact mediating processes in the broader Hegelian sense—in that they have concrete, material effects: they constitute both the reflexive actors and their referring subjects as entities that are vulnerable to laws, infrastructures, and violence.

Thus, my framing of translation encompasses this broader process of mediation in the metaphorical-materialist sense. In clarifying, however, I am compelled to distinguish my position from a prominent set of translational genealogies in post- or nonhuman ethnography and criticism.

GRIDS, EXPLOITS, AND NETWORKS

Arguing for an approach that obviates or at least problematizes the role of translation in nonhuman interactions, a growing genealogy of posthuman anthropology and media theory posits subjects and objects of analysis that imbricate realms of human, animal, natural, and technological emergence. An array of metaphors to describe such subjects and objects abound: cyborg, milieu, actant, grid, network, and parasite are prominent examples:

Cyborg (Haraway 1991; Helmreich 2007)
Milieu (Foucault 2007; Galloway and Thacker 2007; Mackenzie 2010)
Actant, Grid, Network (Latour 1983, 2005)
Parasite (Serres 1982; Derrida 1988)

FIGURE 2. Bus route in Beijing.

Despite a complex and growing analytical epistemology and nomenclature, much of this work insists on post-epistemological, posthuman (even postsemiotic), techno-social ensembles of becoming. These appear to generate possibilities of mobility and encounter between human and nonhuman that are seen as troubling or transcending mediation. This position, at first glance, appears to call forth the liberal narrative of the emancipatory possibilities of information technology and social media, on the one hand, and on the other, a validation of recent theories of technological and object agency as still "in vogue" media anthropological concerns. Both outlooks presume either a kind of prior or virtual radically egalitarian zone of interaction, be it potential radically democratic mass-mediated publics or synchronic vacuums of constant becoming as well as symmetrically colliding actors and actants. Framed as such, the human-animal encounter becomes a foil for two prominent narratives. One contrapuntal manifestation of these emerged during fieldwork in Beijing in 2013. In the summer of 2013, I was waiting with John Rousseau, a Francophone Malagasy who was studying at Aiguo University, to board the 355 bus to get to Renmin University's east gate. Negotiating this urban landscape as newly arrived students with little Chinese, John and I were trying to decipher a bus stop with hundreds of destinations laid out on a green, black, and white grid marked only with arrows and hundreds of Chinese characters (see fig. 2).

As I clumsily tried to read these characters with my still limited Chinese, John pulled out his iPhone and activated the well-known app Pleco. He used the recognition software to instantly translate the relevant characters. Like QR code readers, Pleco accesses a smartphone's camera, recognizing and instantly translating Chinese characters, allowing the user to visually capture and store the translated item in a flashcard for later review. In this way, the entire city of Beijing can be converted into a digital archive for language review later.

The process of incrementally compiling this digital archive allowed us to read the names of all the bus stops we had come to know aurally within our first few months in the city. However, at that time, we were not yet able to recognize them visually. We quickly scanned all the bus stop names into Pleco so we would know which direction to catch the bus from, as well as at which stop to get off at once we had caught the right bus. We were relieved to be standing at the right stop and were fortunate to catch one of the 355 buses as it was arriving. It was getting dark and we were late for a dinner appointment with some other African and Chinese friends, having just returned from a sports meeting at a different university an hour before. Along with a massive, impatient crowd, we pushed on board as the rain began to pour and remained squashed-up against the window as we watched rush-hour traffic visibly escalate on the other side of the bus's window. As digging elbows pushed us right up against the breath-fogged window, John turned to me saying, "Wow, that girl driving the Mercedes-Benz out there is really cute. I'm going to get her number." I thought he was joking until he once again pulled out his iPhone, this time opening WeChat, and started searching the application's local network function for connections that might have the woman's photo. When she accepted his request, John, grinning sheepishly, showed me his phone. Her name was Mingming. The conversation that followed was mediated by a combination of her broken English, his Pleco-assisted Chinese, and WeChat's English translation function that came in handy when Mingming texted in Chinese characters that were beyond our (at the time) somewhat rudimentary language abilities. Eventually, she wanted to know where he was chatting with her from, so she could see her interlocutor, since he did not have a WeChat profile picture of himself, opting instead for a cartoon character as his icon—Doraemon, the time-traveling and earless cyber cat.

As we pulled even with her car, he waved frantically to her from the bus window, trying to get her attention. She turned and must have been curious about the visibly keen black man waving at her, and gingerly waved back. He showed her his WeChat screen on his iPhone and she nodded. What appeared to be initial mutual interest quickly petered out after this, and her car disappeared behind several lanes of traffic ahead of the bus. John tried to contact her on many occasions afterward, but never heard back from Mingming again.

In one popular media narrative, John emerges as a subject whose legibility, history, and ideological landscape becomes nondifferentiable from the emergent potentials of his technological assemblage. He appears to emerge as simultaneous actor-actant in Bruno Latour's nomenclature:

> [T]he actor-network theory (hence A[N]T) has very little to do with the study of social networks. These studies no matter how interesting concerns themselves with the social relations of individual human actors—their frequency, distribution, homogeneity, proximity. It was devised as a reaction to the often too global concepts like those of institutions, organizations, states and nations, adding to them more realistic and smaller set of associations. Although A[N]T shares this distrust for such vague all encompassing sociological terms it aims at describing also the very nature of societies. But to do so it does not limit itself to human individual actors but extend the word *actor*—or *actant*—to non-human, non individual entities. Whereas social network adds information on the relations of humans in a social and natural world which is left untouched by the analysis, A[N]T aims at accounting for the very essence of societies and natures. It does not wish to add social networks to social theory but to rebuild social theory out of networks. It is as much an ontology or a metaphysics, as a sociology. (1996, 369–70)

Analytically, actor-actant formulations present a problem: though they are posthuman analytics, they apparently need to be understood against the backdrop of the negated individual human subject—as the paradoxically presumed-upon primary social unit. Latourian and many postmodern media theorists often present their critique of "rational actor" biases, as though no theorist in the humanistic social sciences has ever considered moving beyond individual-centrism. Even Eurocentric thinkers like Emile Durkheim, Karl Marx, and Max Weber—all of whom have considerably influenced generations of social inquisitors in the global social sciences—would likely balk at Latour's claim to innovation in this regard, particularly given that all three thinkers and their intellectual genealogies have in fact contested the "individual human actor" as the primary unit of analysis for many decades prior to ANT.

Here, a perhaps impertinent question emerges: if John and Mingming are equal actor-actants in relation to their phones and the surrounding traffic assemblage, could we even see—let alone account for—racism and racial ideology as supplying ideological gravity to Latour's account of their colliding on his network? Are there hills and valleys in his grid, and if so what forces allow them to both be felt as well as to stratify actants?

Perhaps actors like John and Mingming would cherish a fluidity of existence where epistemology has no bearing on their passage through the world, but such an experience of fluid subjectivity is reserved for an unmarked few. Being "just an actor-actant" might appear like wondrous oblivion to the marked subject in a marked body. In this sense, ANT emerges as a view of the social that ultimately stratifies those reaching for it—in this case, the materialized epistemology of John's racialization emerges despite the proposition of its "objectively relative" ontology on a posthuman network. It is in this way that sensual, intersubjective phenomenologies problematize even the most logical metaphysics.

In a second prominent media narrative, John—like a twenty-first-century cyber-guerilla—can be seen contesting the cabalistic forces of governmentality and neoliberalism by appropriating the intrinsically democratic, mass-mediated weapons of emancipatory self-fashioning. This trope emerges particularly strongly in Alexander Galloway and Eugene Thacker's *The Exploit: A Theory of Networks*. Masquerading as a kind of intellectual anarchism, Thacker and Galloway ultimately enshrine the privilege of making an argument that can, in their words: "avoid the limits of academic writing in favor of a more experimental, speculative approach" (2007, vii). Not unlike Latour, Galloway and Thacker regard the network itself as an arbitrary commensurator despite the asymmetrical human labor that goes into its construction:

> The nonhuman quality of networks is precisely what makes them so difficult to grasp. They are, we suggest, a medium of contemporary power, and yet no single subject or group absolutely controls a network. Human subjects constitute and construct networks, but always in a highly distributed and unequal fashion. Human subjects thrive on network interaction (kin groups, clans, the social), yet the moments when the network logic takes over—in the mob or the swarm, in contagion or infection— are the moments that are the most disorienting, the most threatening to the integrity of the human ego. (2007, 5)

In this quote, there is a troubling slippage from the exploitative asymmetries of human labor to the exploitable symmetry of an unruly nonhuman network. The signs, "nonhumanity" and "disorientation" do considerable work here to convert the network into something impersonal and out-of-control, thus equivocating an egalitarian exploit. This shames the vulgar humanist or materialist: "One must be an egoistic, anthropocentric narcissist to suggest that networks could be in any way interested or contingent infrastructures." The exploit rhetorically posits: "Now that the intractable network is beyond hegemony, don't we all have equal access?"

In both Latour's and Thacker and Galloway's narratives, translation—as an ambiguously nonagential, yet uncannily vitalist metaphor—emerges as either inherently arbitrary or inherently egalitarian. In their schema, John's techno-social ensemble in the previous interaction either explicates a flat, synchronic grid—agentless symmetrical translation without mediation, or, paradoxically, a super-agential appropriation of an equal opportunity techno-linguistic media assemblage—the hijacking of the means of translation as a radically democratic *exploit*.

However, both of these prominent media narratives elide three important receptional dimensions of translation: (1) "languages" or units of commensuration; (2) ideological space-time or gravity; and (3) sensory-semiotic capacities that make such a translation intelligible. These three dimensions can be understood as register/genre; context or co-text; and conditions of reception (see fig. 3).

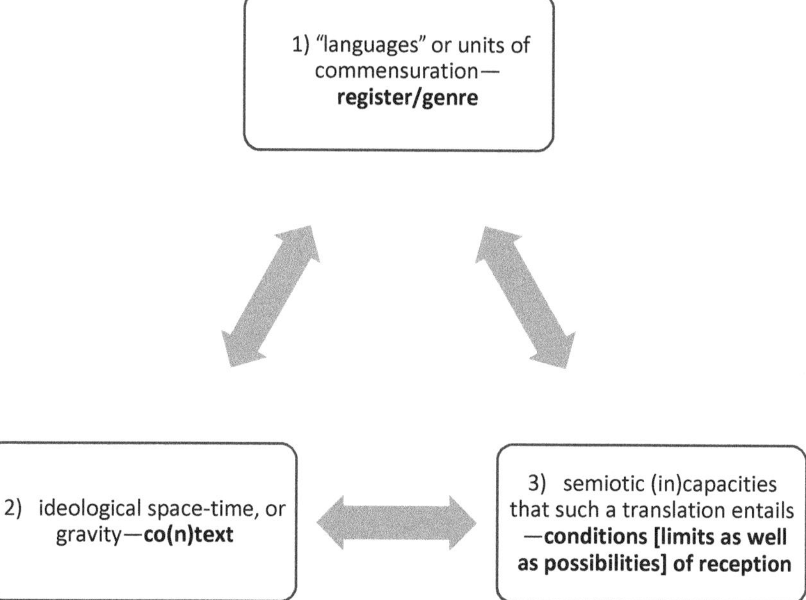

FIGURE 3. Three receptional dimensions of translation.

Together, they extend from what linguistic anthropologists of media have discussed as indexicality (Nakassis 2018; Chumley 2016). However, in articulating some of the more apparent critical theoretical stakes of this analytical approach, I have found the work of Frankfurt School media historian Susan Buck-Morss particularly productive. Buck-Morss points to "numbing" or anesthesia as historically situated, techno-social strategies to diminish shock as a response to industrial modernity. In doing so, she argues for an etymological resuturing of the discourses of aesthetics and anesthetics. Here, she points to a broader contextualization of aesthetics as imbricating a kind of calibration of the sensorium. As she suggests: "the experience of intoxication is not limited to drug-induced, biochemical transformations," in fact, "narcotics" can be "made out of reality itself" (1992, 22). In the meta-debates around the mediation of danger in Beijing's Tiger Park, and in John's recourse to WeChat and the avatar Doraemon in sustaining his interaction with Mingming, we see an analog to Buck-Morss's argument. Western industrial modernity's sensory numbing of twentieth-century urban inhabitants finds its counterpoint in the animal-cyborg ensembles of twenty-first-century mediation—a process that does not unfold outside of an ideological landscape that still stratifies along intersectional lines. Like Buck-Morss's (an)aesthetic dependencies, Chinese netizens and African media users invest in semiotic infrastructures of danger-avoidance and self-curation. In doing so, they recruit variously mediated "natures"—paper tigers, real tigers, and cyber cats alike. Such techno-sensory investments facilitate an analogous protective shielding from the disappointments of cosmopolitan modernity. What, however, does this shielding conceal through its numbing effects? If nature as material metaphor in contemporary China is indeed recruited for anesthesia, what kinds of traumas are being elided and displaced?

FROM NATURAL SEMANTICS TO RACIALIZED PRAGMATICS

In 2013 I began conducting preliminary fieldwork on the racialized interactions between African students and their Chinese interlocutors in Beijing. At this time, one informant—an elite Chinese journalist named Yiwen—offhandedly remarked that she liked Africans "because they are just like animals," mirroring my interaction with Lili in chapter 3. As with Lili, I adopted the default position that this was a racist thing to say. She, like other Chinese informants who had said similar things, balked at my reading and said: "You misunderstand. I think it's wonderful that they [Africans] are so close to nature. We Chinese are nothing, we just eat the world's resources." To be sure, the idea that there exists a kind of originary, authentic subject of nature that contrasts with a compromised Chinese modernity is a fairly pervasive sentiment in urban China.

Understanding how this subjectivity becomes mapped onto black bodies, however, requires an approach that accounts for the ways in which nature is not only recruited but also racialized as a means of mediating that modernity.

Mingming's negation of John could be an open-ended, nonselective act—like the obvious frequency with which black African students are more frequently ignored by Chinese cab drivers compared to their foreign counterparts. Yiwen's nature-black African equivalencies may well emerge from a place of innocent concatenations of categories of alterity, which can be miscontextualized by Anglophone intellectual observers. The issue, however, isn't whether Mingming and Yiwen *are* racist in the semantically flat-footed Euro-American sense. Rather, what is at issue must account for what is pragmatically *experienced:* (a) whether John and others like him face persistent racialized discrimination in China; and (b) how to account for the ideological manifestation of racism in a context that denies that racism is possible because of a hyper-localist analytical exoticism. The question of whether Chinese subjects are racist, as suggested in the previous chapter, problematically assumes that the translation of the meanings of actions are determined by "sign production" and their always elusory intentions. This preoccupation both occludes reception as a vast domain of semiosis and denies the possibility that meanings of signs are transformed through the interaction of persons coming from different participant frameworks.

John and others are not being profiled because they are "dark" or because somehow there is a folk-schema of segmentable "blackness" in China. Black African students are profiled because they are racio-politically black in a more transnational sense, for Chinese cosmopolitan interlocutors are judging them according to imagined international, unmarked horizons of aspirational personhood—with English-language characteristics. Far from being "local," various black subjects have undeniably become a part of the always-shifting, yet always-stratified schema of Chinese urban, class, and racial capital. The question is not whether one *is* black in some essential semantic framework, but rather—in a more pragmatic sense—*for whom* one is black, and *in what ways* this category of racial capital becomes configured through other intersectional vectors of social stratification in an encounter that includes subjects who are not in fact Chinese, but who are undeniably in China and helping to expand a Sinophone world.

To ask "Where is blackness in China?" is as absurd an intellectual question as asking where Europeans' "yellowness" philologically stems from in their perception of East Asian alterities. Furthermore, we are not undertaking study into the visual cognition of racism, but rather the pragmatic and perceptible features of politicized blackness and black experience. It is as inappropriate for a Sinologist to dismiss racism, racialization, and racial capital in China as it is for a scholar of English literature with no experience with the Chinese language to posit calligraphic divinations of the potential meanings of Chinese characters and how they might determine cultural features of Chinese-language speakers. Sinologists are no more equipped to study transnational racial capital than a nonlinguist is to evaluate language features of a language they have no personal or disciplinary experiences with, making use only of their own mother-tongue bias. Perhaps Sinological perspectives, in their current form, are not all that well equipped to undertake the increasingly urgent inquiries into making and translating of China's others?

It is understandable that this is an uncomfortable proposition in an analytical tradition like western Sinology, which has focused on segmentation, differentiation, and exegetic nuance in building an impressive archive around the proposition of quintessence and civilizational integrity, while simultaneously being compelled to enact a conceptual monopoly on every interaction the Sinosphere touches. This compels a number of career Sinologists, at present, to saunter into debates on the racialization of blackness in China, without bothering to engage the substantial archive on transnational black experience and with no awareness that this is significantly different from: (a) the national histories of citizens of different African countries; (b) the ethnic identities within and across them; and (c) the textual semantics of *hei* in the exegesis of Chinese classical texts. Rather, it may be prudent to ask how the historical fact of global-colonial racial capital inflects Sinology's institutional orientations around durability and agreement on the names of things. I am in fact willing to bet my life that such a change in orientation—approaching

Sinology from politically black genealogies of the Global South—will reveal significant disciplinary blind spots.

Two prominent blind spots that are important to this discussion include Occidentalism and semantic relativism; in many ways, the former can be understood as leading into the latter.[3] The unfortunate effect of standardized western languages as the target context for Sinophone and Sinosphere matrixes is that a monolinguistic "dictionary" bias enters the frame when discussing and ultimately essentializing the *names of* the ten thousand things *as* the ten thousand things in themselves. Many Herderian-influenced western Sinologists essentialized this "frozen-in-time" quality as an intrinsic feature of Chinese (Olender 2009). It is apparent, however, that this perception of language was problematically disconnected from Chinese speakers' diverse practices through time down to the present, and stemmed more from western Sinologists' own Lockean biases around what languages are or how languages should work. Though the surface racist forms of this bias have been scraped away, their foundational element persists in semantic relativism. Let's consider two frequently motivated equivalencies: *hei* as the limited semantic range of both "blackness" (of color) and "darkness" (of skin) in China; and *ziran* and *shanshui* as expressions of a semantic "nature" dualism in the Sinosphere.

Here, *shanshui* might be understood as a poetic expression of ethical nature-feeling or "landscape" in classical Chinese art and writing, while *ziran* represents more of a Linnaean biological segmentation of the (scientifically) natural world—a kind of nature without classical poetry. I have encountered the leveraging of these equivalencies mostly when presenting early versions of these chapters to China studies scholars. In such settings, mostly western-trained or Chinese cosmopolitan Sinologists frequently attempted to correct my third-world misconception of what "blackness" and "nature" meant in China by seeking recourse to Han Chinese hyper-localism as a means of erasing black experience in the area sphere of their object of study. The problem with semantic relativism around limited distillation of terms like *shanshui, ziran,* and *hei* (among practitioners of what should be an exegetic tradition) is that the game of defining singular words posits a conceptual Shangri-la, where "Chinese" concepts are hermetically sealed from the world—a recapitulation of Herderianism.

Beyond this political problem of Orientalism in the motivation of *shanshui*'s and *ziran*'s seemingly apolitical semantic range, a foundational semiotic as well as conceptual problem emerges around the fetishization of graphic = semantic continuities in reading the character for *hei* (see fig. 4). The understanding of words like *hei* having a singular apolitical association with some kind of ambiguous "black-dark" gradable and arbitrary color scheme presents not only a misleading one-to-one relation between *hei* as character and *hei* as univocal semantic unit across contexts referring to color, skin tone, and political blackness. It also elides the fact that Chinese subjects of variously stratified class and educational backgrounds can in fact distinguish the lexical differences of *hei*—which are neither frozen in time,

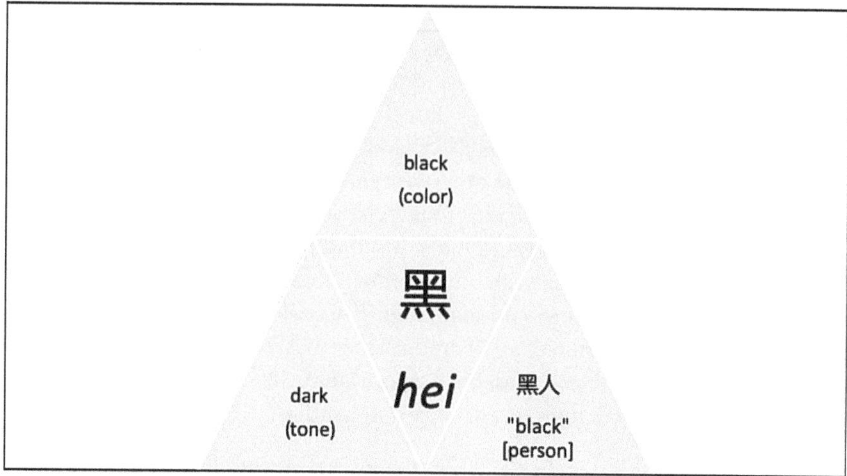

FIGURE 4. Semantically relative associations of *hei*.

nor inter-linguistically isolated—in the same ways English speakers can distinguish the homophones *dark* (as a transcendental state) and *dark* (as a gradable quality). Consider the following sentences:

A) Lili's mother: "Lili's husband became rather dark after their honeymoon."
B) Lili's mother: "Lili's husband is a little dark."

Sentence A suggests that Lili's husband became tanned, and that there is a concern for the degree to which he has been tanned, as tanning can be graded into the limited categorial distinctions of English from dark, to darker, to darkest. In the racial ideologies of many liberal intellectual theaters, race and racialization are interpretable only in these categorial distinctions, which deny categorical racialization as political and equally pragmatic realities. Sentence B, though it might seem to suggest a categorial gradeability in the sense of "a little," in fact presumes upon a categorical thus transcendental darkness even in its Chinese gloss: *yi dian (dian)*. With reference to the previous chapter, Tim's "darkness A" can be changed by degrees, while Adam's "darkness B" cannot. Racism and various kinds of essentialism geared toward social stratification frequently nest categorical ideologies of distinction within a categorial language of potential disavowal. Saying "your husband is a little dark," as in the second sense, implies a categorically nongradable blackness through the absurd and thus deniable equivocation of darkness's categorial gradeability (see Kockelman 2016).

Furthermore, such sematic-relativist fixations occlude what linguist Benjamin Whorf (1956) might describe as the *cryptotypic* articulations that exist within languages or inter-linguistically among members of a speaking community that operate through more than one language. The proposition that racist articulations between blackness and nature don't exist in Chinese in the way they do in English—and that therefore articulations of blackness and nature are meaningless—shares the same conceptual problem as suggesting English lends itself inherently to generational and gender equality because it lacks honorific structures and gendered nouns. As Whorf demonstrated, English shares many covert categories of all kinds of hierarchical structures that were otherwise embedded in the actual grammatical forms of other languages. He referred to these covert categories as cryptotypes. In a similar way, it would be useful to point out that the articulation of nature and blackness in China needn't operate through the semantic ranges of *hei, shanshui,* and *ziran*. In fact, they can even do so in English. Consider the following extract in Michael Sullivan's discussion of an infamous letter to African embassies in Beijing, sent on behalf of the Chinese Students Association (CSA) in 1989. It is an example that demonstrates this cryptotypic articulation handily:

> China whose thousand-year glory and cultural tradition is ineffaceably written in the history of mankind, stands today, because of the great Xiao-Ping's merit in front of a new historical prime. . . . We are walking towards our great aim on a broad road opened to [the] advanced and civilized world. It doesn't mean, however, that we will feed the whole uncultured Africa with the results of our efforts and we will allow any Negro to hang about our universities to annoy Chinese girls and to introduce on our academic grounds manner[s] acquired by life in tropical forests, offending our traditional hospitality and broad mindedness. If . . . there will be no correction in [the] behaviour of idling black students, new and even harder lessons of "friendship" will follow. They [i.e., these lessons] will be based on the experience of Americans, who know very well what to do to curb the Negroes in their country.[4]

If one were reading this extract through the myopic lens of word-production, one might infer that no political meaning resides in phrases like "black students" or "life in tropical forests"—that these are disinterested observations of the skin tones and climactic terroir of the students being described. The reader will hopefully agree that this would not only be an idiotic reading, but also a completely bad faith interpretation that is likely informed by a perspective so mired in racism that it mistakes outright discrimination for an innocent politics of unmarkedness.[5] Again, beyond the obvious political problems of semantic relativism, this letter and countless Sino-African communications like it over the preceding decades should draw our concern not to the semantics of word-production, but rather the more pragmatic dimensions of reception and translation. The writers of the letter wrote the letter in English with the intention that it was meant to be read in English by African diplomats. The letter further recruited a US-specific but transnationally mediated chronotope of race relations, referring to black students as Negroes. This may prompt the conspiracy theorist to infer a CIA plot in the circulation of the letter. However, I have witnessed too many racialized interactions between Chinese and African students that recruit the same contextually peculiar but transnationally intelligible combinations of Anglo racist tropes (even into Chinese) to attribute the content of the letter to US imperialist sabotage—even though such expressions of imperialism are very real in many other contexts. Thus, conjoined interpretations of Anglo-racial blackness and nature as somehow foreign concepts to cosmopolitan Chinese subjects who are cognitively sequestered in their own linguistic prisons of *hei, shanshui,* and *ziran* seems like a fairly obvious recapitulation of the Anglo-colonial mentalese of inscrutability.

A more explicit iteration of this articulation between blackness and nature emerged during an art exhibition in Chengdu, where the exotic imaginary that black Africans index an originary state of nature was literally put on display through a series of photographic juxtapositions by acclaimed Chinese photographer Yu Huiping. His photographic series—titled *This is Africa*—placed African photographic subjects next to those of animal subjects. In defense of artistic expression, and against initial protests directed toward the exhibition, the juxtapositions were praised by Zhao Yixin—president of the China Photographic Publishing House— as "perceptive, smart and visually impactful, capturing the vitality of primitive life." Wang Yuejun, a curator of the museum, also came to Yu's defense, stating that "in Chinese proverbs, animals are always used for admiration and compliment."

Nature again operates as anesthetic against a diffuse but compromised modernity. In the exhibit of *This is Africa*, this framing is perhaps taken a step further. We may understand anti-modernist strategies of synesthesia as necessitating the recruitment of a racialized "blackness of nature." Is this a counterpoint to an unmarked "nature of whiteness" at the core of Chinese and African subjects' emerging cosmopolitan horizon of aspiration? Adding weight to this proposition, it is worth pointing out that blackness-equals-nature equivocations only stand while African subjects in China are not taken as speaking, communicating, urban subjects, that are already extractively incorporated in China's social media matrix. Their participation in this domain bears crucial insights for a critique of posthumanism from the perspective of Afro-Chinese interactions. If Chinese subjects are (syn)aesthetically articulating new discourses of nature and race as a response to an acceleratively anomic modernity; how might we understand African students' (syn)aesthetic approaches to the similarly alienating conditions of educational labor migrancy? Engaging this question, I observed a resonance between the intersectionally compromised dependencies on the Angloscene as demonstrated by Lerato and Damien in chapter 1, and a dimension of social life that some anthropologists have discussed broadly as affect. In situating affect in a discussions of raciolinguistic encounter, I must qualify that I align more with a historical-materialist framing of affect (Berlant 2011; Mazzarella 2017) than a vitalist and post-representational one (Stewart 2007; Massumi 2015). However, my fundamental inspiration in situating affect in Afro-Chinese encounters takes its cue from Frantz Fanon's own permutations in *Wretched of the Earth*.

AFFECTIVITIES OF THE AFRO-CHINESE ANGLOSCENE

In John's smartphone vignette recounted earlier in this chapter, we see a further analog to Buck-Morss's argument. Western industrial modernity's sensory numbing of twentieth-century urban inhabitants also finds its counterpoint in John's and others' commitment to the techno-linguistic ensembles of twenty-first-century social media within the ideological landscape of white, English, cosmopolitan cultural capital. Like Buck-Morss's (an)aesthetic dependencies, John's and others' techno-linguistic investment facilitates an analogous protective shielding from the disappointments of cosmopolitan mobility, while simultaneously committing them to its very means of dissemination—an English-iPhone-mobility ensemble.

Many students like John arrive in Beijing after grueling personal and academic trials only to find many of their Chinese peers aspiring to enter American and European universities. At present, there is a massive and expanding education industry in centers like Beijing, where Chinese aspirational cosmopolitans are learning English as well as taking courses on how to pass European and American standardized exams for university entrance (figs. 5 and 6). Within this language market, many Anglophone African students—almost upon arrival—find themselves in illegal, hence exploitative, English-teaching positions to supplement their somewhat meager stipends. To buy the desirable iPhone, and to acquire the desirable Pleco app, a student will almost certainly teach English, given the absence of alternatives (a theme I explored in chapter 2). Even Francophone African students, like John, will quickly recognize this opportunity, committing themselves more diligently to studying English than Chinese.

Thus, it isn't purely the iPhone and its apps that anesthetize the panic of a bus-schedule comprised of only indecipherable hieroglyphs. It is also the necessarily imbricated ideological space-time of Anglo-cosmopolitanism—the Angloscene chronotope—within which John and Mingming imagine "safety" as long as they commit to that world. I asked John if he was ever worried about getting arrested for teaching English illegally. "Look," he said, "as long as you speak English, no one is going to hurt you." Here, it is more the belief than the reality of John's claim that is important. For many, English indeed appears to provide a literal, protective shielding from discrimination and persecution. But, again, this belief comes with significant compromise.

In *Wretched of the Earth*, Frantz Fanon explores a similar politicization of the sensorium in his discussion of *affectivity:* "In the colonial world," he writes, "the colonized's *affectivity* is kept on edge like a running sore flinching from a caustic agent. And the psyche retracts, is obliterated, and finds an outlet through muscular spasms that have caused many an expert to classify the colonized as hysterical. This overexcited *affectivity*, spied on by the invisible guardians who constantly communicate with the core of the personality, takes an erotic delight in the muscular deflation of the crisis" (1963, 19).[6]

FIGURE 5. Yao Ming studying English.

FIGURE 6. Cowboy-themed ad for English and standardized test prep instruction.

In depicting how the colonial state governs the (re)production of violence through its governed and colonized bodies, Fanon uses this psycho-physical concept as a way of understanding an exploitable capacity for affective interpolation. Here, I hope to suggest that affectivity becomes a way of understanding how phenomena like governance (Xi 2014), hegemony (Gramsci 1975), and essentially the colonization of consciousness (Comaroff 1991) are all attained through managing affect by recruiting a capacity for its calibration—through forms of anesthesia or stimulation. For Fanon, affectivity is manifested through forms of repression—in the Freudian sense ([1920] 2015)—where the colonized subject is constantly dreaming of taking the place of the colonist. This "envy" persists through an ideological "compartmentalization" within, and subsequent to, the colonial order—from outright subjugation and constantly deferred dreams of racial inclusion. This situation creates perpetually "penned-in" colonial and postcolonial subjects who, accordingly, have what Fanon evocatively refers to as "muscular dreams, dreams of action, dreams of aggressive vitality" (1963, 15). For him, these dreams are not of "becoming a colonist, but of replacing him," not only of escaping the colonized hell immediately, but desiring "a paradise within arm's reach guarded by ferocious watchdogs" (16). On the surface, the colonized subject learns not to overstep the limits of this compartmentalization, yet at a deeper level, the colonized subject secretly harbors the dreams of a vital efficacy, engendering self-recognition as animalcules or monsters: "He patiently waits for the colonist to let his guard down and then jumps on him" (16). For Fanon, this figurative "patient waiting" is embodied in muscular tension, spasm, and so-called hysteria of the colonial bodies. In this way, colonial bodies keep on accumulating "aggressiveness," while accumulating tension through a compelled stasis given the ideological and thus "physical" limits of the continually colonized condition.

This reinforced intensity in bodies—through a capacity or susceptibility—for further forceful actions on the part of the colonized, can be understood through Fanon's evocative somatic metaphor as being "kept on edge like a running sore flinching from a caustic agent" (19). Here, affectivity is more than "being emotional," since it imbricates a susceptibility to potential physical forces that transcend emotion as a rational reduction of complex affective states. Through his examples, he shows how—in needing to find "an outlet"—this affective capacity can be "drained of energy" through forms of crisis, the ecstasy of dance, spirit possession, fratricidal struggles, or intertribal conflicts (19). In its self-destructive manifestations, "the supercharged libido and the stifled aggressiveness spew out volcanically" (20). Thus, for Fanon, managing these "outlets" becomes key to maintaining the equilibrium of a social world: "On the way there [to the dance] their nerves 'on edge.' On the way back, the village returns to serenity, peace and stillness" (20).

In contemporary Sino-African encounters, affectivity perhaps no longer manifests through a barely suppressed rage. However, this manifestation—in

Fanon's context—is merely one symptom of affectivity as an exploitable capacity. Perhaps adaptation to transformed modalities of colonial capitalism, in the postcolonial era, necessitate a reconsideration of how affectivity must be (an)aesthetically apprehended, in and beyond the "third world." Here, I suggest that a partial, (an)aesthetic management of this capacity might be at play in Chinese and African informants' persistent commitments to cosmopolitan desire despite encountering considerable obstacles within a landscape of exclusionary "global" cosmopolitan aspiration. I say that it is a *partial management* for two reasons. First, because affectivity—as an intersocial, beyond conscious capacity—thwarts the agential imperatives of rational freedom or capacity to choose, and second, because the (an)aesthetic conditions within which contemporary Chinese and African subjects find themselves to be emplaced complicate the outright manifestation of barely controllable rage in the ways that Fanon described decades ago. This speaks to the ways in which the world has perhaps not decolonized, but rather, that the sensory and semiotic conditions of subjecthood within that world have become compromised.

Thus, affectivity—as a sensory semiotic capacity—can be understood as a volatile nexus of intersocial forces that acts on subjects' not-necessarily-rational, not-necessarily-conscious propensities for reception and action, a space-time emerging between the volatile sensorium and the ideological materialities within which it becomes imbricated. Providing the example of dance, Fanon locates the capacity to calibrate affectivity as the political site of both resistance and control: "[T]he colonized's affectivity can be seen when it is drained of energy by the ecstasy of dance. . . . The dance circle is a permissive circle. It protects and empowers" (19–20). Affectivity is thus a capacity, exploitable either on the part of the colonizer, which renders the colonized more tractable, or on the part of the colonized—as a means of resistance through (an)aesthetic calibration similar to that proposed by Buck-Morss. Here, it is important, that this calibration dialectically draws on the ideological and material conditions at the experiencing subject's disposal—the articulation or anesthesia of histories of capitalist modernity and colonial stratification.

In Fanon's case, it is the dialectical space-time of the colonial encounter that supplies the ideological gravity or indexicality for grounding affectivity's exploitation, mirroring the ways in which the traumas of modernity require the cultivation of (an)aesthetic technologies (Buck-Morss 1992). It is in this way that the very means of emancipation for the postcolonial subject entails either an unlimited unfolding of endlessly limited compromises—perhaps fractally—or the violence of a discourse-ending tabula rasa. Perhaps there should be a reevaluation of the nexus between the sensorium and the semiotic in postcolonial studies' engagement with the analytic of translation. When the meaning of "language" is less overdetermined and the relationship between signs more dialectically considered, perhaps more attention can be given to the pragmatics of postcolonial translation as opposed to semantic fetishism over how to define it. The analyst might then begin to begin to consider language *as* (an)aesthetic technology—where affectivity mediates English, as English mediates affectivity.

In the way that unmarked whiteness, as liberal ideology and horizon of aspiration, both necessitates and occludes the racial stratification of all other racial imaginaries, so too, I argue, the proposition of unmediated encounters necessitates the recruitment of new, silent subalterns. In many ways, this is critical race theory's most important critique of contemporary anthropology's failure to decolonize: That Euro-American anthropology's analytical focus from marginal humans to marginal nonhumans perpetuates the discipline's still-colonial impetus: its continued propensity to privilege speaking for, and representing, those who are unable to speak; its more recent propensity to resist translation as a disciplinary metaphor (in an act of spectacular representational denialism); and, finally, its escalating propensity to actively seek out nonmediation and nonhumans while nonetheless continuing to depict such topics and subjects only in terms of anthropology's own all-too-mediated and all-too-human relativistic proclivities. A translational attentiveness to the (an)aesthetics of mediation attempts a way out of the flat-footed impasse between so-called structural and non-/anti-representational anthropologies of nonhumans. It does so by understanding the sensorium as material, semiotic, as well as fundamentally ideological, and therefore as intersubjectively contingent. This is in fact not a new position, but it does require a translation of an older argument.

THE MEANS OF TRANSLATION

In stating famously that "the forming of the five senses is a labor of the entire history of the world down to the present," the young Karl Marx once pointed to the centrality of the sensorium as a zone for mediating or alienating personhood, an understanding that has informed the ideological centrality of the sensorium for subsequent generations of Marxist scholars.

> [Persons] appropriate [their] total essence in a total manner.... Each of their human relations to the world—seeing, hearing, smelling, tasting, feeling, thinking, being aware, sensing, wanting, acting, loving—in short, all the organs of [one's] individual being, like those organs which are directly social in their form, are in their objective orientation or in their orientation to the object, the appropriation of that object, the appropriation of the human world; the orientation to the object is the manifestation of the human world; it is human efficaciousness and human suffering, for suffering, apprehended humanly, is an enjoyment of self in man. ([1884] 2007, 87)

Since we are "affirmed in the objective world not only in the act of thinking, but with all [our] senses," according to Marx, the capacity to appropriate the means for translating the senses is central to affirming species being (88). The sensorium—a far from depoloticized semiotic and material nexus that is vulnerable to ideological and intersectional stratifications—is thus a grounding point for thinking and producing both human and nonhuman, as well as mediated and unmediated possibilities of personhood. In this regard, personhood does not require the narrow typification of an individuated "human." Since, if we regard the sensorium as the means of production for fashioning more capacious personhoods, then the attempt to wrest control over the translational labor it already performs, is ultimately a claim to that means of production.

5

Ubuntu/Guanxi and the Pragmatics of Translation

Thinking from the South is necessarily an endeavor of translation: between scales of representation and materiality, between ontology and epistemology, and crucially between chronotopes of encounter.[1] As such, thinking from the South, in its very proposition, is compelled to shift the interzone of encounter from the west and a world full of its aspirationally cosmopolitan Others to a more horizontal, and thus ultimately more multilingual, conception of intersubjective *interactions* and collaboratively *translated* personhoods—these being interactions and translations that unfold in a world of mutually negotiated alterities that resist the flat, commensurative relativisms of Anglo multiculturalism in a still-decolonizing world. For a generation of postmodernists, exploring such fraught social interzones of endlessly becoming alterity seemed to induce a representational delirium, leading to an initially ecstatic rejection of so-called structure and translation, eventually culminating in the awkward, privileged avoidance of society and the human altogether. This remains the intellectual equivalent of retreating into a gated community—away from the unsettling discomfort of an increasingly stratified world. Destabilizing this logic, as I began to suggest in the preceding chapter, entails the embrace of translation as an intersubjective imperative and social fact, without the expectation of universal commensurability that remains appropriately impossible in a multilingual world.

In this chapter, I take this approach further and explore the indispensability of translation as social practice not only in the particular instance of Afro-Chinese interactions, but in the broader context of non-western encounters beyond the settler-colonial encounter. This is a step that I hope will be of benefit to many projects of intellectual decolonization that take thinking from the South as their starting point. Demonstrating a pragmatics of postcolonial translation, I analyze the reflexive, intersubjective mediation of Southern African and Chinese "culture" concepts—those of *Ubuntu* and *guanxi*—as my primary example for discussion. I begin with a discussion of affinities between these concepts as they have been written about, or publicly contextualized in some of their respective genealogies. I then move to a discussion of their reflexive translation in contemporary Afro-Chinese encounters. Following this, I conclude with a discussion about how a pragmatics of translation intervenes in a number of popular non-representational or anti-translational literatures in the western social sciences.

In their independent and synthesized contextualizations, *Ubuntu* and *guanxi* share a general feature of "intersubjective interdependency"—a convergence of interpretations that has allowed many African students in China to not only treat the respective cultural ideologies of *Ubuntu* and *guanxi* as malleable enough to permit a translation of one into the other; but also the capacity to reflexively re-purpose the pragmatic deployment of these concepts for limited gains within a still-inequivalent context of encounter and exchange. In line with these observations, and drawing on the shared intersubjective sensibilities of *guanxi* and *Ubuntu*, I understand translation—always simultaneously interpersonal and intertextual—as a pragmatics of mediating incommensurability. Thus, translation is not only an immanent capacity that always entails the acknowledgement of difference in the abstract analytical sense, it should also be understood as a vital and inevitable social process that is both reflexively referred to and relied upon to permit transformations of social and material worlds without reducing cultural concepts—like *Ubuntu* or *guanxi*—to arbitrary propositions under the banner of cultural relativism.

In addition to facilitating the observation of social dynamics, a pragmatics of translation and its contingent translational attunement has implications for methodology and research ethics more broadly. The research orientation such an approach necessitates is that encounters and interactions are never single events, but ultimately encompass a wider social context as well as socio-spatiotemporal trajectories that are evidenced through interactions. What the reader may initially discern as a series of "individual encounters" in the context of an interaction-based ethnography is a misleading understanding of what happens between the ethnographic context and the subsequent representational act of ethnographic writing—historical or anthropological.

"Single" interactions are meant to diagram, with depth, positionalities, contexts, and dispositions that are occupied by a broad range of subjects over time in the ethnographic context. It would be profoundly monolingual—in the Lockean sense—to believe that an ethnographic interaction represents (a) a singular event, and (b) "real" people, since textual representations are extensions of social realities as opposed to the realities themselves. Just as no large-scale quantitative survey will ever capture why subjects, collectively, behave the way they do, an interactional analysis is by its very nature incomplete. This is because no interaction is ever a social isolate—given that they encompass a distillation of language, performances, and ideas that are never, and have never been, the sole authorial objects of interlocutors. Understanding that there is no one-to-one correspondence between the number of interview subjects and the possibilities of their alignments, perspectives, opinions, and personae, it is inevitably the ethnographer who—through mediating between ethnographic context, research institutions, writing, and critical reception—is undertaking the burden of qualitative exploration and evidence-based argumentation. Here, I can only claim that my informants and their social milieu were observed in depth, in a context full of informants, longitudinally, and that I conducted over two hundred interviews over a period of four years. However, should the reading audience really be persuaded by me or any other ethnographer simply saying so in a methodology or a footnote, especially when a chapter that is eight thousand words long can only accommodate a fragmentary representative sample from years of observation and interviews? These are disciplinary and conceptual biases that my work is directly aiming to write against and thus, the interactions explored in this book are precisely a reaction to default ethnographic textures (as they are commensurated in much contemporary American anthropology) that attempt to perform ethnographic multiplicity which ultimately reduces the depth of ethnographic insight.

BEYOND SYNCHRONIC GUANXI

In western anthropologies of Chinese *guanxi* (M. Yang 1994; Bian 1994; Kipnis 1997; Bell 2000), the concept has often been understood through two of its more obvious iterations. First, it might manifest in many Chinese social settings in a variety of modalities, including the exchange of gifts like luxury goods or "red envelopes" (that contain money), patronage and patrimony networks (particularly in government institutions), as well as an array of functional and dysfunctional techniques, tactics, and economies of corruption. This latter kind of *guanxi* has been the central theme and focus of a number of MBA-style courses and guidebooks providing financial guru-like advice on "how to do networking in China." However, this MBA-style *guanxi* caters to a more western and instrumentally inclined understanding of the short-term and transactional appearances of *guanxi*. Critiquing such token essentialisms of *guanxi*—both their self-help appropriations and Orientalisms within Euro-American corporate literature and education—a number of anthropologists of (but mostly not *from*) China have pointed out how such approaches run the risk of reducing *guanxi* to a purely instrumental social practice, lacking specificity in its hyper-local Chinese context. Here, *guanxi's* more ethical or practice-based dimensions appear to be "rescued" by scholars like Andrew Kipnis (1997). For Kipnis, in particular, *guanxi* has a mutually constitutive affinity with another Chinese concept of intersubjectivity, one that is inseparable from *guanxi's* contextual and co-textual meanings: *renqing*. Building on French sociologist, Pierre Bourdieu's (1977) work, Kipnis suggests that *renqing* emerges within a simultaneously 'embodied' and "compassionate" habitus that *guanxi* sustains and is sustained by—intersubjectively—between persons mutually committed to maintaining habitus in a mainly nonreflexive, "beneath conscious" manner. Following Kipnis, *guanxi* exists in a dis-articulable equilibrium with *renqing*. Following his former teacher, anthropologist Judith Farquhar (2002), it can additionally be argued that *guanxi* might do so in ways that are simultaneously particular to, and reiterated through, embodied practices that both constitute and are constituted within an intersocial space-time: that of an anthropologically delineable community, society, or polity (Munn 1986; Bourdieu 1977).

However, at the heart of this rescue attempt by western anthropologists of China, there is a persistent tension between cultural determinism and emergence of the everyday. In much of this west-to-Other anthropology, *guanxi* and *renqing*—still read through an Orientalist gaze—are unproblematically maintained through the work of the everyday. In much of this writing, which negates the dialectical in favor of the linear-descriptive, it is as though *guanxi* were hermetically sealed from the continuous remaking and redefining of its meanings through interactions among those for whom *guanxi* matters. There is still a presupposition that the definer and reader of cultural terms and concepts is able to observe a synchronic durability of *guanxi*, which somehow overshadows, and yet escapes the notice of, those undertaking the labor of *guanxi*'s diachronic maintenance. A way past this contradiction may be attendance to interactional and intercultural contextualizations of *guanxi* that take seriously the reflexive, diachronic mediation of such ideas not only among subjects who believe they own such concepts, but also for their interlocutors who believe they have cultural analogues for the same ideas. Such an approach, to be sure, would be more dialogical and dialectical by its very nature. In this vein, it will be argued that culture concepts like *guanxi* have a vibrant cultural and historical life in Sino-Other encounters that entail third-worldist histories and genealogies.

FROM GUANXI TO UBUNTU

Diverging from the inalienable romance of cultural synchrony, what I argue and demonstrate aligns with a few important (if somewhat marginalized) critical theoretical analyses that have attended to the ways China continues to make itself through making its others—particularly in relation to the play of external and internal forces that are necessarily ideological and political in the making of culture (F. Yang 2015; Rofel 2007; P. Liu 2015; L. Liu 2004; Vukovich 2012). Importantly, such approaches do not provincialize the cultural but understand culture as very much at stake in the vibrant making and contestation of social life under the predatory as well as contradictory conditions of cultural alienation and appropriation that typify the experience of modernity in postcolonial and postsocialist settings. *Guanxi* is both a cultural and (self-)Orientalized culture term that has had a vibrant life in pre- and postsocialist China, and has seen its fair share of colonial translations and reductions. *Guanxi*'s reflexive referability—manifested in a vast range of "*guanxi*-talk" across time, space, and languages—makes it both a contested and ideal lens through which to explicate the tension between intercultural awareness and cultural fetishism that haunts even the most mundane interaction between mutually constituted others, particularly in the context of Afro-Chinese cultural translations.

Guanxi, for many Chinese, thus imbricates a meta-awareness of intersubjectivity as social practice, which is made apparent through *guanxi* talk. *Guanxi*, in this sense shares affinities with the trans–Southern African intelligibility of *Ubuntu* as not only a similar moral and ethical contingency that animates intersubjective relations, mediations, or supernatural efficacies; but once again is an idea that is reflexively accessible through *Ubuntu*-talk. My emphasis in this chapter is on *Ubuntu*-talk as a living, intersubjective object of cultural reference and as a translational analog for *guanxi* in Afro-Chinese encounters. Here, I am *not* engaging *Ubuntu* as analytical proposition in contemporary African and Africa-engaged analytical philosophy, as demonstrated in the debate between Matolino and Kwindingwi (2013), Metz (2014); and the subsequent commentary by Chimakonam (2016). My response to this issue is that—regardless of the logical propositions of the life, death, or afterlives of *Ubuntu* as analytical object—*Ubuntu* remains rehearsed and discursively under continuous maintenance in the "language games" of those for whom the existence of *Ubuntu* remains indispensable. Following Michael Silverstein's (2004, 621–22) elaborate discussion of the discursive maintenance of "cultural concepts," it might be analytically expedient to grant *Ubuntu*'s pragmatic and public materiality as a portable and transmissible discourse object, beyond its suffocating reduction to existential binarism.

In this more public and pragmatic realm, *Ubuntu*'s ethical and co-textual dependency—that is, its reliance on reception as much as representation—has been articulately captured by African language and literary scholar James Ogude: "In the Nguni saying popularized by [Desmond] Tutu, 'Umuntu ngumuntu ngabantu' (a person is only a person in relation to other persons), the idea is that no individual can become a person without the role played by other individuals and by society more wholly and generally. In other words, humans are made to be interdependent with each other. Humans realize and fulfill their selfhood only in interplay with others as a moral and metaphysical destiny" (Ogude 2019, 4).

It is important, however, that the moral and ethical contingencies of *Ubuntu* might also include witchcraft. As with *guanxi, Ubuntu* is as much the condition of possibility for mutually beneficial social relations, as it affords propensities for mutual destruction. Such transcendental ethical propensities have been partially—though not fully—explored in the innovative work of Adam Ashforth, where he frames witchcraft's contingent relationship with *Ubuntu*—witchcraft as a kind of "dark matter" of *Ubuntu* (2005). In his excellent *Madumo: A Man Bewitched* (2000), Ashforth demonstrates this principle at work in the life of his friend and informant Madumo, who must counter the effects of witchcraft directed toward him through his close kin ties, as those very ties are the source of the witchcraft as well as the means for combating it. In Madumo's bewitching, *Ubuntu*—as the mutually constitutive force that engenders one's personhood through others—is the metaphysical infrastructure that permits both the efficacy of witchcraft and commonality of personhood between subjects.

In this vein, anthropologists John and Jean Comaroff (2012, 102) have described *Ubuntu* as "a common African humanity" that has profound consequences for how we understand the nature of reflexive personhood maintenance as a feature of Southern African social life across cultural communities. In popular culture, *Ubuntu* is often explained in English through the phrase, "I exist because you exist," and by a number of commentators including notable public figures like South Africa's Desmond Tutu and Nelson Mandela. This double-edged public life of *Ubuntu* permits insights into exploring the dark side of *guanxi*—namely, *fubai* ("corruption")—a relation that anthropologist Cheryl Schmitz's recent exploration of witchcraft "translation" in the context of Sino-Angolan encounters evocatively suggests but does not quite articulate (2020). With the exception of this excellent work, Chinese and western Sinologists have been somewhat loath to explore the relationship between *guanxi* and its dialectically negating shadow: witchcraft.

By contrast, attention to the everyday governance of China reveals a fairly explicit public awareness of *guanxi*'s corrupting or *fubai* affordances. In both rural and urban settings in the PRC, this public awareness is manifested officially, not only in the form of large-scale anti-corruption campaigns, but also at the marginal scale of everyday policing where public messaging ubiquitously warns passers-by of the inveigling influence of "dark forces" (*heishili*)—referring to criminal, political, or religious fundamentalist underworlds. China observers attuned to the discursive transformations of public anti-corruption advocacy in the PRC would not fail to have noticed a recent historical sequence of anti-corruption political campaigns: starting from the "fighting the tiger" (*dalaohu*) campaign in 2013—metaphorically meaning to persecute corrupted government leaders—and then followed by the "squashing the flies altogether" (*dahu paiying*) campaign, referring to the purging of mid-level corrupt officials, one sees a steady propaganda build-up to eliminating "the dark and evil forces" (*hei e shili*) that began around 2018, targeting kinship-based organized crime. In this discursive shift it would be difficult to miss the escalating degree of insidiousness of these campaigns—from tigers to flies to dark and evil forces—a shift that mirrors the shrinking distance between public criminality and the intimate realm of the "common person" (*putong ren*).

It would be both anachronistic and overly simplistic to view Chinese corruption's witchcraft-like manifestation in relation to *guanxi* as a byproduct of the spectral machinations of neoliberalism operating in the shadows of

Sino-governmentality—particularly given that there is nothing spectral, cabalistic, or "hidden in the shadows" about the PRC's relationship to capital. Rather, outside of western Sinology, there is a much older genealogy of thought exploring the dualistic—both loving and corrupting—dimensions of *guanxi*. This genealogy is associated with (arguably) China's most famous anthropologist, Fei Xiaotong. Contrasting the intersubjective ethical pluralism of Chinese social relations with western social organizational principles based on monotheistic moral centrism, Fei Xiaotong famously outlined what he calls societies with a "differential mode of association." By way of Mencius, he analyzes the interactional basis of intersubjective ethics, while also demonstrating his own pragmatics of translation in analyzing cultural concepts like *guanxi*:

> Mencius replied, "A benevolent man neither harbors anger nor nurses resentment against a brother. All he does is to love him. Because he loves him, he wishes him to have rank. Because he loves him, he wishes him to be rich. [For the emperor to love his brother] was to enrich [his kin] and let him have rank. If as emperor he had allowed his brother to remain a common man, could that be described as loving him?"
>
> A society with a differential mode of association is composed of webs woven out of countless personal relationships. To each knot in these webs is attached a specific ethical principle. For this reason, the traditional moral system was incapable of producing a comprehensive moral concept. Therefore, all the standards of value in this system were incapable of transcending the differential personal relationships of the Chinese social structure. The degree to which Chinese ethics and laws expand and contract depend on a particular context and how one fits into that context. (Fei [1947] 1992, 78)

For Mencius and Fei Xiaotong, interaction and ethics are fundamentally intertwined—there are no ethics without interactions to recruit them, and no interactions without ethical maintenance. Here, Fei Xiaotong also demonstrates the translational implications of web-like contingencies of intersubjective relations decades before Geertz. Elaborating on the ethical capaciousness of *guanxi*, he continues:

> I have heard quite a few friends denounce corruption, but when their own fathers stole from the public, they not only did not denounce them but even covered up the theft. Moreover, some went so far as to ask their fathers for some of the money made off the graft, even while denouncing corruption in others. When they themselves become corrupt, they can still find comfort in their "capabilities." In a society characterized by a differential mode of association, this kind of thinking is not contradictory. In such a society, general standards have no utility. The first thing to do is to understand the specific context: Who is the important figure, and what kind of relationship is appropriate with that figure? (78)

As with *Ubuntu*, persons are maintained through their mutual contingencies—both through their ethical recruitment and through their seemingly contradictory yet ultimately dialectical ethical propensities (Lukács 2010). There is no ethics of *guanxi* without its contingent propensities for corruption, just as there is no *Ubuntu* without its propensity for witchcraft. Conversely, a consideration of Fei Xiaotong and China's contemporary public anti-corruption discourses should prompt us to ask why such similar social insights and intersubjective contingencies have (with few exceptions) not been taken seriously in the context of Southern African governance. Particularly in the context of South African corruption discourse, consideration of Fei Xiaotong's ethical pragmatics would quickly demonstrate the limits of referring to government corruption as antithetical to *Ubuntu* as a naïvely incorruptible intersubjective ethics.

PRAGMATICS OF TRANSLATION

Having highlighted a few grounds for contiguity in discussing *guanxi-Ubuntu* translations, and having speculated about certain grounds for their comparison or shared affinities, a question must be addressed: How do contemporary Chinese and African actors pragmatically bring *guanxi* and *Ubuntu* and their intersubjective underpinnings into a shared field of recognition and reflection? Answering this question necessarily entails identifying and "siting" translation as pragmatic imperative between African and Chinese subjects (Niranjana 1992).

As Tejaswini Niranjana has suggested, the act of translation—considered capaciously—is a political act. As such, political acts are by their nature pragmatic and performative acts in that *doing* and *defining* become inextricable semiotic events. Building on this approach to translation, what follows will draw on a long genealogy of pragmatist thought, including the ideas of several anti-imperialist and third-worldist thinkers, from Du Bois (1903) to Mills and Gerth (1953). At the same time, I must qualify that I understand pragmatist thought as something that is not merely reducible to William James, Charles Peirce, and the Johns (Dewey and Austin), but rather part of a shared humanistic heritage of thought—one in which ideas are understood as constituted through, as well as constitutive of, reflexive processes of mediation. An example of this heritage is demonstrated in the pragmatic sensibility through which Fei Xiaotong interprets the ethical and pragmatic imbrications as well as genealogies of Chinese (and indeed other) intersubjective modalities of social organization—ideas that have been around at least since the early versions of the *Dao De Jing, The Analects*, and *The Mencius.* These genealogies have further been transformed, maintained, and syncretized via Neo-Confucians and a broad range of East Asian literary and historical scholars down to the present.

At the same time, a pragmatics of translation opposes the understanding that culture is the exclusive analytical object of anthropologists who are uniquely situated to identify, translate, and study it. Rather, it prompts us to embrace the fact that cultural translation is an almost mundane reality in most societies that must confront diverse human interactions as their simultaneously ethical and pragmatic foundations—culture *does*, life is *lived*, and translation is *done*, regardless of "loss" or anyone's semiotic nihilism. Actual intercultural, interlinguistic, and intersubjective translations—those happening between persons reflexively invested in receptional and representational labor—are pragmatic translations. Their pragmatic effects and reflexive meta-semantics—that is, their definability as translational events—constitute perhaps the closest thing to a "bounded" or "defined" semiotic subject, object, process, or "event." Understood in this vein, a pragmatics of translation opposes the conventional semantic or metaphysical concern with cultural translation as cause for existential dread and liberal horror in much of the Anglocentric western academy. This position necessarily proposes that we can in fact have pragmatic translatability and intersectional incommensurability at the same time. As the Americans might say: "We can walk and chew gum at the same time." The subsequent discussion provides a unique opportunity to demonstrate an example of what this might look like.

FROM UBUNTU TO GUANXI

Drawing on a key series of interactions that emerged during my dissertation work ([Ke-]Schutte 2018, Ke-Schutte 2019), I will now discuss a situation where mediation between *guanxi* and *Ubuntu* becomes a key site for excavating a pragmatics of translation. In a research period between 2012 and 2016 in Beijing's Haidian district, I frequently observed one informant, Patrice Moji, making statements about his shared cosmopolitanism with various interlocutors: Chinese, African, and white "internationals."[2] He was a senior master's student who had been living in Beijing for a few years. Patrice was one of my informants and regarded himself as a cultural translator between Chinese and African students in Beijing. From these interactions, I gathered that Patrice believed there to be a privileged position of mobility that permitted one to be situated as a translator, that cosmopolitan aspiration was a condition of possibility for translation: "You cannot be a translator unless you have gone from one place to another," he once noted. Elaborating on his claims of cosmopolitanism, he compared Beijing's obvious mass urbanism to the contrasting spaces of both his childhood background in southern Zimbabwe as well as his experiences as an undergraduate student in South Africa—the place where we first met a few years prior while Patrice was an undergraduate.

On one occasion, I learned that Patrice's teacher, Professor Li was holding a banquet for a group of his students. Professor Li, who I also knew as an informant, was a Chinese language and literature professor at Da Hua University—a pseudonym for one of the most elite educational institutions in Beijing. In addition to Patrice, Professor Li had reached out to me with an invitation. During the elaborate dinner—which included Peking duck, double-cooked pork, fried string beans, and a number of other delicacies (with rice only served on request)—Patrice told a story about his grandfather's travels to China and the Soviet Union as a Zimbabwean diplomat. He explained that many in his clan had middle names indicative of his grandfather and family's political alignments: Marx, Mao, Lenin, Fidel, and Trotsky abound on family birth records.

As I have indicated elsewhere, Patrice's overly elaborate setup was very much intentional and directed toward establishing a third-world socialist rapport with Professor Li, given that he desperately needed Professor Li's letter of recommendation to maintain his scholarship at Da Hua University (Ke-Schutte 2019). Before and after the banquet, Patrice reflexively noted that he was building rapport as an instrumentalization of *guanxi*—a conceptual vocabulary he acquired after arriving in China. Patrice's labor was explicated during a climactic moment during the banquet ritual, where participants are meant to toast the professor in brief, laudatory speeches—a common practice during relatively frequent teacher-graduate student gatherings in the Chinese academy. Patrice raised a glass of liquor (*baijiu*) and proclaimed: *Disan shijie da tuanjie!* ("To third-world solidarity!") Acknowledging Patrice, Professor Li responded in deliberate English, while obviously noting my presence as the white anthropologist at the table, whose alignments were uncertain. Looking at me, Professor Li seemed to make up his mind and stated (by way of translation): "Third-world solidarity!" as though Patrice's toast not only required translation, but that I needed to be appraised of who it included (and perhaps who it did not).

I learned from both parties later that Professor Li had in fact written the elicited letter of recommendation. Whether engineered or coincidental, this was taken by Patrice as evidence of both his prowess in managing social relations as well as the ritual efficacy of historical invocation—that he had pragmatically deployed *guanxi* through his own translation of it.

A few days following the banquet, I met with Professor Li to discuss what had transpired. Since *guanxi* was a regular topic of conversation between us and having benefitted on multiple occasions from Professor Li's *guanxi*, I couldn't resist the opportunity to gauge his reflexive awareness of Patrice's engineered hailing. The position he held at his university was officially academic professor; however, due to his social connections and skills in acquiring them, he was more known as a highly talented broker between educational, political, and private sector interactional spaces. In a Chinese bureaucratic setting, he would easily be understood as the *guanxi* artist or manager of an institution—an unofficial, but indispensable position in most Chinese organizations. As I have noted, beyond just being "someone who networks well," a *guanxi* artist is someone who is particularly skilled at recognizing, building, and maintaining *guanxi* relationships (Ke-Schutte 2019). For Professor Li, the emphasis on an aptitude for recognition and reception as imbricated translational processes—rather than on performance and production of instrumentalized rapport—was an important nuance in distinguishing the effective management of *guanxi* from competent networking.

By the accounts of Professor Li's own peers, he was such an excellent manager of *guanxi* "that he was able to send his children to [an Ivy League] university in America."

Perhaps as part of this skill set, Professor Li also mastered a genre of self-exoticism that I had seen him perform with predominantly white visiting scholars and officials from US institutions with whom his institution had formed beneficial ties. In these interactions with his US visitors, he had to manage two performances. On the one hand, he had to advertise China's emerging, cosmopolitan educational status, while on the other, he needed to advertise himself as an expert on socialist political or administrative protocol in China: a translator of otherwise "inscrutable" signs to his American colleagues. This dual performance allowed him to motivate his own indispensability. Beyond his obvious skill at managing *guanxi*, Professor Li was also uncharacteristically keen to engage in a genre of *guanxi* talk, in which he was willing to reflexively discuss making *guanxi* in detail and at length.

He noted that it wasn't merely about giving people money or things, emphasizing that this was "the lowest *guanxi*." Instead, he noted the centrality of contextual self-awareness: "who you are" and "what you have" and that, in turn, this awareness should be extended to "who others are to you." This contextually shifting relationship between you-to-others, and others-to-you, underpins the central question in the *guanxi* interaction: "Why would I spend my time on *guanxi* with others?" Here, he emphasized that in the cultivation of *guanxi* relationships, we needed *to want to spend time on others*. This degree of sincerity, however instrumental it may obviously be, is an essential part of making *guanxi*. "Take you, for instance," he noted to my slight alarm. "You have a good attitude, but as someone from Africa, you are not as useful to me as an American graduate student or professor. [However], you are easier to build a relationship with, and if there is mutual benefit, that is a good thing for both of us. . . . You and I both have to understand and meet our mutual obligations to each other . . . otherwise we sabotage one another" (Ke-Schutte 2019, 328). The importance of sincerity is demonstrated in Professor Li's invocation of attitude. Both seem to matter in calculating whether to commit to a *guanxi* relationship or not, since "attitude" would be a strong indicator of an interlocutor's willingness to reciprocate and maintain the relationship—one that precariously might leave both interlocutors vulnerable to sabotage, or possibly witchcraft.

Seeing an opportunity to shed light on his earlier interaction with Patrice, I asked whether the two of them had a *guanxi* relationship. He responded emphatically that they did not, adding: "I don't mean to sound like a bad person, but he can't offer me anything since he is only a student" (Ke-Schutte 2019, 328). Given that Professor Li wrote many recommendations for his student and also aligned himself—at least performatively—with Patrice's recruitment to third-world solidarity, a question emerges: Is conscious, or, perhaps more accurately, reflexive knowledge about being in a *guanxi* relationship a necessary and sufficient condition to deny its emergence in an interaction?

This question certainly proved to be at stake in Patrice Moji's interpretation of the exchange at the banquet, as well as its aftermath. When I asked him about it, Patrice provided a translation of his own. He understood *guanxi* to be a fundamentally translatable and, in fact, substitutable with another intersocial category drawn from social settings that were mutually intelligible to us: *Ubuntu.* "Look, it [guanxi] is *the same as* Ubuntu." Patrice's own translation attempts an iconizing equivocation of *Ubuntu* as being "the-same-as" *guanxi.*

This iconizing modality of interactions, where the motivation of sameness is at stake, has been evocatively captured in the work of anthropologist Summerson Carr. Interpreting the pragmatist philosopher, Charles Sanders Peirce, she notes the ways in which iconic signs "gain their meaning in a contiguous relation to their object (as in the case of smoke and fire) and also from symbols, which have an arbitrary (that is, conventional) relationship with that which they represent," that—following Peirce—"iconic signs are necessarily 'motivated.'" In this sense icons are "the product of the analogic practices of language users as they selectively establish relationships of likeness . . . [gaining] their meaning not because they naturally resemble some unmediated thing in the world but instead because a community of speakers collectively designates that one kind of thing is like and therefore can come to stand for another" (Carr 2011, 26).

Beyond drawing equivalences between words—since Carr's work is focused on interactional settings where interlocutors have an overlapping language community—Patrice's translation of *Ubuntu* into *guanxi* brings entire notions of intersubjective space-time in relation to one another. The resulting effect is not only the augmentation of the social-semiotic range of *guanxi*, but also that of *Ubuntu.* Furthermore, rather than essentializing both *Ubuntu* and *guanxi*, Patrice's pragmatic translation via iconization of these concepts should perhaps be understood as an attempt to bridge very different theories of social relations that nonetheless allow for intersubjective contingencies and their personhoods: a cultural translation as a transnationally portable resource.

In my own attempt to provoke Patrice's meta-talk of translation—perhaps mirroring what Peter Mwepikeni (2018) has depicted as an abuse of the *Ubuntu* concept to further neoliberal extraction in the guise of Rainbow Nationalism—I responded to his transfiguration with a well-known quip among fellow South and Southern African students: "I thought *Ubuntu* was dead?" (Ke-Schutte 2019, 329). For many post-apartheid and postcolonial subjects, this more cynical take on *Ubuntu* is often suggestive of alienations or anomic disillusionments of various forms (Durkheim [1893] 2013). From the ties of kinship and basic human compassion to a corrosion of cultural forms of belonging and emplacement typified by increasing and destructive commitments to self-interest. These conditions are furthermore understood as eradicating the underlying ethical space-time of *Ubuntu* through which one might be or become a person through other persons (Makgoba 1999, 153). Responding to my pessimism, Patrice noted: "maybe *Ubuntu* is dead for us, but *guanxi* is alive for them" (Ke-Schutte 2019, 329). Pragmatically, Professor Li's letter-writing constituted sufficient evidence—for Patrice—that a translatability between *guanx*i and *Ubuntu* did exist.

Importantly, neither *guanxi* nor *Ubuntu* are terms that can fully represent an inalienable cultural romance for Professor Li and Patrice. On one occasion after a failed meeting with an associate, Professor Li lamented: "You know, *guanxi* has really changed. When I was young, giving a person a ride in a truck or feeding them some dumplings was enough [to secure loyalty for life]. Now [this is] not the case. . . . You know, under Mao, *guanxi* was a lot more real . . . look, I'm not saying [the Cultural Revolution] was a good time, but *guanxi* meant more because it was all [we] had" (Ke-Schutte 2019, 330).

CONCLUSION: FROM A SEMANTICS TO A PRAGMATICS OF TRANSLATION

The preceding interactions with and between Professor Li and Patrice Moji demonstrate a pragmatics of translation—one drawn from an actual micro-interaction (as opposed to those announced, yet seldom demonstrated, by a number of American Foucaultian devotees). This approach contrasts with much current China-Africa related scholarship, particularly research situated in China, which has concerned itself mainly with macro-scale phenomena often providing compelling insights concerning political and economic dimensions of Sino-African interactions (Bodomo 2012; King 2013; Chang et al. 2013; Brautigam 2009; Li et al. 2012; Snow 1989). These studies rigorously attempt to delineate and summarize the various strategic interests of China, African nation states, and a conspicuously silent western audience, often marshaling vast swathes of data to depict very large social formations on a continental scale. As Kenneth King (2013) has noted, however, our picture of the actual people involved in this interaction remains incomplete. This is troubling since, at least from my preliminary research, it appears that what constitutes the capacities for intersubjective personhood is very much at issue in measuring the success or value of an educational development initiative the scale of which is unprecedented on the African continent. "Who Africans are," and "who Africans are capable of being"—to themselves, their sponsors, their communities, as well as other aspirational or elite audiences—depends largely on acquiring and performing capacities to speak, network, and move without cultural constraints in a Chinese world. It is the recruitment of translation in the service of such goals that is at issue in actual face-to-face interactions between Africans and Chinese as non-western interlocutors that must cultivate their own trans-languages (Hanks 2010). But, how does a pragmatics of translation—in the still decolonizing

South—unsettle the post-translational lament of the Northern academic Anglosphere? By way of extended conclusion, I hope to meditate on how a pragmatics of translation might productively engage a number of "settled" assumptions around what Gayatri Spivak once termed "the politics of translation" (1993).

Translation, in the explicitly linguistic sense, has been a central concern for literary theory (Spivak 1993; Sakai 1997) in ways that it has not been for anthropologists, who in the past have borrowed or recruited terms like *mana* or *hau* as disciplinary analytics (Durkheim [1912] 1995; Mauss [1925] 1967), and yet more recently have come to disavow or lament the nihilistic impossibility of translation (Asad 1986). There have been notable critical exceptions, in linguistic anthropology, to both this polemical legacy of translational "borrowing" as well as post-translational "nihilism" (cf. Michael Silverstein 2017, 2004). In their work, Michael Silverstein (2003a) and Greg Urban (1996) have elaborated some of the imbricated problems with both textual "translation" and its "impossibility," demonstrating the limits of actualizing either in the strictly literary sense. The understanding here is perhaps that translation—insofar as it is understood to be a practice of "commensurating meaning" between languages—has analytical limitations when applied to a spoken language and its inextricable context of signification. This is because language, when understood to be inseparable from the life world of its community of users, is always a mutually constituting process rather than an object. Thus, it is more akin to a process, dialogically and semiotically unfolding in the moment to moment of real-time speech (Silverstein 2003a, 1976; Irvine and Gal 2000; Keane 1997, 2007; Agha 2007b; Urban 1996; Bakhtin 1981; Austin 1975). Thus the target and matrix languages in the context of a translation might be seen to be constantly under construction, rendering translation as a stabilization of meaning a somewhat remote goal. Yet outside of the Andersonian language ideologies of the "west," this precariously maintained state of translation and translatability has never been about the stabilization of meaning, but rather the commitment to translational maintenance—both entextualized or interactional. For those committed to the endeavor of translation—like African students and their Chinese teachers in Beijing—the achievement of a translation, however imperfect or fleeting, exists as an unquestionable horizon of possibility, even if a durable permanence or stabilization never emerges.

Of course, in its more metaphorical uses, translation has been a classical concern for scholars of culture more or less up until the *Writing Culture* "crisis" (Clifford and Marcus1986). Given the obvious, if somewhat problematized, resilience of this analytic (Spivak 1993; Derrida 1976; Sakai 1997; Chakrabarty 2000; M. Silverstein 2003a; Urban 1996) and its contestations (Asad 1986; Clifford and Marcus 1986; Abu-Lughod 1991) particularly in the domain of cultural translation, a key question emerges: How is it that a concept so closely associated with the formal uses of language seems to have such a broad purchase for an immensely divergent group of disciplinary concerns?

This question, however, presupposes language as a stable category to begin with—as though we know where language or multilingualism begins and ends. Rather, we should ask how purely linguistically a concept like translation glosses once the analyst unsettles the very category we call language to begin with. However, in the monolingual seminar rooms of Global North, such extensions of translation as metaphor don't even seem worthy of consideration in the work of scholars like Bruno Latour (1996), Adrian Mackenzie (2002), and Stefan Helmreich (2007). As indicated in the previous chapter, translation, in its posthuman framings— and particularly in the case of Latour—bypasses its linguistic and semantic associations in favor of generating the emergent nature of ontological legibility as both the object and outcome of translational or transductional processes that are left bracketed in their analyses. Here, the Southern scholar is compelled to ask: How does Latourian translation understand the relationship between emerging formations of subjectivity that are not in engagement with the translation or translation-defining Global North? In my case, the translational labor of Afro-Chinese interactants on Beijing's university scene would easily disappear in the network of social relations and cultural mediations enveloping subject formation in the definitions of non-representational or post-representational translation. Additionally, how would we do so without considering the fact that these subjects both speak and reflect on translation as reflexive process? Here, the preceding discussion provided a unique opportunity to engage these questions by way of demonstrating how cultural translation cannot be disarticulated from the culturally situated social relations practices, institutions, and infrastructures that translating subjects both performatively constitute and depend on.

However, such primitivist and Orientalist circulations differ drastically from the attempt at cultural translation unfolding between Professor Li and Patrice, and indeed within a great many other Afro-Chinese encounters unfolding at present. Rather, we can understand their respective recourse to *guanxi* and an *Ubuntu* translation of *guanxi* as standing in for a humanistic attempt to disrupt often alienating, machine-like, automatic, and bureaucratic social institutions that surround most other aspects of their interaction: the global inequalities and inevitable racisms that haunt Patrice's educational endeavor, and Professor Li's mostly under-appreciated and "hidden" affective labor in managing it. In the face of their respective but fundamentally unequal alienations of labor and personhood, both *guanxi* and *Ubuntu* can be seen as a refuge—a cultural space-time of reintegration representing transcendent cultural justifications for enduring forms of solidarity. Cultural translation, as a condition of possibility for generating such a cultural space-time, might only then be understood as a way of resisting a contemporary corruption of expectations of mutual obligation—perhaps suggestive of the spectral residue of "organic divisions of labor" within "mechanical divisions of labor" (Durkheim [1893] 2013; Benjamin 2007c). In this way, we might understand *guanxi* and *Ubuntu* as coming to ground third-world solidarity as the romantic promise of a social bondage that mutually excludes the immediate, utilitarian purchase of the first world either by China or Africa. However, such speculative possibilities were less easy to discern, since both interactants were careful to hedge—despite frequent recourse to utopic imaginaries of culture and history—that these terms are not immune to historical forces and reappropriation, and certainly could not unfold in an ideological vacuum. Regardless of apparent obstacles, their attempts at cultural translation persist.

For subjects like Professor Li and Patrice, misrepresentations, misunderstandings, and mistranslations will and certainly do abound, but the attempt at translation—despite the violence of its failures—remains unmitigated between non-western others. These must be accounted for rather than denied, preferably by researchers from the Global South, and building analytical approaches to cultural translation that are drawn from contexts that disrupt, complicate, diversify, and provincialize encounters between the west and its Others. From this standpoint, cultivating a pragmatics of translation will be an important empirical starting point to decolonizing the study non-western, non-Anglocentric interactions and the framing of their polyphonous scales of cultural encounter.

6

____

Liberal-Racisms and Invisible Orders

In the preceding chapters, I have offered an account of the ways in which whiteness, English, and cosmopolitan mobility together form an intersubjective space-time of mediation, an Angloscene, that can be understood as simultaneously reconstituted through, and recruited to, African and Chinese encounters in contemporary Beijing. Throughout, I framed this simultaneous recruiting and reconstituting process as a form of translation—conceptualized more in a dialectical and interactionist sense. In doing so, I drew attention to the historical material condition of decolonization that animates an emergent but far from depoliticized non-western encounter. I further suggested that this approach has important implications for the study of interactions—in both anthropology as well as a variety of disciplines concerned with contact, encounter, and the stratification of social diversity along multiple intersectional vectors.

In reconsidering postcolonial translation in this critical semiotic sense, I have suggested that there are three dimensions to understanding translation or mediation as simultaneously a pragmatic and dialectical concern. I suggested that there is, first, a chronotopic dimension to interactions, in the sense that they require the recruitment and construction of space-time(s) through which units of commensuration and social value—like English, whiteness, or unmarked cosmopolitan mobility—become co(n)textualized. Second, I suggested that such interactions—including but not limited to dialogical speech acts—are intersectionally emplaced (Crenshaw 1991), complicating the possibilities of "taking any line" (Goffman 1959) of interaction by any subject at any time. This is due to the ways in which relationships between race, gender, and sexuality have a propensity to stratify subjects in relation to an emergent ideological gravity of whiteness—even if their presumed national and intersocial chronotopes were very different. Finally, I showed how interactions among subjects—who are variously stratified by aspirationally cosmopolitan horizons and the personhoods these imbricate—have an (an)aesthetic propensity. Here, I reflected that the affective and mimetic capacities of non-white sensoriums—and their techno-linguistic dependencies—become recruited to sustaining a persistent stratification through whiteness—whether by embracing a liberal nonracial cosmopolitanism, or a reconstituted "third world" *imaginaire*—as a means to escape the gravity of white space-time.

The universities and wider settings within which I was able to work during the course of my fieldwork certainly amplified the tensions imbricated by the Anglo-scene—tensions that both promised young Africans and their Chinese interlocutors access to unmarked, cosmopolitan social mobility while simultaneously deferring it. The fact that the means for making and acquiring the ideal future subject of third-world cosmopolitanism was a promise that became continuously elided prompted my observation of (an)aesthesia as a way to mitigate the disjunctive ways in which a cosmopolitan future was constantly being brought closer while being kept at bay. In this way, the interactional space-time of whiteness was very much distilled by the global university and transnational educational matrix within which African and Chinese students found themselves: transforming on- and off-campus interactions as a theater for aspiration and privilege that must (still) be imported from an "enlightened" (perhaps en-whitened) elsewhere. For many educational migrants, adolescence remains endlessly augmented, and adulthood deferred, just to cope with the "youthful" experiences of "exclusion and in-betweenness" that twenty-first-century conditions of mobility and personhood impose on non-western subjects—a concern that has emerged in the work of anthropologist, Constantine Nakassis (2016a).

In his work, Nakassis suggests that the southern Indian university campus's interactional space-time suspends the ideological gravity of stratification acting on his "youthful" Tamil-speaking subjects, "allowing for a moment to pause and play on those hierarchies by figuratively reanimating and deforming them" (228). On campuses in Beijing, such moments of suspension are certainly present, but rather than pointing to a kind of radical, poststructural agency within conditions of neo-liberal compromise, the transformation of experiences of liminality and hierarchy through such moments of suspension have an equal propensity to also reinforce liminality and hierarchy. Transformation in the interactional here-and-now can go in more than one direction. (An)aesthetically, it can open up "spaces for youth sociality, aesthetics, value, and subjectivity" as much as it can compromise such an "opening-up" (228). Thus, it is precisely through commitments to the possibilities of opened-up conditions of youth sociality, aesthetics, value, and subjectivity that we note their dialectical, cruelly optimistic other: how the powerful conditions for historically material and semiotic alienations of personhood become not only equally possible, but also intersectionally inevitable.

I have emphasized throughout that the mediation of intersubjective and mass-mediated icons of personhood—in dialectical interactions—are central to sustaining a pragmatics of postcolonial translation: "the unmarked cosmopolitan," "the Purple Cow," "Sheryl Sandberg," "Oprah Winfrey," and "Trevor Noah."

These archetypes come into intersubjective existence through interactions, and yet are also experienced as both prior to, and impinging upon, African and Chinese encounters. It is this interplay between present and past, interior and exterior, and emergent and transcendent that I have tried to emphasize by framing these encounters as dialectical interactions. Inhabiting this dialectical tension, my informants both attempted to overturn complex stratifications they found themselves in, as well as to recruit them in their favor—thus ultimately compromising themselves through transforming and reinforcing the very conditions of stratification they were attempting to escape. Thus, the recruitment of such archetypes and mass-mediated icons of personhood certainly allowed for a partial suspension from precarious intersubjective tensions. However, the emancipatory propensities of this recruitment and suspension—once committed to on the part of the cosmopolitan aspirant—can also be interpreted as eliding the inaccessibility of cosmopolitan realities through the fetishization of cosmopolitan potentials.

TRANSLATION'S MOBILE ENTANGLEMENTS

The attempt to convert the precarities of mobility into aspirational possibilities entails the recruitment of a universal, perhaps cosmopolitan, register to enact a postcolonial translation—in this case not only English, but also its elided racio-linguistic entailments. Suggesting a similar set of dynamics, Homi Bhabha writes that "culture as a strategy of survival is both transnational and translational. [T]he transnational dimension of cultural transformation"—which I interpret as a salient, although not totalizing dimension of mobility—"turns the specifying or localizing process of cultural translation into a complex process of signification" (1995, 48). For him and many others (Gilroy 1993; Spivak 1993; Nuttall and Mbembe 2008; Butler 1995), this transnational condition disrupts the capacity to reference "the natural(ized), unifying discourse of 'nation,' 'peoples,' 'folk' tradition" (Bhabha 1995, 49). In mobility, there is a transformation in concrete and signifying conditions that disrupt the signs of identity or personhood in their national or local expressions—a theme that becomes salient in transnational encounters. This disruption, for Bhabha, problematizes identity formation by short-circuiting the reading of such signs by changing the national or local context from which they derive their legibility. Since the meanings of signs are contingent on the spatial, temporal, and material totality of their context of utterance—or simply their indexical factors (M. Silverstein 1976)—conditions of mobility necessarily impinge on signs of personhood. To be sure, such disruptions open gaps in taken-for-granted worlds that are unsettled by transnational interactions and their emergent communities of reception and reproduction—where African educational migrants in Beijing and cosmopolitan Chinese graduate students in America all encounter and appropriate various cultural signs, producing perhaps productive ambiguities, curiosities, and forms of mimesis. Or is the Sino-African encounter—an object of analysis to the western media and academic Anglosphere—merely a potential staging ground for Eurocentric multicultural fantasies, or when they fail, racist dystopias?

This book did not seek to argue against novelty or contestation. Rather, it attempted to capture the ideological conditions that both obstruct and perpetuate this fantasy of equal opportunity multiculturalism as an outlook undergirding western intellectual expectations of Chinese and African contemporary encounters. If Sino-African encounters could be genuinely equitable, egalitarian mobility would be a condition of possibility for such encounters. But what kind of mobility is in question? Is mobility an experience, or is it a physical state, objectively delineable, irrespective of the one experiencing it? In this *experience* of mobility, where and how does this experience become legible? In posing such questions, temporality and sequence become key considerations. In the movement or reproduction of language, race, and cosmopolitanism, what exactly does this mobility entail?

Homi Bhabha clearly situates the state of mobility as being in translation, while on the other side of the same epistemic coin, Jacques Derrida and Gayatri Spivak have suggested that it is the state of translation that is a mobile one. There is something happening at the confluence of mobility and translation that appears to generate the solipsism at issue for these thinkers. It is also out of this solipsism (or perhaps dialectic)—of history, meaning, and material conditions—that translation as the primary analytic of postcolonial theory has emerged—and while I do not explicitly enter into a semantic exegesis, it is translation in its postcolonial mode that has haunted my engagement throughout this project.

This necessitates a polemic of sorts, in which I have drawn on, and recontextualized a very particular genealogy of postcolonial theory—in some ways at odds with what I have experienced as its canonical, mostly American, reduction in the US university classroom. In fetishizing the moment of translation and its discursive consequences, Bhabha, Spivak, and Derrida—in a poststructural or deconstructionist mode of postcolonial inquiry—have largely been recruited into the proposition of intellectual equal opportunism within privileged American higher educational settings. I mean no disrespect to these ancestors of postcolonial theory since it is on the foundations of their work that my own critique is constructed. Instead, I am criticizing from a position of frustration at the way in which their work has both been co-opted, and (perhaps unintentionally) lends itself to a still pervasive, extractive logic that underpins many intellectual interventions that sustain social science and humanistic inquiries that simultaneously aim to be both objective and relativist without questioning the condition of possibility for this very proposition. While colonization certainly *transforms the colonizer too*, I feel that a *discourse from nowhere because it is everywhere* approach to postcolonial translation makes power an ultimately arbitrary proposition, where those who don't have it critique it and ultimately reconstitute its persistent salience. It was Erving Goffman—a contemporary of Michel Foucault—who also concluded that hierarchies of power or "interactional orders" ultimately required interactional labor to sustain them. However, Goffman also pointed out that subjects were not equal in their capacity to participate in the maintenance or contestation of hierarchy—there was an ordering of the interaction that emerged as though imposed on it, that made the same marginal subjects perpetually bear the burden of marginality in any interaction, and that this occurred regardless of the unfinalizability of personhood that exists as a default proposition in liberal societies. Even in the more general political writings of Frantz Fanon, Achille Mbembe, and Mao Zedong—working at fundamentally different scales, and out of contrasting settings—a micro-interactional dynamics of stratification is at play in the politics of revolution and decolonization. In his lectures on surveillance at the University of Tunis, Fanon noted the raciolinguistic contingencies of reception (as production) that make the encounters of the colonized with the ideological space-time of the colonizer a far from open-ended one (Browne 2015). In this regard, he preceded both Said ([1977] 2003) and Foucault (2007, 1995, 1982) in noting how subject formation unfolds through "ascending relations of power," as well as how this formation is contingent upon mediated modes of reception, like surveillance.

All of these thinkers point to the dialectical emergence of an ideological gravity where despite the constant propositions of decolonization, modernity, sovereignty, and equal opportunism, marginal subjects of history are stratified so as to bear the seemingly perpetual burdens of blackness, refugee-ness, or Chineseness as liabilities. Regardless of the volatility of semiotic forms—due to the open-ended play of difference and repetition, or the arbitrariness of signs of alterity—there appears to remain a durability in the ideological gravity of stratification: a durability that is pragmatic rather than semantic. Thus, there is no "failure" or "impossibility" of translation as a pragmatic proposition, and indeed no interaction without some attempt at translation. Even if translation fails every time, the interlocutor remains committed to it, thus sustaining translation as a durable social process even if it remains incomplete, hierarchical, and ultimately compromised—a point demonstrated explicitly in chapter 5.

Communicating this has been difficult in my time in the United States—as a graduate student and, later, as a postdoctoral student and faculty member. I can cite my own experiences of teaching postcolonial theory and attempting to make use of it in my research within the evaluatory regime of the American academy. I was constantly informed not only of how "out-of-date" this genealogy was, but also of its lack of theoretical rigor and ethnographic nuance. "More complex" readings of my own postcolonial interlocutors were constantly encouraged, where colonialism suddenly became "not the real concern" of Spivak, who could now "easily be updated with Povinelli (2001), Brown (2005), and Butler (1997)." Fanon was suddenly "not really advocating violence" as a challenge to white liberalism in the shadow of decolonization, and those who would dare to read Fanon in the "wrong way" were suddenly not "exegetic" enough—an accusation recently directed toward South African students voicing Fanon to protest white monopoly capital. Latour, Agamben, Foucault, and *Writing Culture* became almost dogmatically prescribed (or perhaps proscribed) as a theoretical panacea to the "hysterical radicalism" that would dare to challenge the "unmarked" "objectivity" of liberal intellectualism. Masquerading as open-ended and open-minded deconstruction, so many of these accusations against radical hysteria, some of them even of racism, continue to conceal the ideological gravity within which updated translations of postcolonialism unfold.

This both implicit and explicit concealment evidences the existence of vast institutions and regimes of arbitration, not to mention economic systems that are sustained by commitments to translatability and commensuration (Sassen 2014). For example, journalistic and academic institutions of the Anglosphere that are committed to a situated objectivity—and yet speak for all others—are still squarely situated within what Adorno once called the culture industry, yet on a fundamentally more global scale masquerading as intellectual excellence. There are clearly a set of institutional practices that authenticate both legibility and value to Sino-African interactions within a subjective, far from arbitrary, regime of arbitration. There is a lot at stake in translating the cultural and economic value of a China-Africa interaction, and there are certainly those who are the authenticators of such translations. Meta-translators, like anthropologists, not only exercise authority over a translation, but also mastery of the original, the ur-text, and thus authorize an appropriate relationship to history. It is precisely for this reason that anthropologists' situatedness in relation to both their field of study and research subjects should not be elided. "Who are the anthropologists in the field?" is a question many anthropologists these days engage with great relish, eager to perform the genre of narcissistic navel-gazing even while reflexively deriding it. Few, however, need to ask: who are they *to* their field?

As an Afrikaner anthropologist, I felt more at home in my field site of Beijing than I ever did as a graduate student in the United States. I found refuge among my informants in China and elsewhere, learning a language that I still struggle to speak. However, I will maintain that proclaiming "friendships" between myself and my informants within the chronotope of an ethnography is wholly inappropriate, even though such claims have increasingly become commonplace in the English anthropological literature. This representational politics becomes all the more apparent as increasing numbers of non-American and non-white anthropologists must internalize an appropriate affective disposition to their research subjects so as to perform an acceptable "Anthroman" (Jackson 2005). The performance of an appropriate sentiment must be mastered to put an imagined (and thus omnipresent) Euro-American arbiter at ease. We must make our friendships with our informants accessible to our evaluators by mastering a representation of our subjects that we imagine will affectively trigger our teachers' evaluations of us. In my fieldwork, there were and continue to be genuine friendships—meaningful ones—but I have tried, as far as possible, not to make these available to the parasitically voyeuristic imagination of the default monolingual, white, English-speaking public of American anthropology's reading Anglosphere. Proclaiming friendship in the rhetorical service of assuring the reader that one had "genuine rapport with the natives" is disingenuous at best, but it also dismisses possibilities of insight that can only be gained through other kinds of "misanthropic," or (mis)anthropological, social intensities—violence for instance.

During my fieldwork, one personal experience demonstrated the productive insights to be gained from violent, but nonetheless socially intensive, interactions. As a member of a Southern African student soccer team—Azania United—which participated in the competitive inter-Africa league in Beijing, I was at one point deliberately injured by an opposition player who was humiliated by his teammates and Azania United's manager for giving the ball away to "the only white guy on the field." Incensed by this, the freshman from Nong Da (Agricultural University) broke my leg and caused an ACL tear with an off-the-ball revenge foul. As I was recovering from my injuries, my teammates and informants—both Chinese and African—often jokingly told me that I could "walk them off." Toward the end of my fieldwork, I saw the student who had injured me in a university canteen several months later, he looked at me limping, and also jokingly said: "When are you going to come and try to steal the ball from me again?" We had rapport, but were not friends; nor would we ever be "equals" in the relativistic sense. In this regard, violent recognitions can render very different kinds of anthropological insights between increasingly atypical not-quite-native informants and not-quite-native ethnographers, making persistent American ethnographic platitudes, like "my friends, the informants," seem somewhat out of touch with reality and worthy of suspicion by the other social sciences.

In retrospect, "violent recognition" as a constant experience in and beyond the field was likely a strong motivator for my depiction of Fanon's "violence of decolonization" as a mode of translation, where "decolonization . . . sets out to change the order of the world" and "cannot come as a result of magical practices, nor of a natural shock, nor of a friendly understanding" (1963, 36). Here, I understood decolonization not only as "an always as-yet-incomplete project," but also, one that is "translated" in the pragmatist sense I discussed before. By this emphasis on translation, I will further suggest that communicative incompleteness does not mean that translation is either open-ended or arbitrary—for open-endedness and arbitrariness are ultimately visible only from a truly privileged perspective. As I will demonstrate, movement between colonization and decolonization is very much contingent on an ideological context that does not allow for a seamless shift in relations and reappropriations of power, and here I will emphasize that the same is true for disciplinary debates in anthropology and other social sciences—particularly in the privileged domain of the American academic Anglosphere where consensus and passive-aggressive gatekeeping constrain debates in their insistence on a nonconfrontational, analytical equal opportunism. This is an experienced daily reality for any third-world or intersectionally marginalized subject participating in collegial interactions within America's knowledge industry. If our debates are to be relevant, and if we are genuinely committed to decolonizing anthropology—which, I would argue, no amount of privileged relativism can ever accomplish—we may want to consider Fanon's imperative more seriously:

> The Third World has no intention of organizing a vast hunger crusade against Europe. What it does expect from those who have kept it in slavery for centuries is to help rehabilitate man, ensure his triumph everywhere, once and for all. But it is obvious we are not so naïve as to think this will be achieved with the cooperation and goodwill of the European governments. This colossal task, which consists of reintroducing man into the world, man in his totality, will be achieved with the crucial help of the European masses who would do well to confess that they have often rallied behind the position of our common masters on colonial issues. In order to do this, the European masses must first of all decide to wake up, put on their thinking caps and stop playing the irresponsible game of Sleeping Beauty. (1963, 63)

Given that the apex of white imperialism—following Said (2003)—has perhaps shifted from Europe to the elite of America, where privilege is validated by its most prestigious institutions of knowledge—like the University of Chicago and Harvard University, for instance—the semiotic value of Europe and the European in Fanon's words must be understood as a "shifter" (M. Silverstein 1976). This shifter, however, forms an important component in enabling the maintenance of a more transhistorical, transnational, yet implicit white gravity that reiterates the stratification of its constantly thwarted others. In this regard, I understand that the American academy as the driver of a global knowledge industry (followed by an increasing number of transnational franchises) does not operate in an ideological vacuum. I also acknowledge that many of its personnel believe themselves to be fighting the good fight. Here, I hope to have demonstrated the degree to which this remains a compromised belief, while an elite—mostly liberal—American intellectual class remains oblivious to their complicity in stratifying subjectivity far beyond their own imagined, utopian horizons. I argue that this complicit stratification is enabled by many of my elite colleagues and teachers both in underestimating and investing in arguments against an imagined boogeyman of "structure." This is an ultimately lazy intellectual commitment that bypasses the ideological impacts of vast belief systems that are dependent on structure and structural sense. The literary registers and publication industries promoting the most committed poststructural and nonrepresentational work; the mass- and linguistically mediated cosmopolitan horizons of personhood academia itself engenders; the aesthetic and ethical forms that persuade us about the existence of a culturally diverse, but far-from-disconnected Anthropocene—all of these ultimately depend on a significant faith in structure. The dismissal and denigration of postcolonial critiques of Anglo-centric mass media and English monolingualism as simplistic and somehow "less complex" are all significant manifestations of this structural blind spot in western anthropology's relativist yet still monolingual theater of operations. Neither "complex" nor "novel," this critique merely underlines the compromised conditions within which so many American-trained anthropologists are attempting to rescue efficacious agency in the lives of informants who experience neither efficaciousness nor agency. In the following concluding interactional analysis, I hope to not only demonstrate some of the limits of rescuing agency and the situated theater of personhood that informs it. I hope to additionally reveal how the very proposition of liberal subjecthood—emerging in the following interaction through contestations around the term "freedom"—generates the otherwise invisible ideological order within which interactional participants are stratified.

MUTUAL BENEFITS, INVISIBLE ORDERS

As China's contemporary engagement with Africa continues to engender a tension between "mutually beneficial" and hierarchical relations, a number of western journalists have begun to critique China as a modern-day colonizer, restaging Africa as the eternally colonized. This staging recruits Africans as a popular and recent addition to their list of China's subalterns—equating China's relationship with ethnic minorities, who themselves are seeking various degrees of sovereignty, with Africans' historical and political history with Europeans. Given a topical interest in these "colonial" Sino-African encounters, increasing numbers of western journalists have become a prominent presence in a number of ethnographic settings in China and Africa. Through their hyper-legibility, they play a key role in recontextualizing the interactional frameworks that imbricate both African and Chinese actors and their ethnographic voyeurs. But, what does this recontextualization do?

This final, hopefully revealing, account of an interaction in Beijing was mediated by a famous American journalist, who, through her own attempt at "equal" participation in a Sino-African encounter, inadvertently generated the very ideological gravity that inflects Afro-Chinese "interactional orders" (Goffman 1983). I have suggested in preceding chapters, and following Goffman, that interactional orders can be understood as a dialectical, interactionally immanent, ideological stratifications that appear as transcendent to the participants in that interaction. I also theorized such interactions as mediated through linguistic enregisterment. In the interaction that follows, the stratification that unfolds is significantly informed by a set of historical and material conditions assumed to be absent in Sino-African engagements—the absent presence of a recontextualized white space-time.

In 2015, near the end of a stint of fieldwork in Beijing, I attended a talk by a former chief economist of the World Bank, Justin Lin. The talk was hosted at the Beijing branch of an elite American university—one of several Ivy League outposts in the Chinese capital. In attendance were numerous high-profile personnel from state-related financial institutions. Liu Xiaoming, a high-ranking economist who was in charge of the Africa division of one of China's top three foreign-development banks, was among them. Attendees also included a number of journalists like Anne West, a well-known white American writer who had been active for a number of years as a feminist and ethnic minority activist in China. At the end of Lin's talk, there was a Q and A, with many of the questions coming from younger Chinese men, such as: "How does one make the most of a western education as a Chinese man?" Other questions, all of which were posed in English despite the fact that more than 90 percent of the attendees were Chinese, focused on China's future role in a world where not only Chinese labor, but Chinese capital, became central to more countries' development strategies, and the global economy as a whole. Justin Lin emphasized that China was positioned to see different kinds of investment potential compared to past European American investments, "especially in places like Africa."

At this, Lin Xiaoming somewhat overeagerly leaped out of his seat and moderated his own question to Lin: "I am the chief economist for the Africa division of China's Da Qian Bank and we have been struggling with this question for a long time. How is China going to develop Africa when we have seen many failures of development in the past? There are so many obstacles, the most pressing being epidemics, corruption, and civil war." Justin Lin looked genuinely confused by the question, perhaps due to Xiaoming's self-introduction and the contradiction of his question with China's already considerable investments in Africa. Why would an Africa investor for the Chinese government be so opposed to investment in Africa? After a considered pause, Justin Lin responded: "I think your opinion is exaggerated; surely, Africa is a big place with many different strengths in different regions?" Anne West—whom I had met on an earlier occasion through my partner—was sitting next to me at the talk, and commented in a whispered aside: "Are you kidding me?" Feeling incensed by Xiaoming's question, I had the same phrase in mind at the time, but as I would come to learn later, our exasperation stemmed from very different alignments and assumptions about the ideological context within which Sino-African interactions were emplaced. At the end of the talk, as attendees broke into groups with wine glasses in hand, Anne immediately gravitated toward Liu Xiaoming and I followed.

"I really enjoyed your question," Anne said to Xiaoming, who gleefully nodded and said, "Thank you so much, Anne, I am a really big fan of your work." Anne then introduced me as "an expert on China-Africa relations from the University of Chicago" and then immediately stepped back from the interaction, watching. Xiaoming smiled, shook my hand, and told me the name of his Ivy League university where he had studied for an MBA degree in finance. I then asked Xiaoming how often he traveled to Africa for his work. Wasn't it exhausting? He responded that it wasn't all that necessary in his position, but that he had once gone to Tanzania for two weeks. He was proud of the fact that his organization was fortunate in that they were able to work with reliable forecasting data, making use of both Chinese and American think tanks to get the information they need to make "informed policy decisions." As we spoke, and as Anne watched, I increasingly began to feel as though I was being drawn into an American fraternity chronotope of sorts, as his register shifted from professional to American college colloquial. As he commented on the Chicago Bulls' poor basketball performances in recent years and whether I had been following their season, I began to realize that Xiaoming was entering into this register because he thought that I was an American. Confirming this, he then asked—probably noting my inability to engage in basketball banter—"Where in the States are you from?" When I answered, "I'm not from the States," thus confirming his suspicions, and followed up with "I'm from South Africa," Xiaoming's expression and register instantly changed. The interaction stopped dead in its tracks as he said, "Oh" and looked at Anne, as though waiting for further instructions. On cue, she quickly suggested that we should "continue this fascinating conversation" over dinner the following week. Xiaoming eagerly agreed and we exchanged WeChat accounts to arrange the event, which did actually come about a week later.

Anne texted me and my partner a few days before the dinner with Xiaoming, saying that she was bringing one of her ethnic minority informants to the meeting. She then suggested that I "bring one of [my] African friends [to challenge] his assumptions." What Anne meant by Xiaoming's assumptions was "patriarchal Han Chinese ethnocentrism," a theme she had often contextualized in her own work with ethnic minorities in China, and particularly ethnic minority women, and which—in interactions with (particularly male) Chinese government officials— she rarely hesitated to call out. The presence of another—this time African— subaltern would both serve as an opportunity to (perhaps intersectionally) extend her argument beyond China, as well as provide a provocative ethnographic encounter through which to demonstrate it. It is worth noting that, without Anne's mediation, a meeting with Xiaoming would have been an unachievable feat for me, a South African anthropologist. Given my status, interactions with people like Xiaoming are mostly out of the question. When the high-profile Chinese government official and the renowned American journalist discuss their subalterns— ethnic minorities and Africans—it is anthropologists and "their colorful friends" who become the parasites of the journalistic encounter.

In preparation for our meeting, I chose to invite my informant Rousseau Asara—an ambitious finance student from Madagascar studying at one of Beijing's top universities. Through my fieldwork, I came to know Rousseau as both a confident conversational provocateur as well as someone who had obsessively acquired knowledge of Chinese development banks' investment strategies—the topic of his honors thesis. Thus, of all my informants, he was the one most likely to benefit professionally and academically from meeting Xiaoming. Anne and Xiaoming left it to the rest of us to make the arrangements and my partner (fittingly) chose an ethnic minority restaurant in the Haidian district for the setting of the conversation. On the appointed day, Rousseau arrived early, wearing a pink polo shirt and a gold-colored watch, which I had never seen him wear before—possibly to impress Xiaoming. Soon after, Xiaoming arrived wearing a black suit and tie despite the heavily polluted, scorching hot weather—to impress Anne. The rest of us—including Anne, my partner, and Anne's informant—were wearing less "high stakes," casual attire.

From the moment we took our seats inside the air-conditioned restaurant, it was apparent that Xiaoming was uncomfortable, arising perhaps from a perception that he was obviously being set up as the overdressed Beijing government official who had to encounter an array of exotic others in an ethnic minority setting. By contrast, Anne was clearly enjoying herself, enthusiastically commenting on the diversity of ethnic minority dishes in China, before asking Rousseau all about his home country and praising his educational cosmopolitanism. Rousseau, who seemed either oblivious to the tension at the table or determined to ignore it, addressed Xiaoming and said that he admired his institution's development strategy in Africa. This broke the ice somewhat and allowed Xiaoming to emphasize the party line—"mutual benefit should always be win-win, so China is also grateful to Africa." Here, Xiaoming emphasized the "r" in "grateful," as well as nasalizing the first "A" in "Africa" to suggest an American accent, thus emphasizing his education abroad, something he indexed later in the interaction when telling Rousseau that he had "studied the same major, but in the US." After Xiaoming dropped the party line, Anne was quick to interject: "But can Africans move as freely in China as Chinese can in Africa, or Tibet for that matter?" This three-way dynamic set the tone for an exchange that took up almost an hour: Rousseau attempting to network with Xiaoming, who would voice a party-line platitude, which would be scathingly set upon by Anne, who would recruit Xiaoming to the role of privileged Han Chinese, an ethnonationalist patriarch and colonizer of transglobal subalterns.

My partner, Anne's informant, and I watched as Xiaoming would listen thoughtfully to Anne, and then pretend that he did not entirely understand what she was driving at—turning his attention time and again to Rousseau, someone he normally would not have given the time of day, but whom in this encounter represented an escape from an unexpectedly hostile interaction. Another escape tactic presented itself when—as one dish after another arrived in our restaurant booth—Xiaoming somewhat over enthusiastically entered into a mode of connoisseurship, praising "the skill of these people." As a distraction tactic, it backfired when Anne stated: "Well, enjoy it while it lasts," hinting at her own journalistic criticism of the Chinese central government's heavy-handed regulation of ethnic minorities in China. Rousseau, who had by now become aware of and/or fed up with the interactional dynamic, turned to Anne and said: "You know, everybody wants freedom, but maybe everybody doesn't want *your* freedom" (Rousseau's emphasis). At this,

Anne looked visibly flabbergasted, and perhaps even a little betrayed. Rousseau stared at her firmly, standing his ground. It was the first time in the interaction that Xiaoming smiled, and—spotting his gap—suggested that despite a "wonderful evening of important conversations" we should all probably "get some much needed rest." In this way, both the evening and our interactions with Xiaoming came to an awkward end.

In a brief interaction one afternoon following the dinner, Anne voiced her disapproval of Rousseau's views, which to her seemed naïve and uncritical of China's real relationship to its subalterns, suggesting that Africans were "backing the wrong horse." We were standing in her kitchen brewing a pot of tea when she said this. I asked her what horse she thought they should be backing instead. Looking at me over her glasses, she replied: "Whoever guarantees their freedom." "Are you thinking of America?" I asked. Avoiding the question, she emphasized again: "Whoever guarantees their freedom." Irritated, I replied: "It's funny how those guarantees never seem to work out for blacks and indigenous people in your own country." Anne happily conceded this point, but having now proposed both my alignment with Rousseau's argument and her historical alignment with white settler colonialism, I was not invited back for tea. Regardless of what horse I might have been backing, it was clear that I was not backing hers.

Freedom, for Anne, certainly represented the capacity to move without constraint, and in China, she certainly observed a blatant stratification of constraint. Some people are able to move more freely than others both economically and in physical space. In addition, China has a bureaucratic system in place that entrenches these capacities for mobility along ethnic and class lines. However, while holding China accountable for entrenching inequality within a largely invisible global order of value that necessitates inequality, Anne fails to recognize that her capacity for mobility depends precisely on the relative immobility of others—that, in fact, the liberal horizon of egalitarian freedom her criticism of Rousseau presupposes, necessarily requires an outsourcing of the dirty work of stratification on the part of subalterns still willing to throw each other under the bus for the privilege of second place.

RETURNING TO AMERICA: ENCOUNTERING
THE LIBERAL- SUPREMACY COMPLEX

In this final coda, I want to take a step back from the preceding interactional tensions between third-world cosmopolitanism and white space-time as they played out within Sino-African encounters in Beijing and resituate them in the *space* and *time* of writing. I want to reminisce somewhat more freely and recontextualize their revelations of still-compromised ideological conditions of personhood in the early twenty-first century by introducing a final provocation that emerged upon my return to the United States, and during the completion of my degree. Here,

I point to a wider stratification of intersectionality and mobility that I believe animates both this research and the wider context of my work.

In November 2016, following my return from fieldwork, the campus of the University of Chicago, my home institution, was vandalized with neo-Nazi or other white supremacist artifacts. Many people were outraged and upset by the racist paraphernalia littering billboards and buildings, igniting horror among liberal, elite American students and onlookers, and painful familiarity for others. For some, these signs were reiterations of nightmares that were thought to belong to another time. For others, the clumsy wielding of their signifying potential represented further evidence of the laughable ignorance of "open" white supremacy in America. As for myself, I was neither traumatized, nor laughing. The initial impact of American white supremacist gesturing emerged as a dangerous combination of absurdity and trauma, generating a climate of fear for friends, colleagues, and loved ones alike. I was compelled to take these events very seriously, because—for me—they were uncannily familiar.

I have known white supremacy intimately for my entire life: from the time I was a child growing up in apartheid South Africa, into post-apartheid adulthood when the language changed, but the inequalities remained, and all the way to the United States to pursue a graduate degree. What I initially encountered in America was the fresh face of an analogous racial, gender, queer, religious, and class prejudice. When I began my studies in the fall of 2010, during the early Obama years, the blatancy of inequality was rationalized and perpetuated through an ingenious veneer of unmarked (yet default white) liberalism. I recall at the time that it manifested as a self-satisfied narcissism that would shame those who spoke of race or racism, and would school us for thinking that postcolonialism was anything but dead, out-of-date, and "obviously structuralist." Rather than a frothing assertion of ethnocentric pride (the kind I knew far better), whiteness manifested in an unmarked horizon of endless possibilities, basking in liberalism's total victory over oppressions of all kinds. Any complaints to the contrary were dismissed as a misrecognition of "more complex" realities. As suggested earlier, this position was not only perpetuated by white teachers and colleagues in the American academy, but by elite former subalterns who had joined their ranks in the previous decades.

However, in the months following Donald Trump's presidency, it became apparent that both impeccably political, liberal elitism and frothing white supremacist rage ultimately masked the same deep insecurity: a dependency on whiteness as either fetishized or unmarked. Being a "waste of a white skin" is a fear that drives many poor white Americans who imagine themselves to have no other currency, while pretending that race, and therefore whiteness, does not exist has become a pervasive liberal elite strategy for coping with various strata of privilege, even among elite non-whites. This is not a new argument, nor one situated in the liberal intellectual enclaves of the Euro-American academic Anglosphere. Many movements and intellectuals, including the most recent critiques by Black Lives Matter in the United States, and #FeesMustFall in South Africa, have already suggested that this increasingly explicit anxiety among both liberal and racist whites constitutes only a symptom, rather than the engine, of both pervasive and persistent investments in whiteness. From the perspective of a third-world outsider, this is just a quintessentially American expression of the systemic contradictions of white liberalism once revealed by Steve Biko ([1978] 2002), and what might productively be called a liberal-racism complex.

At present, it appears that both American liberals and racists are locked in a frantic battle of self-discovery. On one side are those wildly brandishing heirlooms of mostly imagined ancestors they've never encountered or bothered to fully understand; on the other are those (safety-)pinning an identity—based on guilt, but framed in sanctimony—onto people paternalistically being recruited to be retrospective victims in the making of white saviors. But we must ask: Who is to blame for the loss of identity experienced by whites in America, even though countless non-whites, in non-western places, are (often literally) drowning in white hegemony? How did so many working-class white bodies remain unmarked up until the early hours of November 8, 2016?

Cowardice is an analytically important vector from which to conceptualize a great deal of white supremacist activity in a post-Trump world, not only because so many white supremacists lack the courage to openly address the people they often threaten outside of their communities, often opting for clandestine acts, like vandalism or anonymous cyberterrorism, intimidation, and harassment. Cowardice is indeed more manifest in the obvious lack of impetus to address inequalities among white supremacists themselves—since this is supposedly what their "struggle" (or Kampf) is about. White supremacists in America and Africa alike have always failed to erase structural inequalities in their own self-designated interest groups. In this regard, poor whites fundamentally trouble master-race arguments, whether these are made in America or have been enacted in apartheid South Africa. One neo-Nazi slogan that stood during a number of post-Trump vandalism campaigns was: "No Degeneracy, No Tolerance, Hail Victory."

This slogan was suggestive of the ways in which a certain kind of tolerance was precisely at issue in the post-Trump world, since it is tolerance—of the equal opportunity variety—that has the tendency to oppress. The equal capacity to contest one's conditions of being has been a keystone in the liberal rhetoric of tolerance in America, a stance that has marginalized its working class, people of color, women, non-Christians, and queer communities in unequal but related ways. With the exportation of American-style values of liberal freedom underpinning the expansion of neoliberal globalization in a post–Cold War world, this contradictory pattern has also emerged elsewhere: from the respective class-shaming liberal environmentalism and Han-centric ethnonationalism that has characterized the simultaneous rise of these opposing elements within the Chinese middle and upper classes to the failure of liberal African governments to erase inequalities within a global economic system that ultimately still favors the widening of planetary social inequality and the maintenance of Africa as its dysfunctional space of exception. This is because of the ways in which "tolerance"—manifesting as equal treatment of unequal people—has always reinforced, rather than alleviated, inequality regardless of where it has been applied. Once again, this point has been made over and over again within America, and by many of its greatest thinkers—most of them black intellectuals (Du Bois [1903] 1994; Lorde [1984] 2007; Robinson 1983; hooks 1992). Finally, it is also tolerance that has allowed America's home-grown racism to ferment into the ways we see it manifested now.

The United States, followed by other influential governments like those of BRICS nations, continues to tolerate elite profit over general education—a pattern that many liberal political leaders have perpetuated through their own rational economic divestment from educational equity and social welfare. In this regard, it is ironic that—in the aftermath of November 8, 2016—the United States' liberal elites are somehow shocked that marked white entitlement is threatening unmarked white privilege. In response, many of the American white, educated elite began wearing safety pins that were supposed to symbolize safety to those marginalized by white supremacists. The arguments made in the preceding chapters suggest that however well-intentioned such actions might be, they merely enshrine the unassailability of whiteness through positing the white savior as the only figure that can vanquish the white supremacist. This is a problematic analog to another liberal delusion: that white genocide is the dystopian solution to racism. Not only is this an astoundingly arrogant and racist assumption—that only whites are powerful (or capable) enough to end the problem of whiteness through their own suicide—it also fundamentally underestimates whiteness as a horizon of aspiration that can, as I have demonstrated, operate efficiently without a Caucasian in sight. Whiteness, in the ways I have demonstrated, does not need white bodies.

Herein, perhaps, lies the misunderstood precarity of the world's poor whites—the subconscious realization that whiteness doesn't need them, and is perfectly willing to leave them behind. There is, in the Angloscene and its white space-time, no available category for white failure other than white trash, and this is a far from sympathetic category of personhood. The usual PC rules do not apply, because white, liberal elitism enshrines the rules around whiteness's unmarked unassailability. If one has ever tried racially insulting a white person, one will quickly come to the realization that the only attack that has any effect is the accusation: racist. Bottom-feeding white supremacists who will attempt to get poor whites to buy into hate know this at some level. They have used, and will continue to use, this knowledge to recruit people who feel like white "deplorables" have been branded as such by white elite liberals. In doing so, their victims feel vulnerable, as though a cabal of big white men are the only ones who can preserve a whiteness imagined to be under threat. Such patriarchs of global white supremacy, however, have a fatal flaw: they commit to whiteness not because whiteness is threatened, but because they don't feel white enough. It should be obvious to even the most casual observer that chasing supremacist whiteness is neither transgressive nor empowering since it ultimately undermines the unassailable privileges of unmarked whiteness in the first place. Such flawed commitments to supremacist whiteness, however, have a propensity to anesthetize a far more pervasive ordering of the white liberal-supremacy complex.

A clue as to the ordering of the liberal-supremacy complex may productively emerge through a contemporary recontextualization and exegesis of and postcolonial analytic: subaltern. My use of subaltern (in this book and elsewhere) is precisely not an invocation of a cover-all term. I am not expanding the capaciousness of the term to account for all subjects of discrimination for all time. Instead, drawing on Gayatri Spivak's ([1988] 2010) original invocation of this concept (often misappropriated and misunderstood), my voicing tries to account for its chimeric dimension: the simultaneity of subalternity's both perspectival emergence and structural stratification. This simultaneity frequently emerges in questions like: How do rarified Chinese and African educational elites appropriate English, whiteness, and cosmopolitan mobility in their interactions with one another and yet come to compromise themselves by virtue of never being able to live up to the ideal subject of these appropriations? I understand subaltern in such settings of inquiry as a relational concept.

One is not a subaltern because everyone is potentially a subaltern, nor because certain subjects are intrinsic subalterns of colonial and decolonizing projects. Instead, I argue that subjects become subalterns precisely by virtue of the stratifying terms of commensuration they invoke vis-à-vis one another—terms of commensuration, which by virtue of being less easy to appropriate for some than others, ultimately reveal the limits of a subject's aspirations and their situatedness within an inescapable ideological order of stratification. This is also why I have been concerned throughout with the dynamics of interaction in intersectional (gender, race, class), interlinguistic, and transnational encounters. While intersectionality has traditionally been studied in English-speaking and/or settler colonial societies, such encounters, under conditions where Anglocentric whiteness may seem absent, precisely explicate the contradictory formation of subalternity.

Non-western encounters reveal how whiteness and Englishness—despite their seemingly absent embodiments—persistently come to manifest in perspectival yet always stratifying ways. This is the case for both those seeking refuge *through* unmarked whiteness, as well as for those seeking refuge *from* hegemonic whiteness. It is in this way, I have shown, that African and Chinese actors who attempt to pursue a novel cosmopolitan mobility have little choice but to appropriate signs that compromise this pursuit—where would-be translators, using the master units of commensuration, become the others of their own translation.

In studying the race-language tensions that imbricate Chinese and African interactions, the preceding chapters have demonstrated the enduring relevance of critical and postcolonial theories in unpacking the contradictory conditions that often generate intersectional vectors between inequalities of language, race, gender, sexuality, class, and mobility. Here, translation emerged as an intersubjective, interactional, and dialectical process—apparent in the ways ideological formations like whiteness, English, and cosmopolitan mobility are commensurated into subcategories of broader racial or mobility types. This commensuration is certainly attempted by various culture industries not only in China, but also the postcolonial contexts African students in Beijing *arrive from* (Africa), as well as the centers many of their Chinese interlocutors aspire to *go to* (Europe or America). Here, typifications like race, language, and mobility enable a great deal of alienating institutional labor in relation to their subtypes—whiteness, English, and cosmopolitanism.

In the example of race, a liberal educational discourse (particularly in the settler-colonial west) would insist on the vulgar color differences between white, black, brown, beige, and various other racialized phenotypes as being of an arbitrary nature. In doing so, additional colors are often thrown in for rhetorical effect: blue, green, and so on. For an example, consider sentences like: "I don't care if you are black, white, blue, or purple." In this liberal western educational schema, racism emerges as irrational and therefore unthinkable. The force of this argument stems from ignorantly motivating the equality or equivalence between subtypes of race via the broader type of Race. This generates a familiar deductive logic:

> *If races are arbitrarily equivalent, then race as a measure of alterity does not*
> *(or should not) exist.*
> And therefore:
> *If race is not real, then racism cannot (or must not) exist.*

In an imagined transnational, cosmopolitan space-time, the deductive circuit of race often diagrams a kind of liberal nonracialist ideology:

This schema is internalized by not only liberal whites in the west, but also elite, or aspirationally elite, Chinese and African subjects in Beijing, who would align themselves to this logic of racial arbitrariness. What this kind of diagramming suggests is a common sense within which white bodies predominate as protagonists on advertising billboards in China, Africa, and other non-western countries, but then become rationalized as arbitrary, because it could always have been some*body* else: an arbitrary body or skin. Yet, what this reasoning also allows is for a white body to become the unmarked, default inhabitant of an aspirational cosmopolitan, transglobal social landscape. For many African and Chinese subjects in Beijing, this liberal nonracial common sense also allows different experiences of stratification to be—temporarily—elided or concealed until they emerge as experiences of infrastructural racism.

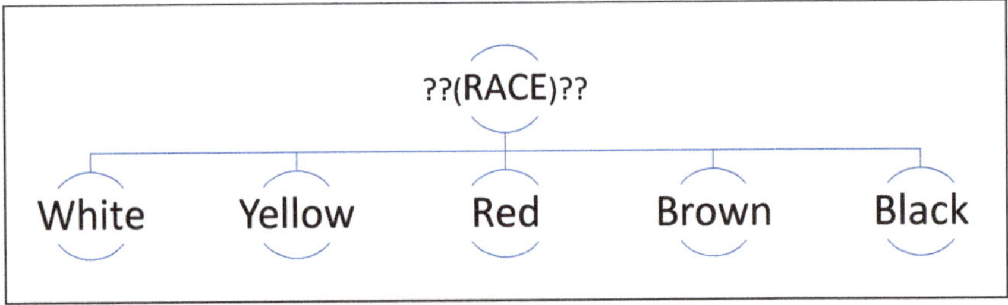

FIGURE 7. Racial arbitrariness.

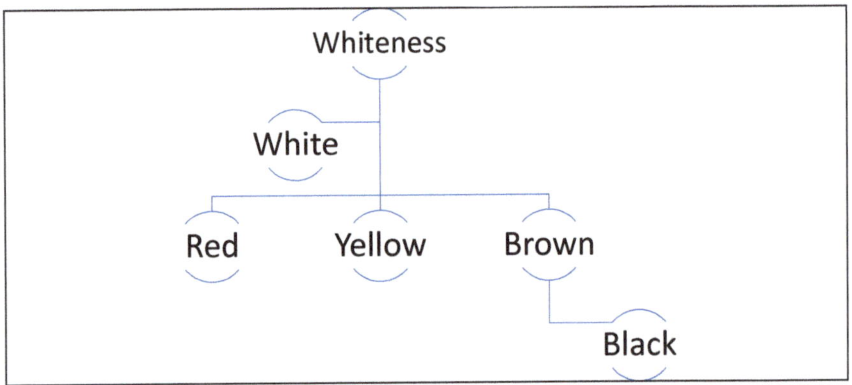

FIGURE 8. Infrastructural racism.

Figure 8 contrasts the previous liberal aspirational ideal of racial arbitrariness with the experienced dimensions of a global infrastructural racism that was prevalent among variously stratified informants. For them, and many others in the decolonizing world, it is whiteness—as an aspirational horizon—rather than race that mediates racism. It is perhaps an understatement to suggest that there is a significant experiential, and thus material, gap between figures 7 and 8. Indeed, the obvious semantic and logical concerns with these propositions have been explored and problematized at length in the work of Charles Mills (1997, 1998) and Kwame Appiah (1989, 1992). Recasting their concerns, this book has explored the pragmatic and performative consequences of these ideas in non-western social interactions that are presumed to be decolonized.

At this point I wish to draw attention to a more general semiotic contingency that underpins this gap between rational arbitrariness and the social stratifications it enables in the postcolonial politics of race, one that is also mirrored in the politics of language. As the political stratifications of whiteness are occluded by relativizing race, so too the material and cultural inequalities imbricated by English are enabled by relativizing language. In the contemporary settler colonial world,

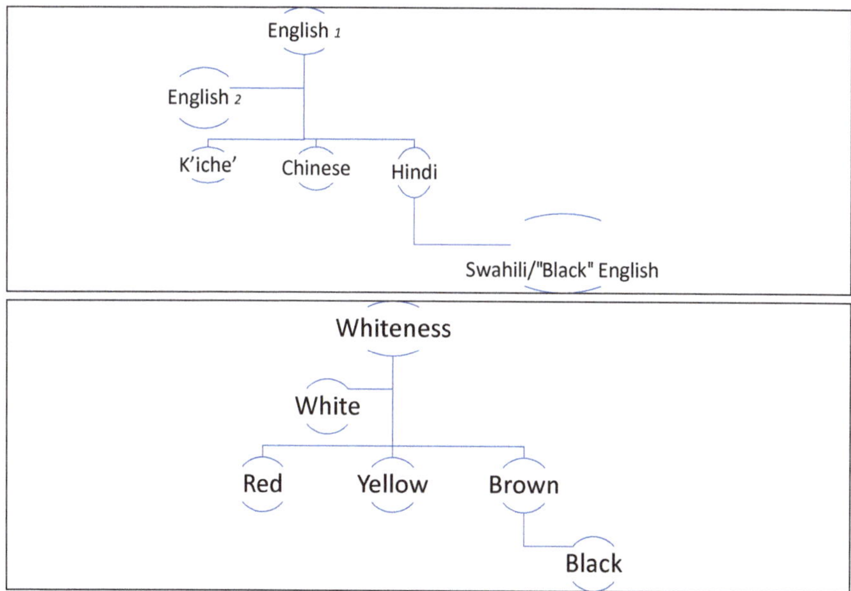

FIGURE 9. Mirroring pragmatic stratifications of English and whiteness.

the arbitrariness of language has been easier to accept than the political arbitrariness of race—even though disciplines like cultural anthropology have long played a considerable role in advocating the relativism of language and race through the analytic of culture (Trouillot 2003, 100; Baker 1998). In China and much of the decolonizing world, the picture is somewhat different: that the racial, in itself, often seems an arbitrary consideration compared to other modalities of differentiation—primary among these is the politics of language and ideas (Vukovich 2019; Ngũgĩ 1994; Spivak 1993). My goal, throughout, is to draw attention to a broader pragmatics of stratification that mutually encompasses language and race, while drawing attention to what language and race occlude. I reveal this pragmatics by disconnecting the relationship between type and subtype in the respective schemas of English as a subtype of language and whiteness as a subtype of race. In doing so, I suggest that English and whiteness transcend their typifications as language and race, mutually constituting an imbricated and encompassing horizon of aspiration—an Angloscene—that comes to compromise the very subjects seeking to exploit their associated signs of symbolic value and cultural capital. Consider the following juxtaposition of the pragmatic stratifications of English and whiteness (fig. 9), with the respective relativistic ideologies of race and language (fig. 10).

The disjuncture between figures 9 and 10 is apparent in the outrage over racial discrimination that was boiling over on at least three continents at the time of writing: riots against a racist American president, protests against white monopoly capital in South Africa, and claims of China's increasingly racist treatment of its

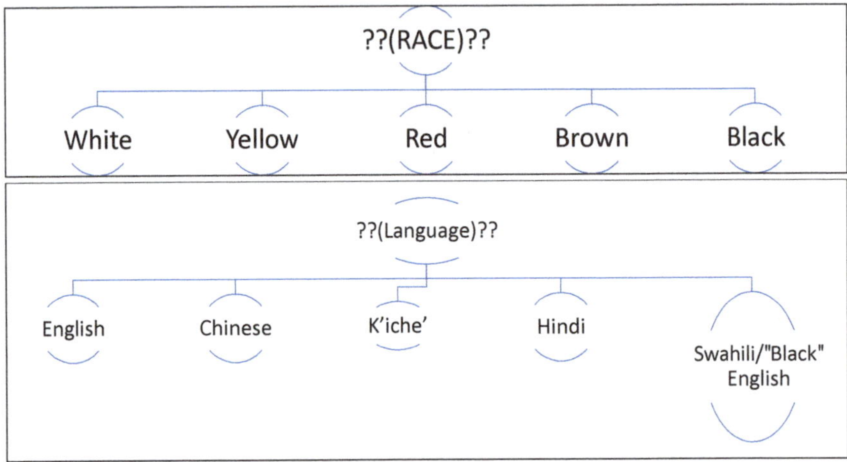

FIGURE 10. Mirroring relativist ideologies of race and language.

ethnic minority or black others. However, one of the ways in which this tension between racial arbitrariness and liberalism manifests across these different contexts—albeit in different ways—forms an important component of the arguments made throughout: if all these *tokens* of race have a genuine sameness, insofar as they are culturally relative or linguistically arbitrary, then why is the broader *type*—race—not obviated, given that race is the unit of commensuration through which its own iconicity and alterity is translated? Thus, if race is discursively arbitrary: why does it pragmatically exist, how is it felt intimately as well as discriminately, and how does it differentially stratify all those produced or occluded by its gaze? These questions remain unsolved and will likely haunt Afro-Chinese, Afro-Asian, and third-worldist encounters in the turbulent decades to come. However, it is my hope that the preceding chapters and interactions provide a starting point for undertaking an honest postcolonial discussion about race and language in the non-western conversations, interactions, and encounters that will necessarily define the twenty-first century. To this end, Audre Lorde left us a profound injunction as a productive point of departure: "Advocating the mere tolerance of difference . . . is the grossest reformism. It is a total denial of the creative function of difference in our lives. Difference must be not merely tolerated, but seen as a fund of necessary polarities between which our creativity can spark like a dialectic. Only then does the necessity for interdependency become unthreatening."[1]

INTRODUCTION

1. "Lunar New Year: Chinese TV gala includes 'racist blackface' sketch," *BBC World*, February 16, 2018. www.bbc.com/news/world-asia-china-43081218.

2. For many, *zhongzuqishi* translates as "racial discrimination," but may also be interpreted as "ethnocentric discrimination."

3. In bringing together Anglocentrism, cosmopolitanism, and whiteness I take a number of contemporary ethnographic texts as inspiration (Pennycook 2007; Blommaert 2014; Mbembe and Nuttall 2008; Rofel 2007; Appadurai 2011; Gilroy 1993; Hage 2000; La Dousa 2014; Nakassis 2016a), however most of these works focus on one or two of the vectors I attempt to connect.

4. Here I am thinking of literatures in postcolonial and critical race theory that have attempted to voice a relationship between discursive forces and social inequality at a "micro-interactional" level (Lorde [1984] 2007; Crenshaw 1991; Butler 1999; Robinson 1983; Mbembe 2001; Fanon 1963, [1952] 2008; Said [1977] 2003; Derrida 1976; Foucault [1966] 2002; hooks 1981; Spivak 1976; Bhabha 1994).

5. Walter Rostow, famous for his *The Stages of Economic Growth: A Non-Communist Manifesto* (1960) in many ways laid down a conceptual apparatus bookended by Melville Herskovits's institutional deployments of Boasian cultural relativism in African (Area) Studies and Wilbur Schramm's expansion of developmentalism in the founding of communication studies as a strategically funded soft power discipline. Schramm's *Mass Media and National Development: The Role of Information in the Developing Countries* (1964) and his founding of the discipline of communication studies were explicitly aligned with the promotion of western democratic developmentalism as a counter to socialist and third-worldist internationalism in the Global South. In fact, Schramm's classic text opens with a criticism of African socialists for committing to anti-technological backwardness in their

rejection of communicative development initiatives promised by NATO countries and the UN in favor of accepting support from China and the Soviet Union in the wake of the decolonization sweeping the African continent after 1945. For his part, Herskovits, though publicly critical of treating newly decolonized African states as Cold War proxies, supplied one of the key arguments for depoliticizing black internationalism in general and black radicalism in the US in particular, by deploying cultural relativism in the service of advocating for originary African subjectivity in black American experience (Gershenhorn 2007)—a move that ultimately delegitimized (then) contemporary struggles for political equality vis-à-vis white Americans who noticeably were not saddled with the same delegitimizing "cultural" baggage as unhyphenated "Americans" (Smith et al. 2009). I would argue that, in retrospectively placing black Americans in Africa—by endowing black Americans with cultural authenticities that are withheld from American whites—Herskovits was ultimately engaging in the apartheid equivalent of creating intellectual Bantustans—distant spaces where one could claim that cultural sovereignty resides, while denying local sovereign rights of mobility to black subjects on the basis of their "authentic" inhabitance of retrospectively reimagined distant spaces. Furthermore, Herskovits and others' deployment of cultural relativism, in an elective affinity with Weber's intellectual recruitment to developmentalism, remains traceable in the institutional templates and funding structures that still maintain area studies disciplines, often in the face of extreme political abuses of this weaponization of "culture."

6. In distinguishing between rational and irrational, I am being critical of rational actor theory as a specter that still haunts the social sciences in general and the undergraduate classroom in particular.

7. See the excellent translations and exploration of He Zhen's genealogy in Lydia Liu, Rebecca Karl, and Dorothy Ko's excellent volume (2013).

8. This is (or should be) as apparent to linguistic anthropologists (M. Silverstein 2003b; Agha 2003) as it is to critical race theorists concerned with intersectionality's conceptual underpinnings (Crenshaw 1991; Lorde [1984] 2007).

9. Patrice Lumumba was a central figure in African decolonial struggle history. He was also president of the Democratic Republic of Congo (DRC). Lumumba was assassinated through a coordinated effort on the part of a number of political opponents, both at home and abroad. The US sanctioned the assassination; Belgium helped organize it (De Witte 2001).

10. I am referring here to the historical theorist and methodologist, Leopold von Ranke (2011).

11. My emphasis.

12. My emphasis.

1. CHRONOTOPES OF THE ANGLOSCENE

1. A version of this chapter appeared in *positions: asia critique* as "Made in Others' Wor(l)ds: Personhood and the Angloscene in Afro-Chinese Beijing," and appears courtesy of their afforded permissions. See Ke-Schutte (forthcoming). All rights reserved. Republished by permission of the copyright holder and the Publisher, Duke University Press. www.dukeupress.edu.

2. One thinks here of the work of Brian Larking (2008), Aihwa Ong (1999), Arjun Appadurai (1996), and Julie Chu (2010) all of whom suggest contrapuntal complexity but where mobility, mediation, and semiotics/language are somewhat segmented.

3. I am thinking here not only of Bourdieu's (1986) "forms of capital," but of the intellectual legacy that has come to use this term as a shorthand.

4. This incorporates a significant cross section of ethnographic work including, but certainly not limited to: H. Wu (1998), James Farrer (2002), Lisa Rofel (2007), Julie Chu (2010), Judith Farquhar and Qicheng Zhang (2012), as well as John Osburg (2013).

5. While these paradoxical tropes are fairly pervasive, a neat distillation emerges in journalist Bill Hayton's popular book *The Invention of China* (2020).

6. In the context of language, this kind of discursive domination is evocatively explored in Maurice Olender's *Languages of Paradise* (2009)—an enormously underrated survey of philological history and early linguistics.

7. To be sure, all repetition is difference, but it would be important to recall that Deleuze ([1968] 1994) also asserted the inverse.

8. David Borenstein, "Rent-a-Foreigner in China," *New York Times*, April 28, 2015, www.nytimes.com/video/opinion/100000003652442/rent-a-foreigner-in-china.html.

9. Tongue, an emphasis, is added to the end of a sentence to express annoyance and is a borrowing from Southern African languages that use "clicks." They are also a widely used interlinguistic phenomenon, even being used by many white English and Afrikaans speakers to express extreme annoyance.

10. See Bourdieu ([1986] 2011), Ngũgĩ (1994), Cohn (1996, 1987), and Errington (2008).

2. THE PURPLE COW PARADOX

1. In language (Spivak [1988] 2010; Butler 1999; Gal 1991), in mobility (Parreñas 2001; Morokvasic 2014; Ehrenreich and Hochschild 2004; Sassen 2003), and in race (Crenshaw 1991; hooks 1981; Lorde [1984] 2007; Puar 2007).

2. See Michel Foucault (2007, 1982) and Kimberlé Crenshaw's (1991) respective arguments that deploy the analytic of micro-interactions at fairly different sociohistorical scales.

3. Particularly as Bakhtin's ideas are expressed in *Dialogic Imagination* (1981) and *Toward a Philosophy of the Act* (1993, with M. Holquist).

4. Current citation around the concept points to a convergence of texts (Agha 2003, 2005; M. Silverstein 1976, 2003b). My use throughout mostly draws on Agha's formulation, but I am indebted to both genealogies in considering enregisterment's place within the broader semiotic frameworks of linguistic anthropology.

5. John and Jean Comaroff's (1993, 2009) pieces capture the dialectical tension that emerges between the seemingly contradictory horizons of cosmopolitan modernity and revolutionary consciousness in postcolonial settings.

6. Here I am referencing Weber's (2002) formulation as a concept, horizon, object, or figure of personhood that is nameable and referable, and yet never fully attainable or perceivable in its totality.

7. WeChat is a Chinese social networking platform that plays a key role in mediating urban and social life in China. Access to western social media platforms, like Twitter and WhatsApp, is made possible by installing a VPN to bypass the Chinese firewall.

8. See Mahajan (2009); Mbembe (2014); Kamanzi (2015); and Naiker (2016).

9. See Erving Goffman's (1981) summary of the concept as well as Asif Agha (2005) and my own (Ke-Schutte 2019) different deployments of "footing."

10. The advantage of this technique, drawing on the use of "pair-part" notation in more conventional sociolinguistic analyses, is that it attempts to represent the overlapping of multiple voices in their temporal sequence. In doing so, I take inspiration from an ethnomusicological transcription technique, called "pulse notation," developed by ethnomusicologist Andrew Tracey (1970). I have also included other auxiliary speech events—marked by square brackets [ ]—that unfold during the interaction. My goal in using this graphic mode of representation is to capture moments during an interaction when actors voice—through vocalization, focus, or gesture—ideological alignment or disalignment with a main speaker, but through this process subordinate themselves.

11. In the Gramscian sense (Gramsci 1975).

3. WHO CAN BE A RACIST? OR, HOW TO DO THINGS WITH PERSONHOOD

1. Lisa Rofel's (2007) evocative work captures this intersectional relationship between gender, class, youth, and constrained mobility extremely well.

2. Here I am thinking in particular of Crenshaw's (1991) and hooks's (1981, 1992) inspiring work.

3. James Griffiths and Shen Lu, "Outrage Erupts over 'Racist Detergent Ad,'" *CNN*, May 28, 2016, www.cnn.com/2016/05/27/asia/chinese-racist-detergent-ad.

4. Francis Scott, "You Thought the Chinese Advert Was Racist . . . Wait until You See the Italian Commercial That Inspired It," *Daily Mail*, May 28, 2016, www.dailymail.co.uk /news/article-3614152/You-thought-Chinese-advert-racist-wait-Italian-advert-inspired-it .html.

5. Euphonik, "ziRight iGals [Official Video] ft. Bekzin Terris, Khaya Dlanga," YouTube, May 3, 2016, www.youtube.com/watch?v=qpylxEJfGqo.

6. Trevor Noah, "'Surfing AIDS'—Trevor Noah—(That's Racist) LONGER RE-RELEASE," YouTube, June 6, 2019, www.youtube.com/watch?v=BMf5—QPyNw.

7. For an expended deployment of dynamic figuration, see Michael Silverstein's (2004) framing of the term.

8. Trevor Noah, "Trevor Noah: Daywalker 2.0—Oprah's School in South Africa," YouTube, March 19, 2012, www.youtube.com/watch?v=YcyuIKzpYJQ.

9. Noah, "Trevor Noah: Daywalker 2.0."

10. This term was initially used to define the mixed-raced descendants of Dutch colonialists, slaves, and Khoisan people in what was called the "Cape region" of South Africa during the Dutch occupation. It later became used under British colonial conditions and within the apartheid state to classify any communities or individuals that could fit into neither white nor black categories as defined within the rubric of the apartheid-colonial matrix (Saul and Bond 2014).

4. HOW PAPER TIGERS KILL

1. Mao Zedong, "On The Question of Whether Imperialism and All Reactionaries Are Real Tigers," *Selected Works of Mao Tse-tung* (Beijing: Foreign Languages Press, 1958). www .marxists.org/reference/archive/mao/selectedworks.

2. Laura Zhou, "Woman in Serious Condition after Tiger Attack Kills Mother in Beijing Wildlife Park," *South China Morning Post*, July 25, 2016, www.scmp.com/news/china/society/article/1994494/woman-serious-condition-after-tiger-attack-kills-mother-beijing.

3. I am thinking in particular of Wang Mingming's brilliant work exploring Occidentalist biases in Sinology.

4. Cited from Michael Sullivan's excellent exploration of racial nationalist dimensions of anti-African protests in late 1980s China.

5. See Zheng Churan's excellent article, "China Has no Problem with Racism, and That's a Problem," *Supchina*, February 23, 2018, https://supchina.com/2018/02/23/china-has-no-problem-with-racism-and-thats-a-problem.

6. My emphasis.

5. UBUNTU/GUANXI AND THE PRAGMATICS OF TRANSLATION

1. A version of this chapter (Ke-Schutte 2022) appeared in the collection *Changing Theory: Concepts from the Global South*, edited by Dilip Menon, and appears courtesy of permissions afforded by Routledge.

2. As with the preceding chapters, the names of the subjects represented have been anonymized. However, given that certain naming practices for socialist families of African subjects constitute an important aspect of the analysis, I chose names in this particular chapter that mirrored this practice of diagramming historical socialist alignments. Fortunately, such alignments are so prominent in Afro-Chinese histories of nonalignment that finding similarly glossing alternatives did not prove difficult.

6. LIBERAL-RACISMS AND INVISIBLE ORDERS

1. From Audre Lorde's classic essay, "The Master's Tools Will Never Dismantle the Master's House," in *Sister Outsider* (Lorde [1984] 2007), 111.

BIBLIOGRAPHY

Abrams, Dennis. 2017. "Kenya's Ngũgĩ wa Thiong'o on the Politics of Translation." *Publishing Perspectives*, April 26, 2017. https://publishingperspectives.com/2017/04/ngugi-wa -thiongo-on-translation.

Abu-Lughod, Lila. 1991. "Writing against Culture." In *Recapturing Anthropology: Working in the Present*, edited by Richard G. Fox, 466–79. Santa Fe, NM: School of American Research Press.

Achebe, Chinua. 1965. "English and the African Writer." *Transition* 18:27–30.

Adamson, Bob. 2004. *China's English: A History of English in Chinese Education*. Hong Kong: Hong Kong University Press.

Agamben, Giorgio. 1998. *Homo Sacer: Sovereign Power and Bare Life*. Stanford: Stanford University Press.

Agha, Asif. 2003. "The Social Life of Cultural Value." *Language and Communication* 23:231–73.

———. 2005. "Voice, Footing, Enregisterment." *Journal for Linguistic Anthropology* 15 (1): 38–59.

———. 2007a. "Recombinant Selves in Mass-Mediated Space-time." *Language and Communication* 27:320–35.

———. 2007b. *Language and Social Relations: Studies in the Social and Cultural Foundations of Language*. Cambridge: Cambridge University Press.

Alden, Chris. 2007. *China in Africa*. Zed Books: London.

Alim, H. Samy, John R. Rickford, and Arnetha F. Ball, eds. 2016. *Raciolinguistics: How Language Shapes Our Ideas about Race*. New York: Oxford University Press.

Allen, Jafari S., and Ryan C. Jobson. 2016. "The Decolonizing Generation: (Race and) Theory in Anthropology since the Eighties." *Current Anthropology* 57 (2): 129–48.

Althusser, Louis. 1971. *Lenin and Philosophy and Other Essays*. London: New Left Books.

Anderson, Benedict. 1983. *Imagined Communities: Reflections on the Origin and Spread of Nationalism*. London: Verso.

Appadurai, Arjun. 1996. *Modernity at Large: Cultural Dimensions of Globalization.* Minneapolis: University of Minnesota Press.

———. 2011. "Cosmopolitanism from Below: Some Ethical Lessons from the Slums of Mumbai." In *The Johannesburg Salon: Volume 4*, edited by Lara Allen and Achille Mbembe, 32–43. Johannesburg: Johannesburg Workshop in Theory and Criticism.

———. 2016. *Banking on Words: The Failure of Language in the Age of Derivative Finance.* Chicago: University of Chicago Press.

Appiah, Kwame Anthony. 1989. "The Conservation of 'Race.'" *Black American Literature Forum* 23 (1): 37–60.

———. 1992. *In My Father's House: Africa in the Philosophy of Culture.* Oxford: Oxford University Press.

Arnaut, Karel, Jan Blommaert, Ben Rampton, and Massimiliano Spotti, eds. 2016. *Language and Superdiversity.* New York: Routledge.

Arrighi, Giovanni. 1994. *The Long Twentieth Century: Money, Power, and the Origins of Our Times.* London: Verso.

Asad, Talal. 1986. "The Concept of Cultural Translation in British Social Anthropology." In *Writing Culture: Poetics and Politics of Ethnography*, edited by James Clifford and George E. Marcus. Berkeley: University of California Press.

Ashforth, Adam. 2000. *Madumo, A Man Bewitched.* Chicago: University of Chicago Press.

———. 2005. *Witchcraft, Violence, and Democracy in South Africa.* Chicago: University of Chicago Press.

Augé, Marc. 1995. *Non-Places: Introduction to an Anthropology of Supermodernity.* Translated by John Howe. London: Verso.

Austin, John L. 1975. *How to Do Things with Words.* Cambridge, MA: Harvard University Press.

Bakhtin, Mikhail M. 1981. *The Dialogic Imagination: Four Essays.* Austin: University of Texas Press.

———. 1984. *Problems of Dostoevsky's Poetics.* Edited and translated by C. Emerson. Minneapolis: University of Minneapolis Press.

———. 2004. *Speech Genres and Other Late Essays.* Austin: University of Texas Press.

Bakhtin, Mikhail M., and Michael Holquist. 1993. *Toward a Philosophy of the Act.* Austin: University of Texas Press.

Baldwin, James. 1963. *The Fire Next Time.* New York: Dial Press.

Baldwin, Kate A. 2002. *Beyond the Color Line and the Iron Curtain: Reading Encounters Between Black and Red, 1922–1963.* Durham: Duke University Press.

Ballantine, Christopher. 2000. "Gender, Migrancy, and South African Popular Music in the Late 1940s and 1950s." *Ethnomusicology* 44 (3): 376–407.

Balso, Judith. 2019. "Paper Tiger." In *Afterlives of Chinese Communism: Political Concepts from Mao to Xi*, edited by Christian Sorace, Ivan Franceschini, and Nicholas Loubere, 161–67. Acton, Australia: ANU Press and Verso.

Bassnett, Susan, and Harish Trivedi. 1999. *Postcolonial Translation: Theory and Practice.* London: Routledge.

Bell, Duran. 2000. "Guanxi: A Nesting of Groups." *Current Anthropology* 41 (1): 132–38.

Benjamin, Walter. 2007a. "The Task of the Translator." In *Illuminations*, edited by Hannah Arendt, translated by Harry Zohn, 69–82. New York: Random House.

———. 2007b. "Theses on the Philosophy of History." In *Illuminations*, edited by Hannah Arendt, translated by Harry Zohn, 253–64. New York: Random House.

———. 2007c. "The Work of Art in the Age of Mechanical Reproduction." In *Illuminations*, edited by Hannah Arendt, translated by Harry Zohn, 217–52. New York: Random House.

Berlant, Lauren. 2011. *Cruel Optimism*. Durham: Duke University Press.

Bhabha, Homi. 1994. *The Location of Culture*. New York: Routledge.

———. 1995. "Freedom's Basis in the Indeterminate." In *The Identity in Question*, edited by John Rajchman, 47–62. New York: Routledge.

Bian, Yanjie. 1994. "Guanxi and the Allocation of Urban Jobs in China." *China Quarterly* 140:971–99.

Biko, Steve. 1978. *I Write What I Like: A Selection of His Writings*. London: Heinemann Publishers.

———. 2002. *I Write What I Like: Selected Writings*. Reprint, University of Chicago Press.

Blommaert, Jan. 2010. *The Sociolinguistics of Globalization*. Cambridge: Cambridge University Press.

———. 2014. "Sociolinguistics and English Language Studies." In *The Routledge Companion to English Studies*, edited by B. Street and C. Leung, 131–45. London: Routledge.

Bodomo, Adams. 2012. *Africans in China: A Socio-Cultural Study and its Implications on China-African Relations*. New York: Cambria Press.

———. 2020. "Historical and Contemporary Perspectives on Inequalities and Well-Being of Africans in China." *Asian Ethnicity* 21 (4): 526–41.

Bourdieu, Pierre. 1977. *Outline of a Theory of Practice*. Translated by Richard Nice. London: Cambridge University Press.

———. [1986] 2011. "The Forms of Capital." In *Cultural Theory: An Anthology*, edited by Imre Szeman and Timothy Kaposy, 81–93. West Sussex: Wiley-Blackwell.

Braudel, Fernand. 1972. *The Mediterranean and the Mediterranean World in the Age of Philip II: Volume I*. Translated by Siân Reynolds. New York: Harper and Row.

Brautigam, Deborah. 2009. *The Dragon's Gift: The Real Story of China in Africa*. Oxford: Oxford University Press.

Brown, Wendy. 2005. *Edgework: Critical Essays on Knowledge and Politics*. Princeton: Princeton University Press.

Browne, Simone. 2015. *Dark Matters: On the Surveillance of Blackness*. Durham: Duke University Press

Bucholtz, Mary. 2010. *White Kids: Language, Race, and Styles of Youth Identity*. London: Cambridge University Press.

———. 2016. "On Being Called Out of One's Name." In *Raciolinguistics: How Language Shapes Our Ideas about Race*, edited by Samy H. Alim, John R. Rickford, and Arnetha F. Ball. New York: Oxford University Press.

Buck-Morss, Susan. 1992. "Aesthetics and Anaesthetics: Walter Benjamin's Artwork Essay Reconsidered." *October* 62 (Autumn): 3–41.

Burke, Timothy. 1996. *Lifebuoy Men, Lux Women: Commodification, Consumption and Cleanliness in Modern Zimbabwe*. Durham: Duke University Press.

Butler, Judith. 1993. *Bodies That Matter: On the Discursive Limits of Sex*. New York: Routledge.

———. 1995. "Subjection Resistance, Resignification: Between Freud and Foucault." In *The Identity in Question*, edited by J. Rajchman. New York: Routledge.

———. 1997. *Excitable Speech: A Politics of the Performative*. New York: Routledge.

———. 1999. *Gender Trouble: Feminism and the Subversion of Identity*. London: Routledge.

———. 2008. "Sexual Politics, Torture, and Secular Time." *British Journal of Sociology* 59 (1): 1–23.

Callon, Michel. 1986. "Some Elements of a Sociology of Translation: Domestication of the Scallops and the Fishermen of St Brieuc Bay." In *Power, Action and Belief: A New Sociology of Knowledge*, edited by John Law, 196–233. London: Routledge and Kegan Paul.

Carillo Garcia, Beatriz. 2004. "Rural-Urban Migration in China: Temporary Migrants in Search of Permanent Settlement." *PORTAL Journal of Multidisciplinary International Studies* 1 (2): 1–26. https://epress.lib.uts.edu.au/journals/index.php/portal/issue/view/4.

Carr, E. Summerson. 2011. *Scripting Addiction: The Politics of Therapeutic Talk and American Sobriety*. Princeton: Princeton University Press.

Carr, E. Summerson, and Michael Lempert, eds. 2016. *Scale: Discourse and Dimensions of Social Life*. Berkeley: University of California Press.

Chakrabarty, Dipesh. 2000. *Provincializing Europe: Postcolonial Thought and Historical Difference*. New Jersey: Princeton University Press.

———. 2005. "Legacies of Bandung: Decolonization and the Politics of Culture." *Economic and Political Weekly* 40 (46). www.epw.in/journal/2005/46/perspectives/legacies-band ung.html.

Chan, Stephen, et al. 2013. *The Morality of China in Africa*. New York: Zed Books.

Chigumadzi, Panashe. 2015. "Why I Call Myself a 'Coconut' to Claim My Place in Post-Apartheid South Africa." *Guardian*, August 24, 2015. www.theguardian.com/world/2015 /aug/24/south-africa-race-panashe-chigumadzi-ruth-first-lecture.

Chimakonam, J. O. 2016. "The End of Ubuntu or Its Beginning in Matolino-Kwindingwi-Metz Debate: An Exercise in Conversational Philosophy." *South African Journal of Philosophy* 35 (2): 224–34.

Chu, Julie. 2010. *Cosmologies of Credit: Transnational Mobility and the Politics of Destination in China*. Durham: Duke University Press.

Chumley, Lily. 2016. *Creativity Class: Art School and Culture Work in Postsocialist China*. Princeton: Princeton University Press.

Clifford, James, and George E. Marcus, eds. 1986. *Writing Culture: Poetics and Politics of Ethnography*. Berkeley: University of California Press.

Cohn, Bernard. 1987. *An Anthropologist among the Historians and Other Essays*. Delhi: Oxford University Press.

———. 1996. *Colonialism and Its Forms of Knowledge: The British in India*. Princeton: Princeton University Press.

Cole, Jennifer. 2010. *Sex and Salvation: Imagining the Future in Madagascar*. Chicago: University of Chicago Press.

Comaroff, Jean, and John L. Comaroff. 1991. *Of Revelation and Revolution: Christianity, Colonialism and Consciousness, Vol. 1*. Chicago: University of Chicago Press.

———. 1993. *Modernity and Its Malcontents: Ritual and Power in Postcolonial Africa*. Chicago: University of Chicago Press.

———. 1999. *On Personhood: An Anthropological Perspective from Africa*. American Bar Foundation.

———. 2009. *Ethnicity, Inc.* Chicago: University of Chicago Press.

———. 2012. *Theory from the South or, How Euro-America is Evolving Towards Africa*. London: Paradigm Publishers.

Crenshaw, Kimberlé. 1989. "Demarginalizing the Intersection of Race and Sex: A Black Feminist Critique of Antidiscrimination Doctrine, Feminist Theory, and Antiracist Politics." *University of Chicago Legal Forum* 1 (8): 139–67.

———. 1991. "Mapping the Margins: Intersectionality, Identity Politics, and Violence against Women of Color." *Stanford Law Review* 43 (6): 1241–99.

Crovitz, L. Gordon. 2014. "Chicago Teaches Beijing a Lesson." *Wall Street Journal*, September 28, 2014. www.wsj.com/articles/l-gordon-crovitz-chicago-teaches-beijing-a -lesson-1411944905.

De Witte, Ludo. 2001. *The Assassination of Lumumba*. London: Verso.

Deleuze, Gilles. [1968] 1994. *Difference and Repetition*. Translated by Paul Patton. New York: Columbia University Press.

Derrida, Jacques. 1976. *Of Grammatology*. Translated by Gayatri Spivak. Baltimore: Johns Hopkins University Press.

———. 1988. "Signature Event Context." In *Limited Inc.*, translated by Samuel Weber and Jeffrey Mehlman, 1–24. Evanston, IL: Northwestern University Press.

Dixon, Kerryn. 2011. *Literacy, Power, and the Schooled Body*. London: Routledge.

Dreyer, Edward L. 2007. *Zheng He: China and the Oceans of the Early Ming Dynasty (1405–1433)*. New York: Pearson Longman.

Du Bois, W. E. B. [1898] 2000. "The Study of the Negro Problems." *Annals of the American Academy of Political and Social Science* 568:1–23.

———. 1903. *The Souls of Black Folk*. Chicago: A. C. McClurg.

Durkheim, Emile. [1893] 2013. *The Division of Labour in Society*. London: Palgrave Macmillan.

———. [1897] 1979. *Suicide: A Study in Sociology*. Translated by John A. Spaulding and George Simpson, edited by George Simpson. New York: Free Press.

———. [1912] 1995. *The Elementary Forms of Religious Life*. Translated by Karen E. Fields. New York: Free Press.

Ehrenreich, Barbara, and Arlie R. Hochschild. 2004. *Global Woman: Nannies, Maids, and Sex Workers in the New Economy*. New York: Henry Holt.

Epstein, Debby, and Deborah, L. Steinberg. 1995. "Hetero-Sensibilities on the Oprah Winfrey Show." In *(Hetero)sexual Politics*, edited by Mary Maynard and June Purvis, 95–107. London: Taylor and Francis.

Erkens, Rainer, and John S. Kane-Berman. 2000. *Political Correctness in South Africa*. Johannesburg: South African Institute of Race Relations.

Errington, Joseph. 2008. *Linguistics in a Colonial World: A Story of Language, Meaning and Power*. Oxford: Blackwell Publishing.

Evans, Martha. 2016. "The Last Heroic TV Star? Nelson Mandela's Funeral Broadcast, Social Media, and the Future of Media Events." In *Global Perspectives on Media Events in Contemporary Society*, edited by Andrew Fox, 141–57. Hershey, PA: IGI Global.

Fanon, Frantz. [1952] 2008. *Black Skin, White Masks*. New York: Grove.

———. 1963. *The Wretched of the Earth*. New York: Grove.

———. 1964. "Lumumba's Death: Could We Do Otherwise?" In *Toward the African Revolution: Political Essays*, edited by Françoise Maspero, translated by Haakon Chevalier. New York: Grove.

Farquhar, Judith. 2002. *Appetites: Food and Sex in Post-Socialist China*. Durham: Duke University Press.

Farquhar, Judith, and Qicheng Zhang. 2012. *Ten Thousand Things: Nurturing Life in Contemporary Beijing*. New York. Zone Books.

Farred, Grant. 2009. "Not the Moment After, but the Moment Of." *South Atlantic Quarterly* 108 (3): 581–98.

Farrer, James. 2002. *Opening Up: Youth Sex Culture and Market Reform in Shanghai*. Chicago: University of Chicago Press.

Fei, Xiaotong. [1947] 1992. *From the Soil: The Foundations of Chinese Society*. Berkeley: University of California Press.

Ferdjani, Hannane. 2012. *African Students in China: An Exploration of Increasing Numbers and Their Motivations in Beijing*. Stellenbosch: University of Stellenbosch Center for Chinese Studies. http://hdl.handle.net/10019.1/70764.

Ferguson, James. 1999. *Expectations of Modernity: Myths and Meanings of Urban Life on the Zambian Copperbelt*. Berkeley: University of California Press.

Fields, Karen E., and Barbara J. Fields. 2012. *Racecraft: The Soul of Inequality in American Life*. New York: Verso.

Flores, Lisa. 2018. "Towards an Insistent and Transformative Racial Rhetorical Criticism." *Communication and Critical/Cultural Studies* 15 (4): 349–57.

Foucault, Michel. [1966] 2002. *The Order of Things*. London: Routledge Classics.

———. 1982. "The Subject and Power." *Critical Inquiry* 8 (4): 777–95.

———. 1995. *Discipline and Punish: The Birth of the Prison*. New York: Vintage Books.

———. 2007. *Security, Territory, Population*. Translated by Graham Burchell. New York: Palgrave Macmillan.

Frankenberg, Ruth. 2001. "The Mirage of an Unmarked Whiteness." In *The Making and Unmaking of Whiteness*, edited by Birgit B. Rasmussen, Eric Klinenberg, Irene J. Nexica, and Matt Wray, 72–96. Durham: Duke University Press.

Frazier, R. Taj. 2014. *The East is Black: Cold War China in the Black Radical Imagination*. Durham: Duke University Press.

Frekko, Susan E. 2009. "'Normal' in Catalonia: Standard Language, Enregisterment, and the Imagination of a National Public." *Language in Society* 38 (1): 71–93.

French, Howard W. 2014. *China's Second Continent: How a Million Migrants Are Building a New Empire in Africa*. New York: Random House.

Freud, Sigmund. [1920] 2015. *Beyond the Pleasure Principle*. New York: Dover Publications.

Gaetano, Arianne M. 2004. "Filial Daughters, Modern Women: Migrant Domestic Workers in Post-Mao Beijing." In *On the Move: Women and Rural-to-Urban Migration in Contemporary China*, edited by Arianne M. Gaetano and Tamara Jacka, 41–79. New York: Columbia University Press.

Gal, Susan. 1991. "Between Speech and Silence: The Problematics of Research on Language and Gender." In *Gender at the Crossroads of Knowledge: Feminist Anthropology in the Postmodern Era*, edited by Micaela di Leonardo, 175–203. Berkeley: University of California Press.

———. 2015. "Politics of Translation." *Annual Review of Anthropology* 44:225–40.

Galloway, Alexander R., and Eugene Thacker. 2007. *The Exploit: A Theory of Networks*. Minneapolis: University of Minnesota Press.

Geertz, Clifford. 1973. *The Interpretation of Cultures: Selected Essays*. New York: Basic Books.

———. 1977. "Found in Translation: On the Social History of the Modern Imagination." *Georgia Review* 13 (4): 788–810.

Gershenhorn, Jerry. 2007. *Melville J. Herskovits and the Racial Politics of Knowledge*. Lincoln: University of Nebraska Press.

Gershon, Ilana. 2017. *Down and Out in the New Economy: How People Find (Or Don't Find) Work Today*. Chicago: University of Chicago Press.

Gilley, Bruce. 2017. "The Case for Colonialism." *Third World Quarterly*. DOI: 10.1080/01436597.2017.1369037.

Gilroy, Paul. 1992. *There Ain't No Black in the Union Jack*. London: Routledge.

———. 1993. *The Black Atlantic: Modernity and Double-Consciousness*. Penguin.

Godin, Seth. 2009. *Purple Cow: Transform Your Business by Being Remarkable*. New York: Portfolio.

Goebel, Rolf J. 1995. "China as Embalmed Mummy: Herder's Orientalist Poetics." *South Atlantic Review* 60 (1): 111–29.

Goffman, Erving. 1959. *The Presentation of Self in Everyday Life*. New York: Doubleday Press.

———. 1979. "Footing." *Semiotica* 25 (1–2): 1–30.

———. 1981. *Forms of Talk*. Philadelphia: University of Pennsylvania Press.

———. 1983. "The Interaction Order: American Sociological Association, 1982 Presidential Address." *American Sociological Review* 48 (1): 1–17.

Gramsci, Antonio. 1975. *Prison Notebooks, Vol. 2*. New York: Columbia University Press.

Gray, Chris H., Steven Mentor, Heidi J. Figueroa-Sarriera. 1995. *The Cyborg Handbook*. London: Routledge.

Gupta, P. 2014. "#CancelColbert Activist Suey Park: 'This is Not Reform, It's Revolution.'" *Salon*. www.salon.com/2014/04/03/cancelcolbert_activist_suey_park_this_is_not_reform _this_is_revolution.

Hage, Ghassan. 2000. *White Nation: Fantasies of White Supremacy in a Multicultural Society*. London: Routledge.

———. 2009. "Waiting out the Crisis: On Stuckedness and Governmentality." In *Waiting*, edited by Ghassan Hage, 97–106. Carlton: Melbourne University Press.

Hanks, William F. 2010. *Converting Words: Maya in the Age of the Cross*. Berkeley: University of California Press.

Haraway, Donna J. [1984] 1991. *Simians, Cyborgs and Women: The Reinvention of Nature*. New York: Routledge.

———. 2016. *Staying with the Trouble: Making Kin in the Chthulucene*. Durham: Duke University Press.

Hayton, Bill. 2020. *The Invention of China*. New Haven: Yale University Press.

Helmreich, Stefan. 2007. "An Anthropologist Underwater: Immersive Soundscapes, Submarine Cyborgs and Transductive Ethnography." *American Ethnologist* 34 (4): 621–41.

Hevi, Emmanuel J. 1963. *An African Student in China*. New York: Praeger.

Hill, Jane H. 2009. "Language, Race, and White Public Space." In *Linguistic Anthropology: A Reader*, edited by Alessandro Duranti, 479–92. Oxford: Wiley-Blackwell.

Hobsbawm, Eric. 1962. *The Age of Revolution: Europe: 1789-1848*. New York: World Publishing.

———. 1975. *The Age of Capital: 1848-1875*. New York: Vintage Books.

———. 1987. *The Age of Empire: 1875-1914*. London: Weidenfeld and Nicolson.

hooks, bell. 1981. *Ain't I a Woman: Black Women and Feminism*. Boston: South End Press.

———. 1992. *Black Looks: Race and Representation*. Boston: South End Press.

———. 2013. "Dig Deep: Beyond Lean In." *Feminist Wire*, October 28, 2013. www.thefemi
nistwire.com/2013/10/17973.

Hubbert, Jennifer. 2019. *China in the World: An Anthropology of Confucius Institutes, Soft Power, and Globalization*. Honolulu: University of Hawai'i Press.

Hughes, Dana. "Cops Probe Body of Dead Newborn Found at Oprah Winfrey's School." *ABC News*, February 18, 2011. http://abcnews.go.com/International/troubles-oprah
-winfreys-school-south-africa/story?id=12950275.

Hunter, Mark. 2010. *Love in the Time of AIDS: Inequality, Gender, and Rights in South Africa*. Bloomington: Indiana University Press.

Inoue, Miyako. 2006. *Vicarious Language: Gender and Linguistic Modernity in Japan*. Berkeley: University of California Press.

Irvine, Judith T., and Susan Gal. 2000. "Language Ideology and Linguistic Differentiation." In *Linguistic Anthropology: A Reader*, edited by Alessandro Duranti, 402–34. Malden: Blackwell.

Jacka, Tamara. 2015. *Rural Women in Urban China: Gender, Migration, and Social Change*. London: Routledge.

Jackson, John L. 2005. *Real Black: Adventures in Racial Sincerity*. Chicago: University of Chicago Press.

———. 2010. *Racial Paranoia: The Unintended Consequences of Political Correctness*. New York: Civitas Books.

Jacquemet, Marco. 2005. "Transidiomatic Practices: Language and Power in the Age of Globalization." *Language and Communication* 25 (3): 257–77.

Jobson, Ryan. 2020. "The Case for Letting Anthropology Burn: Sociocultural Anthropology in 2019." *American Anthropologist* 122 (2): 259–71.

Kamanzi, Brian. 2015. "'Rhodes Must Fall'—Decolonisation Symbolism—What Is Happening at UCT, South Africa?" *Postcolonialist*, March 29, 2015. http://postcolonialist.com
/civil-discourse/rhodes-must-fall-decolonisation-symbolism-happening-uct-south
-africa.

Keane, Webb. 1997. *Signs of Recognition: Powers and Hazards of Representation in an Indonesian Society*. Berkeley: University of California Press.

———. 2007. *Christian Moderns: Freedom and Fetish in the Mission Encounter*. Berkeley: University of California Press.

Kerr, Myhana M. 2018. "Black in Beijing: How Transient Black Foreigners Create Community in China." Anthropology Honors Projects. https://digitalcommons.macalester
.edu/anth_honors/32.

[Ke-]Schutte, Jan H. 2018. "Third-World Cosmopolitanism in White Spacetime: Intersectionality and Mobility in Sino-African Encounters." PhD diss., University of Chicago.

Ke-Schutte, Jay. 2019. "Aspirational Histories of Third World Cosmopolitanism: Dialectical Interactions in Afro-Chinese Beijing." *Signs and Society* 7 (3). https://doi.org/10.1086/704011.

———. 2022. "Ubuntu/Guanxi." In *Changing Theory: Concepts from the Global South*, edited by Dilip Menon, 33–50. London: Routledge.

———. 2023. "Made in Others' Wor(l)ds: Personhood and the Angloscene in Afro-Chinese Beijing." *positions: asia critique*.

King, Ambrose Yeo-chi. 1991. "Kuan-hsi and Network Building: A Sociological Interpretation." *Daedalus* 120 (2): 63–84.

King, Kenneth. 2013. *China's Aid and Soft Power in Africa: The Case of Education and Training*. Woodbridge: James Currey.

Kipnis, Andrew. 1997. *Producing Guanxi: Sentiment, Self and Subculture in a North China Village*. Durham: Duke University Press.

Kiyosaki, Robert T., and Sharon Lechter. 1997. *Rich Dad, Poor Dad: What the Rich Teach Their Kids about Money—That the Poor and Middle Class Do Not!* New York: Warner Books.

Kockelman, Paul. 2016. "Grading, Gradients, Degradation, Grace Part 1: Intensity and Causality." *Hau: Journal of Ethnographic Theory* 6 (2): 389–423.

La Dousa, Chaise. 2014. *Hindi Is Our Ground, English Is Our Sky: Education, Language, and Social Class in Contemporary India*. New York: Berghan Books.

Latour, Bruno. 1983. "Give Me a Laboratory and I Will Raise the World." In *Science Observed: Perspectives on the Social Study of Science*, edited by Karin Knorr-Cetina and Michael Mulkay, 141–69. London: Sage.

———. 1996. "On Actor-Network Theory: A Few Clarifications." *Soziale Welt* 47:369–81.

———. 2005. *Reassembling the Social: An Introduction to Actor-Network Theory*. Oxford: Oxford University Press.

Lee, Benjamin. 2018. "Deriving the Derivative." *Signs and Society* 6 (1): 225–55.

Lempert, Michael. 2016. "Interaction Rescaled: How Buddhist Debate Became a Diasporic Pedagogy." In *Scale: Discourse and Dimensions of Social Life*, edited by E. Summerson Carr and Michael Lempert, 52–69. Berkeley: University of California Press.

Leonard, David J., and Lisa A. Guerrero, eds. 2013. *African Americans on Television: Raceing for Ratings*. Denver: Praeger.

Li, Anshan, Haifang Liu, Huaqiong Pan, Aiping Zeng, and Wenping He. 2012. *FOCAC Twelve Years Later: Achievements, Challenges and the Way Forward (Discussion Paper 74)*. Beijing: Peking University School of International Studies in cooperation with Nordiska Afrikainstitutet.

Li, Darryl. 2019. *The Universal Enemy: Jihad, Empire, and the Challenge of Solidarity*. Stanford: Stanford University Press.

———. 2021. "Aid as Pan-Islamic solidarity in Bosnia-Herzegovina: Toward an Anthropology of Universalism." *American Ethnologist* 48 (3): 231–44.

Liu, Lydia H. 2004. *Clash of Empires: The Invention of China in Modern World Making*. Cambridge, MA: Harvard University Press.

Liu, Lydia, Rebecca Karl, and Dorothy Ko, eds. 2013. *The Birth of Chinese Feminism: Essential Texts in Translational Theory*. New York: Columbia University Press.

Liu, Petrus. 2015. *Queer Marxism in Two Chinas*. Durham: Duke University Press.

Longmore, Laura. 1966. *The Dispossessed: A Study of the Sex-Life of Bantu Women in and around Johannesburg*. London: Corgi Books.

Lorde, Audre. [1984] 2007. *Sister Outsider: Essays and Speeches by Audre Lorde*. Berkeley: Crossing Press.

Lukács, Georg. 2010. *Soul and Form*. New York: Columbia University Press.

Mackenzie, Adrian. 2002. *Transductions: Bodies and Machines at Speed* London; New York: Continuum.

———. 2010. *Wirelessness: Radical Empiricism in Network Cultures*. Cambridge, MA: MIT Press.

Mahajan, Vijay. 2009. *Africa Rising: How 900 Million African Consumers Offer More Than You Think*. Upper Saddle River, NJ: Pearson Education.

Makgoba, Malegapuru, ed. 1999. *African Renaissance: The New Struggle*. Cape Town: Tafelberg and Mafube.

Manning, H. Paul. 2001. "On Social Deixis." *Anthropological Linguistics* 43, (1): 54–100.

Massumi, Brian. 2015. *Politics of Affect*. Cambridge: Polity Press.

Marx, Karl. [1884] 2007. *Economic and Philosophic Manuscripts of 1844*. Translated by M. Milligan. New York: Dover Publications.

———. 1972. *Capital: A Critique of Political Economy, Vol. 1*. New York: Vintage Press.

Matolino, Bernard, and Wenceslaus Kwindingwi. 2013. "The End of Ubuntu." *South African Journal of Philosophy* 32 (2): 197–205.

Mauss, Marcel. 1967. *The Gift: Forms and Functions of Exchange in Archaic Societies*. New York: W. W. Norton.

———. 1985. "A Category of the Human Mind: The Notion of the Person; The Notion of the Self." In *The Category of the Person: Anthropology, Philosophy, History*, edited by Michael Carrithers, Steven Collins, and Steven Lukes, 1–25. Cambridge: Cambridge University Press.

Mazzarella, William. 2004. "Culture, Globalization, Mediation." *Annual Review of Anthropology* 33:345–67.

———. 2017. *The Mana of Mass Society*. Chicago: University of Chicago Press.

Mbembe, Achille. 2001. *On the Postcolony*. Berkeley: University of California Press.

———. 2003 "Necropolitics." *Public Culture* 15 (1): 11–40.

———. 2008. "Aesthetics of Superfluity." In *Johannesburg: The Elusive Metropolis*, edited by Achille Mbembe and Sarah Nuttall, 37–67. Durham: Duke University Press.

———. 2014. "Decolonizing Knowledge and the Archive." *Platform for Experimental Collaborative Ethnography*, August 14, 2018. https://worldpece.org/content/mbembe-achille-2015-%E2%80%9Cdecolonizing-knowledge-and-question-archive%E2%80%9D-africa-country.

Mbembe, Achille, and Sarah Nuttall. 2008. "Introduction: Afropolis." In *Johannesburg: The Elusive Metropolis*, edited by Achille Mbembe and Sarah Nuttall, 1–36. Durham: Duke University Press.

McKaiser, Eusebius. 2013. "The Unbearable Whiteness of Being." *IOL*, June 10, 2013. www.iol.co.za/the-star/the-unbearable-whiteness-of-being-1529686.

Mendoza-Denton, Norma. 2008. *Homegirls: Language and Cultural Practice Among Latina Youth Gangs*. Oxford: Blackwell.

Metz, Thaddeus. 2014. "Just the Beginning for Ubuntu: Reply to Matolino and Kwindingwi." *South African Journal of Philosophy* 33 (1): 65–72.

Mills, C. Wright, and Hans Gerth. 1953. *Character and Social Structure: The Psychology of Social Institutions*. New York: Harcourt, Brace.

Mills, Charles W. 1997. *The Racial Contract*. Ithaca: Cornell University Press.

———. 1998. *Blackness Visible: Essays on Philosophy and Race*. Ithaca: Cornell University Press.

———. 2017. *Black Rights/White Wrongs: The Critique of Racial Liberalism*. London: Oxford University Press.

Munn, Nancy. 1986. *Fame of Gawa: A Symbolic Study of Value Transformation in a Massim (Papua New Guinea) Society*. Cambridge: Cambridge University Press.

Mwipikeni, Peter. 2018. "Ubuntu and the Modern Society." *South African Journal of Philosophy* 37 (3): 322–34.

Naiker, Camalita. 2016. "From Marikana to #FeesMustFall: The Praxis of Popular Politics in South Africa." *Urbanisation* 1 (1): 53–61.

Nakassis, Constantine. 2012. "Brand, Citationality, Performativity." *American Anthropologist* 114 (4): 624–38.

———. 2016a. *Doing Style: Youth and Mass-Mediation in South India.* Chicago: Chicago University Press.

———. 2016b. "Linguistic Anthropology in 2015: Not the Study of Language." *American Anthropologist* 118 (2): 1–16.

———. 2018. "Indexicality's Ambivalent Ground." *Signs in Society* 6 (1): 281–304.

Ngũgĩ wa Thiong'o. 1994. *Decolonizing the Mind: The Politics of Language in African Literature.* Portsmouth, NH: Heinemann.

Niranjana, Tejaswini. 1992. *Siting Translation: History, Poststructuralism, and the Postcolonial Context.* Berkeley: University of California Press.

Ogude, James. 2019. *Ubuntu and the Reconstitution of Community.* Bloomington: Indiana University Press.

Okihiro, Gary Y. 2016. *Third World Studies: Theorizing Liberation.* Durham: Duke University Press.

Olender, Maurice. 2009. *Languages of Paradise: Race, Religion, and Philology in the Nineteenth Century.* Translation by Arthur Goldhammer. Cambridge, MA: Harvard University Press.

Onslow, Sue, ed. 2009. *Cold War in Southern Africa: White Power, Black Liberation.* London: Routledge.

Opondo, Sam O. 2015. "Biocolonial and Racial Entanglements: Immunity, Community, and Superfluity in the Name of Humanity." *Alternatives: Global, Local, Political* 40 (2): 115–32.

Osburg, John. 2013. *Anxious Wealth: Money and Morality among China's New Rich.* Stanford: Stanford University Press.

Paglia, Camille. 1990. *Sexual Personae.* New Haven: Yale University Press.

Pan, Lin. 2015. *English as Global Language in China: Deconstructing the Ideological Discourses of English in Language Education.* Heidelberg: Springer International Publishing.

Parreñas, Rhacel S. 2001. *Servants of Globalization: Women, Migration and Domestic Work.* Stanford: Stanford University Press.

Peirce, Charles S. 1955. *The Philosophical Writings of Peirce.* New York: Dover.

Pennycook, Alastair. 2007. *Global Englishes and Transcultural Flows.* Routledge: London.

Pines, Jim. 1992. *Black and White in Colour: Black People in British Television Since 1936.* London: British Film Institute.

Piot, Charles. 2010. *Nostalgia for the Future: West Africa after the Cold War.* Chicago: University of Chicago Press.

Povinelli, Elizabeth. 2001. "Radical Worlds: The Anthropology of Incommensurability and Inconceivability." *Annual Review of Anthropology* 30:319–34.

Puar, Jasbir K. 2007. *Terrorist Assemblages: Homonationalism in Queer Times.* Durham: Duke University Press.

Ranke, Leopold von. 2011. *The Theory and Practice of History.* Edited by Georg G. Iggers. London Routledge.

Robinson, Cedric J. 1983. *Black Marxism: The Making of the Black Radical Tradition.* Chapel Hill: University of North Carolina Press.

Rofel, Lisa. 2007. *Desiring China: Experiments in Neoliberalism, Sexuality, and Public Culture*. Durham: Duke University Press.

———. 2012. "Between Tianxia and Postsocialism: Contemporary Chinese Cosmopolitanism." In *Routledge International Handbook of Cosmopolitanism Studies*, edited by Gerard Delanty, 443–51. London: Routledge.

Rosa, Jonathan. 2016a. "Standardization, Racialization, Languagelessness: Raciolinguistic Ideologies across Communicative Contexts." *Journal of Linguistic Anthropology* 26 (2): 162–83.

———. 2016b. "Racializing Language, Regimenting Latinas/os: Chronotope, Social Tense, and American Raciolinguistic Futures." *Language and Communication* 46 (3): 106–17.

———. 2016c. "From Mock Spanish to Inverted Spanglish: Language Ideologies and the Racialization of U.S. Latinas/os." In *Raciolinguistics: How Language Shapes Our Ideas about Race*, edited by Samy Alim, John Rickford, and Arnetha Ball, 65–80. Oxford: Oxford University Press.

Rostow, Walt Whitman. 1960. *The Stages of Economic Growth: A Non-Communist Manifesto*. Cambridge: Cambridge University Press.

Sahlins, Marshall. 2013. "China U: Confucius Institutes Censor Political Discussions and Restrain the Free Exchange of Ideas. Why, Then, Do American Universities Sponsor Them?" *The Nation*, October 30, 2013. www.thenation.com/article/archive/china-u.

———. 2015. *Confucius Institutes: Academic Malware*. Chicago: University of Chicago Press.

Said, Edward. [1977] 2003. *Orientalism*. London: Penguin.

Sakai, Naoki. 1997. *Translation and Subjectivity: On "Japan" and Cultural Nationalism*. Minneapolis: University of Minnesota Press.

Sandberg, Sheryl. 2013. *Lean In: Women, Work, and the Will to Lead*. New York: Knopf, Borzoi Books.

Sassen, Saskia. 2003. "The Feminisation of Survival: Alternative Global Circuits." In *Crossing Borders and Shifting Boundaries, Volume 1: Gender on the Move*, edited by Mirjana Morokvasic, Umut Erel, and Kyoko Shinozaki, 59–78. Opladen, Germany: Leske und Budrich.

———. 2014. *Expulsions: Brutality and Complexity in the Global Economy*. Cambridge, MA: Harvard University Fellows.

Saul, John S., and Patrick Bond. 2014. *South Africa—The Present as History: From Mrs Ples to Mandela and Marikana*. Woolbridge, Suffolk: James Currey.

Saussure, Ferdinand de. 2011. *Course in General Linguistics* New York: Columbia University Press.

Sautman, Barry. 1994. "Anti-Black Racism in Post-Mao China." *China Quarterly* 138:413–37.

Schmidt, Carl. 1996. *The Concept of the Political*. Chicago: University of Chicago Press.

Schmitz, Cheryl. 2020. "Kufala! Translating Witchcraft in an Angolan–Chinese Labor Dispute." *HAU: Journal of Ethnographic Theory* 10 (2): 473–86.

Schramm, Wilbur. 1964. *Mass Media and National Development: The Role of Information in the Developing Countries*. Stanford: Stanford University Press.

Segal, Gerald. 1992. "China and the Disintegration of the Soviet Union." *Asian Survey* 32 (9): 848–68.

Serres, Michel. 1982. *The Parasite*. Translated by Lawrence Schehr. Baltimore: Johns Hopkins University Press.

Silverstein, Michael. 1976. "Shifters, Linguistic Categories, and Cultural Description." In *Meaning in Anthropology*, edited by Keith H. Basso and Henry A. Selby, 11–55. New York: Harper and Row.

———. 1998. "Improvisational Performance of Culture in Realtime Discursive Practice." In *Creativity in Performance*, edited by R. Keith Sawyer, 265–312. London: Ablex.

———. 2003a. "Translation, Transduction and Transformation: Skating Glossando on Thin Semiotic Ice." In *Translating Cultures: Perspectives on Translation and Anthropology*, edited by Abraham Rosman and Paula G. Rubel, 75–108. Oxford: Berg Publishers.

———. 2003b. "Indexical Order and the Dialectics of Sociolinguistic Life." *Language and Communication* 23 (3–4): 193–229.

———. 2004. "'Cultural' Concepts and the Language-Culture Nexus." *Current Anthropology* 45 (5): 621–52.

———. 2014. "Voice of Jacob: Entextualization, Contextualization, and Identity." *ELH* 81 (2): 483–520.

———. 2017. "The Fieldwork Encounter and the Colonized Voice of Indigeneity." *Representations* 137 (1): 23–43.

Silverstein, Michael, and Greg Urban. 1996. "The Natural History of Discourse." In *Natural Histories of Discourse*, edited by Michael Silverstein and Greg Urban, 1–20. Chicago: University of Chicago Press.

Silverstein, Paul A. 2005. "Immigrant Racialization and the New Savage Slot: Race, Migration, and Immigration in the New Europe." *Annual Review of Anthropology* 34:363–84.

Smith, Adam. [1776] 2000. *The Wealth of Nations*. New York: Random House.

Smith, Llewellyn, Vincent Brown, and Christine Herbes-Sommers. 2009. *Herskovits at the Heart of Blackness*. Vital Pictures. 57 mins. www.kanopy.com/product/herskovits-heart -blackness.

Snow, Philip. 1989. *The Star Raft: China's Encounters with Africa*. Ithaca: Cornell University Press.

Spivak, Gayatri. [1988] 2010. "Can the Subaltern Speak?" In *Can the Subaltern Speak?: Reflections on the History of an Idea*, edited by Rosalind C. Morris, 21–78. New York: Columbia University Press.

———. 1993. *Outside in the Teaching Machine*. London: Routledge.

Stephey, M. J. "Top Ten Oprah Controversies: Scandal in South Africa." *Time*, May 25, 2011. http://content.time.com/time/specials/packages/article/0,28804,1939460_1939452 _1939416,00.html.

Stewart, Kathleen. 2007. *Ordinary Affects*. Durham: Duke University Press.

Torres, Sasha, ed. 1998. *Living Color: Race and Television in the United States*. Durham: Duke University Press.

Tracey, Andrew. 1970. "The Matepe Mbira Music of Rhodesia." *African Music* 4 (4): 37–61.

Trouillot, Michel-Rolph. 1995. *Silencing the Past: Power and the Production of History*. Boston: Beacon Press.

———. 2003. *Global Transformations: Anthropology and the Modern World*. New York: Palgrave Macmillan.

Tsing, Anna Lowenhaupt. 2005. *Friction: An Ethnography of Global Connection*. Princeton: Princeton University Press.

———. 2015. *The Mushroom at the End of the World: On the Possibility of Life in Capitalist Ruins*. Princeton: Princeton University Press.

Urban, Greg. 1996. "Entextualization, Replication and Power." In *Natural Histories of Discourse*, edited by Michael Silverstein and Greg Urban, 21–44. Chicago: University of Chicago Press.

Van Onselen, Charles. 1982. *Studies in the Social and Economic History of the Witwatersrand, 1886–1914, Vol. 2: New Nineveh*. Johannesburg: Ravan Press.

Vertovec, Steven. 2007. "Super-diversity and Its Implications." *Ethnic and Racial Studies* 30 (6): 1024–54.

Vukovich, Daniel. 2012. *China and Orientalism: Western Knowledge Production and the P.R.C.* Oxford: Routledge.

———. 2019. *Illiberal China: The Ideological Challenge of the People's Republic of China*. Singapore: Palgrave Macmillan.

Wallace, Michele. 1992. "Negative Images: Toward a Black Feminist Cultural Criticism." In *Cultural Studies*, edited by Lawrence Grossberg, Cary Nelson, and Paula A. Treichler, 654–71. London: Routledge.

Wang, Mingming. 2014. *The West as the Other: A Genealogy of Chinese Occidentalism*. Hong Kong: Chinese University Press.

Weber, Max. 2002. *The Protestant Work Ethic and the Spirit of Capitalism*, edited and translated by Peter Baehr and Gordon C. Wells. New York: Penguin.

White, Hylton. 2013. "Materiality, Form, and Context: Marx contra Latour." *Victorian Studies* 55 (4): 667–82.

Whorf, Benjamin Lee. 1956. *Language, Thought, and Reality: Selected Writings of Benjamin Lee Whorf*. Cambridge, MA: MIT Press.

Williams, Raymond. 1965. *The Long Revolution*. Hammondsworth: Penguin.

Wiredu, Kwasi, and Kwame Gyekye. 1992. *Person and Community: Ghanaian Philosophical Studies*. Washington, DC: Council for Research in Values and Philosophy.

Wirtz, Kristina. 2014. *Performing Afro-Cuba: Image, Voice, Spectacle in the Making of Race and History*. Chicago: University of Chicago Press.

Woolard, Kathryn, Aida Ribot Bencomo, and Josep Soler Carbonell. 2014. "What's So Funny Now? The Strength of Weak Pronouns in Catalonia." *Journal of Linguistic Anthropology* 23 (3): 127–41.

Wu, Hung. 1998. "Ruins, Fragmentation and the Chinese Modern/Postmodern." In *Inside/out: New Chinese Art*, edited by Gao Minglu and Norman Bryson, 59–66. Berkeley: University of California Press.

Yamashita, Michael. 2006. *Zheng He: Tracing the Epic Voyages of China's Greatest Explorer*. Vercelli, Italy: White Star.

Yang, Fan. 2015. *Faked in China: Nation Branding, Counterfeit Culture, and Globalization*. Bloomington: Indiana University Press.

Yang, Ke. 2008. "Preliminary Study on the Use of Mobile Phones among Migrant Workers in Beijing." *Knowledge, Technology and Policy* 21 (2): 65–72.

Yang, Mayfair. 1994. *Gifts, Favors and Banquets: The Art of Social Relationships in China*. Ithaca: Cornell University Press.

Xi, Jinping. 2014. *The Governance of China*. Beijing: Foreign Language Press.

Zhang, Lulu. 2015. "Swedish University Closes Europe's 1st Confucius Institute." China.org.cn, January 12, 2015. http://china.org.cn/world/2015-01/12/content_34537642.htm.

Žižek, Slavoj. 1989. *The Sublime Object of Ideology*. London: Verso.

Founded in 1893,
UNIVERSITY OF CALIFORNIA PRESS
publishes bold, progressive books and journals
on topics in the arts, humanities, social sciences,
and natural sciences—with a focus on social
justice issues—that inspire thought and action
among readers worldwide.

The UC PRESS FOUNDATION
raises funds to uphold the press's vital role
as an independent, nonprofit publisher, and
receives philanthropic support from a wide
range of individuals and institutions—and from
committed readers like you. To learn more, visit
ucpress.edu/supportus.